servants of the saints

SAMENLEVINGEN BUITEN EUROPA / *Non-European Societies*
waarin opgenomen / *including*
ACTUELE ONDERWERPEN / *Occasional Papers*

onder redactie van / *edited by*
prof. dr. A. J. F. KÖBBEN (Amsterdam), prof. dr. R. A. J. VAN LIER (Wageningen)
prof. dr. G. W. LOCHER (Leiden) en prof. dr. L. H. JANSSEN S.J. (Tilburg)

SAMENLEVINGEN BUITEN EUROPA / *Non-European Societies*

ACTUELE ONDERWERPEN / *Occasional Papers*

DR. R. A. M. VAN ZANTWIJK

servants of the saints

THE SOCIAL AND CULTURAL IDENTITY
OF A TARASCAN COMMUNITY IN MEXICO

ASSEN 1967

VAN GORCUM & COMP. N.V. – DR. H. J. PRAKKE & H. M. G. PRAKKE

The publication of this work was made possible through a grant from
the Netherlands Organisation for the Advancement of Pure Research (Z.W.O.)

Printed in the Netherlands by Royal VanGorcum Ltd., Assen

"Non-Western cultures, however much subject to western influences, will never become
identical with our own civilisation"

A. J. F. KÖBBEN

(from: Van Primitieven tot Medeburgers, Assen, 1964, p.93)

table of contents

acknowledgements

A scientific publication is rarely the outcome of a single person's work. Many people have directly or indirectly contributed to this study and the list is so long that it is out of the question to name them all. Although naturally I feel grateful to all who have in one way or another assisted me in my investigations or in improving the text of this study, I may perhaps be excused for restricting my acknowledgements to those who rendered me the most essential assistance in the preparation of this book.

First of all I wish to express my great gratitude to Prof. Dr. J. van Baal, who presented me for my degree. His continuous interest and valuable support were a great encouragement, while his assistance contributed to the essential improvement of the original manuscript. I also owe him a great debt of gratitude for the facilities granted by him as Director of the Department of Anthropology of the Royal Institute of the Tropics.

I am deeply indebted to Prof. Dr. A. F. J. Köbben, to whose initiative I owe the fact that I was twice sent out to Mexico. He also gave his thorough comments on the manuscript, which were valuable contributions to the ultimate text.

Acknowledgements are also due to the members of the Directorate of Crefal, particularly to the Director, Prof. Lucas Ortiz, for their substantial help in the field investigations in and around Ihuatzio during the three years of my study.

My grateful acknowledgements are due to Prof. Dr. Miguel León-Portilla of the University of Mexico, at the time Director of the Instituto Indigenista Interamericano, for his voluntary help in supplying me with information and publications on the subject of *indigenismo*.

I am also grateful to the Instituto Nacional Indigenista of Mexico, especially to its Director, Dr. Alfonso Caso, for the information received on development projects in areas of predominantly Indian populations and for the opportunities, so readily given, to come and see for myself the work done by the Institute.

My obligations are due to Prof. and Mrs. H. Hoetink for their accurate correction of the Spanish summary of this study.

Four of the students who participated in the research distinguished themselves by their great devotion and persistence, giving much of their leisure time to collect supplementary data; their names deserve special mention: Nelly González García, Graciela Oviedo Jofre, Rafael Domínguez Gavidia and Flavio Galicia Aguilar.

I want to express my appreciation to Mrs. W. H. P. M. van Es-Jacobs for the devotion shown by her in translating the Dutch text of the book into English.

Finally I am greatly indebted to the Netherlands Organisation for the Advancement of Pure Research for the financial support which made the publication of this English translation possible.

This study was first published as an academic thesis in Dutch in 1965. The present English edition is intended to make the results of the cultural-anthropological investigations carried out by the author in the Lake Tarscan area between 1960 and 1963 accessible to a larger public.

I   *general introduction*

This work is the outcome of a social cultural study of the largest Lake Tarascan village, Ihuatzio. The study was carried out between November, 1960 and November 1963, when I worked for the Regional Centre of Fundamental Education with a view to Community Development in Latin America (henceforth to be referred to as 'Crefal', which is an abbreviation of its Spanish name), established at Pátzcuaro, Michoacán. I taught seminars in social sciences and their relationships to community development projects. My students consisted of about seventy Latin American officials. A number of these students were directed by me in their field training, which took place in the municipality of Tzintzuntzan. Crefal is a joint venture of the Mexican Government, Unesco and some other international organisations. The Mexican Government had given permission for Crefal to concentrate the field training of the above-mentioned students in five municipalities located around Lake Pátzcuaro. Tzintzuntzan is one of these municipalities and the Tarascan village of Ihuatzio with approximately 2.000 inhabitants is attached administratively to it (see map 1).

During these three years I could spend two days a week doing my research in Ihuatzio, part of which could be combined with my work for Crefal. For about a third of the time that I devoted to my own investigations I could rely on the co-operation of at least three of the students. They rendered considerable assistance especially in collecting numerical data.

The choice of the area and the subject of my study was mainly determined by four factors:

1 The Director of Crefal was greatly interested in a social anthropological

study of one of the larger villages in the so-called 'zone for practical work', particularly with regard to the difficulties which were being encountered in the execution of the projects of technical assistance in the area.

2   There exist three good ethnographic studies of communities in the area of Tarascan culture. One of them, Beals' study of Cherán (Beals, 1946), describes a village in the Sierra Tarasca; the other two studies, one of Tzintzuntzan (Foster, 1948), the other of the municipality of Quiroga (Brand, 1951) are mainly concerned with mestizo populations.[1]

3   These and other studies of Tarascan or mestizo communities in the Modern Tarascan area supply ample information on their material culture.

4   I was staying in one of the low-lying parts of the town of Pátzcuaro. Transportation facilities and the desire to make the most of the time available for my researches necessitated the choice of an area not too far away from the place where I lived.

Personally I was then interested in finding an explanation for the difficulties encountered in the execution of community development projects, resulting from the differences between the social structure of the group that was to be stimulated into developing social economic activities of their own and that of the society from which the leaders of such projects originated.

A first reconnaissance of the area where Crefal operated had already revealed that such problems especially existed in the village of Ihuatzio. This was one of the main reasons which led to the selection of Ihuatzio as the object of my study. Another important argument in favour of Ihuatzio as compared with other Lake Tarascan villages where Crefal experts and students operated, was the fact that it had been one of the three pre-Spanish Tarascan administrative centres. Furthermore it is the only one of the three that has remained a pure Tarascan community down to our own days, while Tzintzuntzan and Pátzcuaro, the other two Tarascan capital towns, are now chiefly inhabited by mestizos. Owing to the important political and religious position of Ihuatzio in pre-Spanish times more data are available about the historical background of this village and its residents than of any other Tarascan community eligible for my study. The last but by no means least important motive for selecting Ihuatzio was based on the results of the preliminary investigations I had made during the first month (December, 1960). It then seemed to me that the social

MAP I   THE LAKE PÁTZCUARO AREA

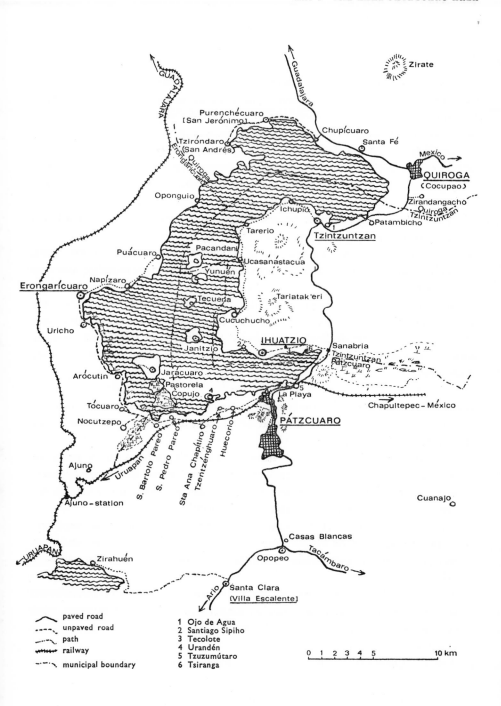

organisation of the community had retained more autochthonic Indian elements than that of any of the other villages. This conclusion also contained a warning that the situation in Ihuatzio might be typical of this village only, and that many results of my study might prove to be unsuitable for generalisation as characteristic of all Lake Tarascan communities, or of the entire Tarascan population of Michoacán. A better insight into the specific position of Ihuatzio was subsequently gained from the results of a short comparative study of some aspects of the social organisation of the villages of San Jerónimo Purenchécuaro and Cucuchucho. A much more extensive comparative study was made on Yunuén Island with the object of ascertaining the differences which might exist between the social organisation of a Tarascan community whose main occupations are farming and handicrafts, and that of a village mainly consisting of fishermen's families.

As the community on Yunuén Island numbered no more than thirty or forty families, a fair amount of exact data could be collected within a comparatively short time. The same study also revealed social differences within one and the same cultural area, which may be due to the variety of sizes of the communities in the area.

The conditions under which my investigations were conducted were favourable in some respects, but not in most, and on the whole they were far from ideal. Favourable factors were:

1   The fact that the population of Ihuatzio is fairly familiar with the presence of strangers in the village. Crefal experts and students have worked there at more or less regular intervals. Some of their activities, however, constituted an unfavourable factor (see no. 7 below).

2   The material support given to me and my students by the Crefal directory. They provided motor vehicles for transportation by land and by water, as well as sufficient equipment, such as beds, blankets, cooking utensils, office supplies, etc.

3   The enthusiastic co-operation of my student-assistants. Twenty-two students participated in the investigations; eleven of them in Ihuatzio, nine on Yunuén Island, one in San Jerónimo Purenchécuaro and one in Cucuchucho.

4   The co-operation of the 15th Indigenous Development Brigade,[2] who

started their activities in Ihuatzio in May 1962 under the direction of an
ex-student of Crefal of the year 1961.

5   The fairly long period of time (about three years) over which my study
could be extended.

There were several factors which exercised an unfavourable influence on the
progress of my study:

1   The ordinary Crefal courses take place between March, 1st and December,
1st of each year. During five or six weeks in September and October
lecturers and students were away on excursions to various parts of Mexico;
so my student-assistants had scarcely seven months in each year to attend
lectures and receive their field training. As had been said, field work was
done on two days each week. No students were available between December, 1st and April, 1st.

2   There was a fresh batch of students every year, so that three different
teams aided in the investigations.

3   The students came from various Latin American countries, and during
the first year of my research there was not a single Mexican student in
the Ihuatzio group. Students usually found it very difficult to be assimilated into the life of the local community. Often teamwork did not agree
with them, and they found it hard to subject themselves to the inevitable
regulations.

4   Most of the student-assistants had never participated in a social anthropological study. Most of them could, indeed, boast a fairly wide experience with Indian and rural populations in their own countries, but six
weeks' field training at the commencement of the Crefal academic year
proved to be insufficient as a theoretical basis.

5   The amount of work required by the general Crefal project made it
impracticable for the students and myself to stay at Ihuatzio overnight
as often as we liked. The students could do this once a week on an
average, but opportunities for me to stay there were very rare.

6   All student-assistants had great difficulty with the Tarascan language,
except one student, whose mother tongue it was. Although no more than
0.6 per cent. of the population of Ihuatzio are monolingual Tarascans,
the other 99.4 per cent bilingual residents often used the language-barrier

as an excuse to conceal a great part of their thoughts and activities. Of course it was impossible for the students to master this difficult language to any appreciable degree during the short space of time available to them, and in spite of my much longer stay in the area I managed to acquire only some passive knowledge of the language, barely enough to follow the main trend of a conversation.

7   There was some discontent among the inhabitants of Ihuatzio over previous activities of Crefal workers in the village. There had been a dispute between some specialists from the Crefal Centre and the Roman-Catholic priest over the Crefal chicken project, which will be described in a later chapter. Another dispute between Crefal experts and traditional officials in Ihuatzio resulted from a course organised by Crefal for un-official village leaders. Some of the students or experts had given definite undertakings and made many more vague promises, which did not materialize, thus enhancing the existing suspicion of the population. This legacy of vain promises, which were often impossible to realize, hampered our study substantially.

8   In the second and third years of our work field training was extended to the whole municipality of Tzintzuntzan. During the first year our activities had been confined to the separate communities and villages, according to the method followed when Crefal still had a different programme of training. When the Centre started to organise its field activities on the basis of administrative territorial units (municipalities), the long-standing land-disputes between Ihuatzio and the municipal capital town of Tzintzuntzan were brought to a head again. As it was necessary for the same persons who had been working in Ihuatzio to co-operate closely with the municipal authorities of Tzintzuntzan, what confidence we had won in the first year was at first lost again almost completely.

9   Some of the foregoing reasons may account for another difficulty. Most of our informants in the village of Ihuatzio appeared to be reluctant to co-operate. Less than thirty per cent. of them gave the same answers to the same questions asked three months later. An equally small number of people gave the same answers to the same questions asked by different interviewers. A similar disappointing lack of co-operation was at first noticed on Yunuén Island, but as it was a small population, which made

it easier to check the data collected, the problem was soon solved. The Ihuatzio community, being more than ten times as large, presented much graver problems. Most of the residents were reluctant to discuss matters connected with their social organisation, religion, and economic relationships. For a long time my work was seriously hampered by a general suspicion on the part of the population, who seemed to resent our intrusion.

10 During a later stage of the study the inhabitants often identified the work that my student-assistants did, with the activities of the Governmental Development Brigade. Some people then refused to co-operate or even opposed our work (see chapters VI and IX).

11 Finally the lack of scientific literature on the subject of my study can be mentioned as an a priori negative factor. This lack was twofold. First the supply of good instructive literature in the field of social science written in Spanish was inadequate, which interfered with the proper training of the students. Furthermore the Crefal library at Pátzcuaro appeared to be greatly deficient especially in literature dealing with the historical background of the Tarascan people. The 'Relación de Michoacán' for instance, a work of essential value for this study, I could only consult before my departure to Mexico and after my return to Holland. During their participation in my investigations the student-assistants were assigned tasks according to their individual talents and experience. The agrarian engineer was requested to collect chiefly quantitative agricultural data, the female social worker obtained information concerning housing and the composition of families, etc. The students' part in the interpretation of the data was only of secondary importance.

The following is a list of the student-teams who participated. Each participant's country is added in brackets.

I *In Ihuatzio:*
Summer, 1961:   1 female social worker (Argentina)
                            1 student of home economics (Ecuador)
                            1 agriculturist (Ecuador)
                            1 sanitory inspector (Panama)
                            1 educationist (Bolivia);

April to November, 1962:   1 female social worker (Argentina)
                           1 educationist (Bolivia)
                           1 director of an Indian development brigade
                           (Mexico);
April to October, 1963:   1 female social worker (Chile)
                           1 head of an Indian boarding-school (Mexico)
                           1 alphabetisation expert (Venezuela).

II   *On Yunuén Island:*
Summer, 1961:   1 female social worker (Peru)
                           1 horticulturist (Mexico)
                           1 sanitary inspector (Guatemala)
                           1 teacher (El Salvador)
                           1 inspector of schools (Peru);
April to October, 1962:   1 female social worker (Venezuela)
                           1 female social worker (Ecuador);
April to September, 1963: 1 female social worker (Peru)
                           1 inspector of schools (Nicaragua).

III   *In San Jerónimo Purenchécuaro:*
August, 1962:   1 social worker (Mexico).

IV   *In Cucuchucho:*
Summer, 1963:   1 graduate student of sociology (Mexico).

Of these twenty-two assistants seven were Indians; there were four Mexican
students: two of them, who were stationed in Ihuatzio one after the other,
were Aztecs; the other two, one of whom worked on Yunuén Island and the
other in Purenchécuaro, were of Tarascan descent, but only the latter spoke
Tarascan. He was also the only student who did not work under my daily
supervision, because the village was not located in the Tzintzuntzan area.
During August, 1962 he came to Pátzcuaro once a week to report his progress.
In that month one of the students in Ihuatzio visited him twice in Purenchécuaro.

When I began my study of Ihuatzio the principal object was to detect the causes underlying the people's passive opposition to the socio-economic projects, which had been started by Crefal experts and students several years before. We suspected that several of the problems were due to the peculiar social organisation of the community, or rather by the fact that the Crefal people were ignorant of it. Our supposition was soon confirmed. As often happens, however, the original objectives of the study fell into the background, as some aspects of it were so fascinating that I was induced to study them more thoroughly than I had at first intended. The ethnohistorical aspect of the study of the social organisation and structure of the Ihuatzio community assumed increasing importance, when interesting remnants of typically pre-Spanish forms of organisation could be traced, so that I felt the need for an extensive study of Tarascan, Aztec and colonial sources.

After the summer of 1961 we abandoned the method previously applied by Crefal teams, who interviewed people from questionnaires which they had in their hands. Whenever we made use of questionnaires, we first learned the questions by heart. All my assistants kept a diary, from which they wrote filing-cards every two or three days. These cards were filed according to a comparatively simple system specially designed for Crefal.[3] In addition my student-assistants submitted monthly surveys of their work in the villages.

The description of community-life in Ihuatzio and its historical background is preceded by a brief summary of the geographical setting and the natural resources of the village, as well as of some aspects of its material culture and its economy.

Ihuatzio, or 'place of the Coyote', is situated on the Bay of Ihuatzio, the southeastern bend of Lake Pátzcuaro. The village extends about two kilometres along the lake frontage. Its three main streets are parallel to the shore and are crossed by three important side-streets. There are some twenty-five narrow streets and pathways leading from the main streets to the settlements scattered all over the outskirts of the village. The church with its enclosed front court and the adjacent square form the centre of the village. The church is clearly visible from the opposite lake-shore, where Pátzcuaro lies. North of the village rises the majestic Mount Tariata k'heri; at the foot of it, pretty high above the village, are the ruins of the pre-Spanish town of Ihuatzio with its five temples, which seem to look down haughtily upon the now rather insignificant village lying in the shade of abundant trees as if to hide its shame. Only the Roman-Catholic church rises above the green carpet and seems to enjoy looking at its pre-Columbian rivals, conquered long ago. Yet the conqueror did not emerge from the battle unspoilt, for the churchtower is crowned by a big stone coyote, which, according to legend, is the image of the pre-Spanish god of the village. The façade of the church is adorned by two relief sculptures, one representing the Sun, the other the Moon, the two chief Tarascan gods.

Next to and in front of the church are the residence of the Roman-Catholic priest and the house of the Prioste (a native official). A stone wall separates the three structures from the rest of the village. Two gates give access to the enclosure. Opposite the northern main entrance to the enclosed front-court of the church or 'temple' ('templo') are two schools standing side by side. The school buildings are outwardly indistinguishable from ordinary houses. The western building is the State school, the eastern the private Roman-Catholic school. Next to the eastern entrance to the front-court of the church is the Jefatura de Tenencia, the 'Sheriff's office' with the lock-up. In front of it is a more or less triangular open space with a basketball court at a lower level than the street.

The first thing that strikes a visitor to Ihuatzio is the abundance of boulders in and around the village. Although they can be a nuisance especially to the farmers, they are useful as material to build walls around fields and gardens. These primitive fences are seen everywhere. The stones are simply piled up, and no cement or any other material is used to hold them together. These walls have the advantage that during the rainy season the water can pass through easily. Owing to the irregularity of the terrain solid walls would convert the enclosed sites into large basins, which would couse water damage to the buildings. Boulders are also used for building sheds, stables and the foundations of houses, while the main streets are paved with them. The walls of the houses and other structures are built of white adobe bricks, made locally in several places in and around the village. Only the church is entirely made of stone.

All houses, except the very small ones, have an attic to store maize and tools. It is called 'tapanco', which is an Aztec word. The roofs are supported by wooden beams. Open spaces between the beams allow the smoke from the fireplace to escape between roof and walls, and fresh air to enter. There are no chimneys; the houses are roofed with tiles or with corrugated iron sheets. None of the houses is roofed with tejamanil (small wooden shakes), as they are in the Sierra Tarasca.

Sometimes on sunny days the villagers dry large quantities of tule-reeds in the southern corner of the plaza. The bay bordering the village used to supply all the tule needed for the production of mats (petates) and baskets. Gradually these tule-grounds have become almost exhausted, and the petateros have to walk about ten kilometres eastward to the hamlet of Chapultepec to obtain their material. About half of the occupational population is regularly occupied in the production of tule mats for sale. Occasionally mats are made for private use. Earnings are very low, tule-weavers receiving 3.5 or 4 pesos (U.S. $ 0.28-0.32) per mat. Housewives, after finishing their household work, can finish one mat per day. When tule-weaving is the husband's only occupation, they can produce three mats a day between them. Allowance should be made for the time needed to cut, transport and dry the reeds. Now that their own tule-grounds are exhausted the petateros have to pay the inhabitants of Chapultepec a small sum of money for the right to cut reeds. Some weavers buy tule from Lake Tarascans who still have a good supply of it, but then they have to pay 7 pesos for a quantity needed for three mats. Once a week an intermediate trader comes to buy mats and carry them to Toluca; every fortnight another trader buys the majority to sell the mats on various markets. The villagers say that the two traders monopolize the trade in Ihuatzio and Cucuchucho, and that they have agreed to keep the prices down. In addition to large mats the weavers also make small table mats to put plates and pots on, baskets and all sorts of other woven articles of popular art, such as figures of angels, crucifixes, figures of men and women busy with various activities. The production of other furniture is negligible. Wooden articles, such as tables, chairs, boxes, etc. for private use are occasionally made in the village, but most of the earthenware and stoneware has to be bought at Tzintzuntzan.

Clothes are chiefly made in the village itself, the cloth is bought elsewhere. A little more than half of the male population still wears the 'calzón' (the traditional long white cotton trousers), mostly of local make. Others wear blue jeans or khaki trousers bought in Pátzcuaro. Most adult men wear huaraches, leather or rubber sandals (often with soles cut from car-tyres), which are also bought in Pátzcuaro. In the rainy season many people wear the traditional Xuhrku, a raincape made from palm leaves. This garment may be of pre-Spanish origin. Old as well as young men, and some women wear hats. The hat-style worn in Jarácuaro is the most important; it is the traditional palm-straw hat worn in Michoacán; it is beautiful, long-lasting and waterproof. But, as in other parts of Mexico, more and more people in Ihuatzio prefer the cowboy hat from Texas, which is very popular today, especially among the mestizos. Many men and boys wear 'gabanes', woollen blankets with an opening for the head. In other parts of Michoacán this garment is usually called 'zarape' or 'tilma', the latter being an Aztec word. There are many kinds of gabanes for sale in the market in Pátzcuaro; they vary in quality, size and patterns, but as a rule they are richly decorated with fine patterns. They are made in several Tarascan mountain villages and are woven on primitive hand looms.

Women generally wear the traditional pleated skirts, which custom dates back to colonial times. Girls make one before they get married. Originally the skirt was so wide that a young mother could use some of the cloth from her own skirt to make the first clothes for her baby daughter. This material, a thick woollen cloth, as well as the material for blouses and aprons is imported. Blouses and aprons are decorated with rich embroidery, often in European style. Flower patterns are the most popular. The long shawl or 'rebozo' is also part of a woman's costume. Sometimes babies are carried on the back in a fold of the rebozo. These shawls are bought in Pátzcuaro; the traditional woollen belts are sometimes made in Ihuatzio. They are worn by males as well as females.

Nearly one fifth of the economically productive age-group of the population of the village is engaged in farming. Landownership is partly private, partly communal.

The land on the slopes of Mount Tariatak'heri which face Ihuatzio, is the communal property of the village. In the course of this century the increasing population has cut all of the abundant forests that used to crown the mountain; consequently there is now a great shortage of firewood in the village.

These common lands comprise 1487 hectares of almost entirely deforested and eroded mountain slopes, which yield very little profit. Ninety-six private landowners hold 601 hectares in all, making individual holdings 626 ares each on an average, not including the houselots. Nearly every household-head in the village, including those men not chiefly engaged in farming, possesses a houselot, which yields a modest harvest for private consumption. A division of the population according to the main sources of income will ignore these houselots. Of a test sample of 37 farmers 36 cultivated maize, 33 brown beans, 17 wheat, 7 broad beans, 1 French beans, while one farmer grew cattle food. Maize and brown beans are widely cultivated, and with 'chile' (pepper) they form the main parts of the national diet. In Ihuatzio wheat is an important crop compared with quantities produced in other Indian villages in Mexico. The houselot-gardens often have fruittrees, such as chayotes,[4] zapotes,[5] gourds, tejocotes,[6] and duraznos,[7] while edible cacti and other vegetables are also grown as welcome additions to the daily diet.

Some stock-raising does occur in the village, although it is always of secondary importance. Our sample of 60 families gave the following numbers of stock: 43 head of cattle, 25 pigs and 21 horses. These data obtained from informants may be considered as representing between 50 and 70 per cent. of the actual possessions, because random tests revealed that many inhabitants of the village had not had their animals entered in the official registers in order to avoid having to pay tax on them. Of course our informants only mentioned their legal possession of livestock. The total number of fowls in the sample was 1569, mostly chickens. In 1961 no more than 18 Ihuatzio chicken-farmers had joined the Crefal regional co-operative society of chicken-farmers. Individual stocks averaged 300 chickens, making 5400 birds in all. This form of chicken-farming is on the whole a profitable business. Ten hens lay 6 eggs a day on an average during the economically best months. New members received 200 young hens (afterwards increased to 250) to start with. After five or six months these hens begin to lay eggs. During a period of 18 months (after which the hens are killed) members earned an average net amount of 20 pesos per hen. Between 1960 and 1963 the individual annual earnings derived from chicken-farming ranged from 3.000 to 8.000 pesos. For most of the farmers this was a considerable addition to their ordinary income.

Six men in the village kept bees, and participated in another Crefal controlled credit-scheme. Between 1960 and 1963 nett profits earned in this business ranged from 800 to 1.500 pesos a year, exclusive of the home consumption of honey.

Only 4 per cent. of the occupational population of Ihuatzio are fishermen, but they are a comparatively important group, because they maintain many more relations with other Lake Tarascans than the rest of the villagers. Their occupation brings them into contact with the island populations, mainly fishers, and with many fishermen from other villages located on the lake shore. As all fishermen in the area are Tarascans, they form an Indian group with characteristic bonds of their own, which are manifested in some traditions, for instance the ceremonial shooting of ducks on November, 1st in the bay of Erongarícuaro, and the traditional dividing of the fishing-grounds to which they subject themselves.[8]

Of the Lake Pátzcuaro area it can be said that during the last decade fishing as a basic economic occupation has been slowly declining. According to the people themselves the waterlevel of Lake Pátzcuaro has fallen considerably since the eruption of the new volcano Parícutin, which began to be formed in the Tarascan mountains in 1943. According to popular theory the volcanic ashes which dropped into the lake choked the eggs of the fish. Other causes of the steady decrease in the fish stock are for instance the limited rainfall, and the increase in the population of the islands, which resulted in more intensive fishing. The critical economic situation which developed gradually on the islands and in some lake-side villages has continued to the present day. The inhabitants of Janitzio Island have found a new source of income now that increasing numbers of tourists visit their island. The population of Jarácuaro is raising the production of straw hats, while on the islands of Yunuén and La Pacanda Crefal came to the rescue with their chicken project. But in several other villages the only solution left to the male inhabitants was 'bracerismo', i.e. temporary emigration as seasonal workers to the north of Mexico or to the United States.

Lake Pátzcuaro is fished by more than 700 men, so that, making allowance for the shortage of seines in Ihuatzio, we may estimate the share of the village in this industry at about 4 per cent.

Hunting is rare and of little economic value. Only the fishermen have their interesting tradition of the ritual duck-hunting, which takes place, if possible, on November 1st. On that day hundreds of men in canoes assemble in the

Bay of Erongarícuaro to shoot ducks. These are offered as food for the dead the next day during the feast which is celebrated in their honour, especially on Janitzio Island. Although many men use shotguns, a great many still have bird spears and the famous pre-Spanish spear-throwers. The Tarascan name for the latter instrument is tzʌpahqui, but it is more generally known by its Aztec name of atlatl.

The fishermen of Ihuatzio are one of the village groups who maintain regular contacts with the mountain (Sierra) Tarascans. They mostly meet them at the market of Erongarícuaro, a village situated on the western lake shore. The market dates back to pre-Spanish times and is based on the mutual need of the inhabitants of the lake and mountain villages to exchange some of their products. The people from the lake area have fish, which the mountain people lack. The latter, however, have firewood, which is much in demand among the Lake Tarascans, as wood is scarce in their area. Long ago this gave rise to the custom of exchanging fish and firewood at the market of Erongarícuaro. Although today the village of Erongarícuaro is almost entirely inhabited by mestizos, the Sunday market is a predominantly Indian affair. Originally the two main products, fish and firewood, were exchanged exclusively on a barter basis. In the course of time these transactions have been adapted to a monetary economy, for the intermediary traders think in terms of money only. When today firewood is exchanged for fish and the two parties agree that the quantities do not represent the same value, they will soon settle the difference in money.

Dug-out canoes are for sale in Erongarícuaro; they are made in the back country and in the area around the village, and are used by the Lake Tarascans.

Another group maintaining many relations with other Tarascan communities is the musicians of Ihuatzio. The village has a number of bands, which are very famous among the Tarascans of the Lake area and even among Tarascans in the Sierra Tarasca. They are hired on many occasions by the chiefs and official authorities of other Tarascan places to take part in the festivities.

Many women in Ihuatzio, in addition to their household duties, do some extra work, which yields them a modest income. In our test sample of 60 families or 267 persons (a good 14 per cent. of the total population) there were 80 women of the economically active age-group (15 to 65). Only six of them did no work other than their household duties; 28 were tule-weavers, one was a trader, and 45 were makers of maize cakes (tortilleras). Many women of the last group went daily from door to door or to the market in Pátzcuaro to sell their cakes.

Young children also have to do their share of work, light jobs at first. So with the limited means of production at their disposal the villagers make good economic use of the available labour.

Trade between members of the village community is insignificant. There are seven shops, nearly all of which are groceries. A good deal of buying and selling takes place outside the shops: for instance the sale of land, pigs, chickens, trees, fishing nets. The external trade of the villagers affords them a link chiefly with the intermediate buyers of the products of tule-weaving and with the markets of Pátzcuaro and Tzintzuntzan, where they sell tule mats and other woven articles. In Pátzcuaro they also sell maize cakes, fish, fat stock, fruit and surpluses of other crops.

Most of the household equipment and clothes are bought in Pátzcuaro, kitchen utensils in Tzintzuntzan.

The Tarascan communities on the islands and around the lake have to deal with two water problems. First drinking water is scarce or difficult to transport to the places where it is needed. Second the winding shore of the lake delays communication between many villages. A great many people of Ihuatzio cross the bay in canoes, when they go to Pátzcuaro, which lies directly opposite to Ihuatzio. It takes them half an hour to make this journey of about three kilometres; the same time it takes the dilapidated bus, which runs twice a day from Cucuchucho to Pátzcuaro. Compared with other villages in the neighbourhood Ihuatzio has quite a lot of water suitable for domestic use. There are 116 wells, scattered all over the village, but many of them are uncovered, and dirty rainwater can run freely into them, making the water unfit for direct human consumption. During the rainy season many wells contain so much water that the women can do the washing at home, but in the dry season they have to go to the lake-side with their washing.

To the north, west and south of the village mountains and the lake form natural barriers to free communication with the outside world. Only the east side is open, and so this is where the sandy road leaves the village. It is five kilometres long and in bad repair. It connects Ihuatzio with the hacienda 'El Tecolote', the hamlet of Tziranga and the ex-hacienda 'Sanabria'. Here it runs into the federal asphalt road from Pátzcuaro to Tzintzuntzan, which at Quiroga joins

The ceremonial centre. The Priostería has a slogan of the Sinarquistas painted on it. In the background is the parish church, with the coyote-god on the tower and reliefs of María de Guadalupe, the Sun and the Moon on the façade. Part of the remaining walls of the Gwatapera can be seen in the bottom right-hand corner.

The Jefatura de Tenencia, east of the ceremonial centre. In the background the lake is visible with Pátzcuaro on the opposite shore.

the main roads to Guadalajara and Mexico City. West of Ihuatzio the same sandy road is a mere pathway leading to Santiago Sipiho and to Cucuchucho 3 kilometres further on.

Data on the number of inhabitants of Ihuatzio vary a great deal. According to the municipal registers in Tzintzuntzan the village of Ihuatzio had 1800 inhabitants in 1961. The Federal 'Brigade for the assistance of the indigenous population', which has operated in the village since April, 1962, estimated the population in September, 1962 at between 3600 and 4000 persons. The village State school gave the same figures. But these figures are gross exaggerations. In November, 1962, after a general population census, the Brigade amended the data, stating a total population figure of 1863 persons, 948 men and 915 women.

The leaders of the wapánekwas (indigenous social groups) stated for September, 1962: 432 families. In the sample of 60 families I had taken the average family-size was 4.45 persons, which also yields a total number of nearly two thousand.

Our sample consisted of 133 males and 134 females. Of these 77 men and 73 women belonged to the age-group of potentially economic value (15 to 65 years). The ability to do manual work is diminished by an inadequate diet of indifferent quality, while the people are rather poorly protected against the unfavourable climatic conditions.

As has been said, the village is attached administratively to Tzintzuntzan. In 1930, when General Cárdenas became governor, the new municipality of Tzintzuntzan was formed by combining parts of the then adjacent municipalities of Pátzcuaro and Quiroga. Ihuatzio had previously belonged to Pátzcuaro, Tzintzuntzan to Quiroga. The municipality of Tzintzuntzan was called into being entirely on sentimental grounds: the most important Tarascan capital historically ought to be a separate administrative entity. Since Tzintzuntzan and Ihuatzio came to belong to the same municipality there have been disputes between the two places over the boundaries of their communal lands.

The following are additional data collected in co-operation with the 15th Indigenous Development Brigade.

1   *Population:*

Total number	1863 persons	(100%)
men	948	(51%)
women	915	(49%)
persons younger than 6 years	368	
boys among them	226 (61%)	
girls among them	142 (39%)	
persons between 6 and 14 years	441	(23%)

2   *Illiteracy:*

males older than 6 years	722	
illiterate	270, or	37%
females older than 6 years	773	
illiterate	443, or	57%
Of the age-group 6-14 years	239 persons were illiterate	54%

3   *Housing:*

Total number of families	432	(100%)
possessing table(s)	155	36%
,, chair(s)	266	61%
,, bed(s)	232	53%
	(many people do not sleep in the beds they have)	
,, a radio	74	17%
,, a sewing-machine	50	11%
,, a flat-iron	20	5%
living in houses with earthen floors		93%
,, ,, ,, ,, cement floors		4%
,, ,, ,, ,, floors of other material		3%

having	electric light	40%
,,	a well	28%
,,	a lavatory	11%
,,	a raised fireplace	11%
,,	window(s)	8%

4   *Occupations* (only the main occupation is given):

tule-weavers	52%
farmers	20%
fishermen	4%
chicken-farmers	3%
beekeepers	1%
tortilleras, peones (farmhands), traders, etc.	20%

5   *Clothing:*

persons	wearing	trousers:	437
,,	,,	calzones:	511
,,	,,	shoes:	239
,,	,,	huaraches:	598
,,	going	barefooted:	1026

(658 persons older than 6 years, that is 44% of all persons older than 6 years).

Notes to the General Introduction:

[1] These studies have resulted from the so-called 'Tarascan project', a series of ethnological and geographical researches in Michoacán, executed under the auspices of the Institute of Social Anthropology of the Smithsonian Institution (Washington D.C.) in co-operation with the Escuela Nacional de Antropología (Mexico, D.F.). See the bibliography.

[2] Brigada de Mejoramiento Indígena no. 15. One of the teams of the Departamento de Asuntos Indígenas, a section of the Secretaría de Educación (Ministry of Education). These units have the same objectives as the Misiones Culturales, the cultural missions, which are engaged on develop-

ment projects in the rural districts of Mexico. The basic idea of these programmes of social welfare is that the rural populations need to have further education facilities, if their social conditions are to be improved. Members of the brigades and missions are expert craftsmen and minor sanitary officials, who under the direction of a teacher have to give training and render assistance to the inhabitants of the areas where they operate. The only task of such teams is to assist the population, they do not carry out public works.

³ See Van Zantwijk, 1963 a, chapter X.

⁴ A kind of thorny gourd; quite fit to eat (Aztec: chayotl).

⁵ A kind of soft apple (Aztec: tsapotl).

⁶ A kind of crab-apple (Aztec: texokotl).

⁷ A kind of apricot.

⁸ There are two main fishing techniques employed by the lake fishers, net-fishing, and fishing with a fishing-rod or sometimes simply with a line. There are three different kinds of nets: the trawl net, the butterfly net, and the largest net, which is commonly known by the Tarascan name of 'warukwa'. Solórzano rightly says that this is commercially the most important net. The fish get caught in the mesh with their gills. The nets are cast in the way of migrating fish, which owing to their rapid movements get stuck in the mesh (Solórzano, 1951, p. 53). Several fishermen on the islands of Janitzio, Pacanda and Tecuena have these big nets, which they use to close off bays or parts of the lake with an irregular shoreline, where in the spring the fish come to lay their eggs, or at other times, in smaller numbers, in search of food. In his book Solórzano confuses the two kinds of nets when he uses the Tarascan word chirémekwa for both of them. In Spanish they are called chinchorro and chinchorro grande respectively, which may have led Solórzano to think that in Tarascan also there is only one name for both the trawl net and the largest net. The lake fishers, however, call only the smaller net, the trawl net, 'cherémikwa', while the large seine is called 'warukwa', a term which is not found in Solórzano's book. Yet he gives a precise description of both nets; so we shall now quote him, only correcting the points where he is mistaken: "Trawl nets and seines are composed of sections of 500 meshes each lengthwise. Four such sections, 2000 meshes, form a separate part of the net, referred to as 'parada' by the fishermen. These paradas may be 25 to 30 m. long when the nets are used to catch small whitefish, or 40 to 50 m. for nets to catch white fish. Widths vary from 50 to 60 centimetres for the smaller net (cherémikwa), and from 1 to 1½ m. for the warukwa. . Some nets may be shorter than stated above; meshes may also vary in size. The nets are cast vertically one by one. Both kinds of nets consist of four parts, with measurements peculiar to each kind. The head and foot ropes of the small trawl net consist of 8 strands of no. 16 thickness, while the two warps of the warukwas consist of 8 plaited strands of the same material. Instead of lead the fishers attach to either of the two kinds of nets small stones, tied with strong hemp thread to the foot rope at intervals of 12-15 cm. As floats they use a variable number of rectangular or cylindrical pieces of pinewood, also firmly attached to the nets with rope" (Solórzano 1961; pp. 53-54).

The ownership of a large seine gives a fisherman some degree of economic security. The owner's position is comparable to that of a large land-owner, who has to employ labourers to cultivate his lands. The wages usually given to the helpers consist of part of the catch: the owner keeps half of it, the other half is divided equally between the helpers. A remarkable fact is that on Janitzio

Island owners of seines have found a new occupation as skippers of boats which take tourists to the island, because they could afford to buy large motorboats. They leave the use of their nets, and fishing in general almost entirely to 'tenants'. In Ihuatzio only one fisherman has a seine.

Seine-making demands a lot of work and great financial sacrifices. It takes a fisherman five or six weeks, working at it daily, to finish a trawl net. Working in his leisure hours, he needs about six months to finish a large seine. The yarn needed to make one seine costs him about 1500 pesos, and only 20 pesos to make the much smaller trawl net. The two smaller nets are much less useful. With them the fisherman catches enough fish for himself and his family, and usually there is little left for sale.

Butterfly nets, or waromútakwa, can only be used when there is no wind blowing. Mostly they are only used to catch 'charal', the smallest kind of lake fish, which forms the main part of the daily diet of the islanders. After six hours' fishing 5 or 6 kilos of charales are caught on an average, but sometimes the owner returns home almost empty-handed.

The lake contains other species of fish of less economic value, such as tirus, chegua and choromu, which are found in abundant quantities, particularly in the Bay of Ihuatzio and in the neighbourhood of Jarácuaro. The smaller trawl net, the cherémikwa, is also used to catch these fish, but less charales (not more than 2 kilos after 7 or 8 hours' fishing).

Two species of fish have a higher economic value than any other fish: the so-called white fish, and bass. In Ihuatzio white fish is chiefly caught with the trawl net, or with a fishing rod, while bass is caught either with a fishing rod or simply with a line. The islanders eat hardly any white fish, as these fetch high prices in the market at Pátzcuaro.

Fishermen can claim no title to any part of the lake, but due regard is paid to the exclusive fishing rights that some people have in places rich in fish. People in lake shore villages also own a strip of water bordering their lands. This right is always acknowledged by others. Apart from that there is a general rule that the first man to cast his nets in a certain place has in fact a right to the place as long as he continues to fish there.

Many inhabitants of Ihuatzio have one or more canoes, but only a few people have canoes large enough to transport animals, chicken-food, or building materials such as adobe, or to collect tule and other articles. The owners of large canoes may rent them to other villagers.

It is very difficult to assess the economic significance of the fishing industry in Lake Pátzcuaro in general and in Ihuatzio in particular. Catches vary a good deal; monthly catches differ, while annual catches also show considerable differences. Moreover, luck and individual skill play an important part, as results obtained by individual fishermen vary a lot. Trade in fish is irregular, which makes it difficult to estimate the commercial value of the industry. Traders operate on the lake, preferring to buy charales and white fish direct from the fishers. The fish is sold in various markets in the interior. Several fishers sell direct to consumers, taking the fish to the market in Pátzcuaro, where prices vary according to the ancient law of supply and demand. During Lent prices rise sharply, soon to fall again, but they keep fluctuating throughout the year. The great demand for fish during Lent does a lot of harm to the fish resource in the lake, as it coincides with the period in which the fish lay eggs; consequently a large number of fish are eliminated before they have spawned (Solórzano, 1961; pp. 53-54). There is no doubt that something must be done about this situation; urgent measures are required to improve the basic livelihood of the fishers of the lake area.

A survey of catches from 1954 to 1958 made by the Pátzcuaro office concerned, though not complete, provides an overall idea of the fall in catches by registering the quantities of fish sent to other parts of the country.

The data by no means represent the total catches, as they do not include the fish sold in the markets of Pátzcuaro and Erongarícuaro. Yet they are in fair agreement with the data obtained from informants on Yunuén Island and in Ihuatzio, who told us that 1955 and 1956 were the last years of good catches.

Quantities in kilograms of fish from Lake Pátzcuaro sent to markets in the interior (cf. Solórzano, 1961; p. 60):

	1954	1955	1956	1957	1958
January	5.463	615	3.091	1.335	4.417
February	3.064	1.831	–	1.128	335
March	–	2.505	115	–	1.715
April	–	–	–	–	–
May	–	–	30	–	–
June	1.225	7.185	7.449	5.194	3.190
July	8.686	10.267	6.719	2.557	3.345
August	8.713	10.819	4.511	1.786	1.115
September	6.846	9.808	3.909	647	1.675
October	5.129	9.352	4.707	1.554	1.334
November	4.544	5.775	3.926	2.622	625
December	5.841	5.884	4.692	–	–
Total	49.541	64.041	39.149	17.843	17.751

the cultural-historical background of the Lake Tarascans

In this description of the cultural-historical background of the Lake Tarascans the author will confine himself to indicating and commenting on those documentary and traditional aspects which may promote a better understanding of the social organisation of the inhabitants of Ihuatzio today.

Records concerning the pre-Spanish history of Michoacán are rare. There exists only one great work of directly indigenous origin which aims at giving more or less complete information on the Tarascan state, namely the 'Relación de las Ceremonias y Ritos, Población y Gobierno de los Indios de la Provincia de Mechuacán' (Description of the Ceremonies and Rites, Population and Government of the Indians of the Province of Michuacán), now mostly called 'Relación de Michoacán' for short. This work was written around 1540 by a Spanish priest as a translation and perhaps a revision of Tarascan basic texts taken down from the lips of former Tarascan government officials and priests in Tzintzuntzan who had survived the Spanish conquest. The original work consisted of three parts dealing with the religion, history and administrative institutions of the Tarascan state respectively. Unfortunately the whole of the first part except one page is lost. Neither has any trace been found of the original Tarascan texts on which, according to the anonymous Spanish translator, the work was based. The Spanish translator and reviser must have been a person with a rare scientific mind, for nowhere in the parts of the work now known to us are there any moralizing comments on Tarascan institutions, such as are often noticed in the writings of Spanish priests of those days; even the great Sahagún could not refrain from making them in his standard work on the Aztecs. Evidently the 'Relación' is an objective and, as its author remarks, as exact a translation as possible of the information obtained in Tzintzuntzan. The texts on which the 'Relación' is based were, like the Relación itself, written shortly after the Spanish conquest. Unlike the Aztecs and other Mexican peoples the Tarascans evidently had no historiographers in pre-Spanish times. Probably they did develop and use some simple forms of registration to record tributes received, crops from their lands, spoils of tribal wars, the number of families in the village wards and other similar data, but real libraries with books on religion, the calendar, history and other fields of knowledge were most probably unknown to them. Apart from the controversial Codex Arantza[1], which is sometimes said to be of pre-Spanish origin, not a single document is known from the Tarascan territory that could claim to be a record of pre-Conquest Tarascan history.

In addition to the 'Relación de Michoacán' there are a few smaller historical documents of indigenous origin dealing with pre-Spanish times. Among them the 'Lienzo de Jucutacato' is especially interesting. Like many post-Conquest Aztec codices this document contains a combination of pictorial writing and accompanying texts written in Roman letters. A remarkable thing is that the texts in the 'Lienzo', which is a document coming from the heart of the Tarascan territory, should be in a Náhuatl dialect. The pictures and the texts deal with the migrations of one of the population groups of Michoacán during pre-Spanish times.[2] A comprehensive paper on this document was written at the beginning of this century by Eduard Seler.[3]

Interesting complements to the 'Relación de Michoacán' are to be found in the 'Relación de Tancítaro' of the year 1580, which describes conditions in the southern Sierra Tarasca.

Other historical writings, including archival documents, have only been of incidental importance in the preparation of this study, so that they need not be taken into consideration in this general discussion.

During the time immediately preceding the coming of the Spaniards the ancestors of those inhabitants of Michoacán who are now called Tarascans, formed the dominant group in a state extending over almost the whole modern state of Michoacán, as well as parts of the modern states of Guerrero, Guanajuato and Querétaro (see map 3). The Tarascan state was bounded to the east and south by the territory of the Aztecs or Mexi'ka', to the west by the Aztec-controlled regions of Zacatollan and Coliman and to the north by the Chichi-mecapan, the territory of the Chichimecs, then considered an uncivilized people, who were divided into many administrative units and tribal organi-sations. The territory controlled by the Tarascans was about 70.000 sq.km., which is a little more than twice the size of the Netherlands. From the data accumulated by Cook and Borah we may conclude that in 1520 this Tarascan state had at least one and a half or two million inhabitants.[4] If the estimate of Mendieta y Núñez, who assumes the number of pure Tarascans in 1520 to be 200.000 is correct, they would have formed scarcely ten per cent. of the total population of the empire dominated by them. Apart from the question of whether this percentage is correct or not, it is an undoubted fact that at the beginning of the 16th century there existed in Michoacán besides the Tarascans several other, ethnically different population groups. Without the places where there were Tarascan military garrisons and some isolated settlements of Tarascan officials and landowners in the conquered areas the range of the Tarascans was only about twice as large as it is today.

To the south and east of Pátzcuaro the areas inhabited by them extended a little further than the present limits; this is also the case north of a line from Xacona to Capula. In pre-Conquest times, however, this region of about 20.000 sq.km. was by no means exclusively inhabited by Tarascans. From the Relación de Tancítaro, the Villa Señor report[5] and other historical documents it appears that they lived there together with Nahuatlacas (Nawatlaka') and Tecos (Tekoecha). It is quite likely, however, that around 1520 the latter two groups were no more than important minority groups in the Tarascan nuclear area. The Relación de Michoacán also states that some villages in the centre of Michoacán had a population of 'nahuatlatos' (Náhuatl-speaking people).[6] Some Aztec sources contain a fairly detailed description of an episode from the early history of the country, when Tarascans and Mexitin lived together on the shores of Lake Pátzcuaro.[7] These sources as well as folk tales today suggest that in any case Tzintzuntzan – called Huitzitzillan (Witsitsillan) by the Aztecs – and probably also Ihuatzio, which in the Relación de Michoacán is indicated by the Aztec name of Coyuacan (Koyuwâkan), were originally inhabited by Náhuatl-speaking people. Furthermore the Lienzo de Jucutacato points to Toltec influences in the Uruapan and Lake Pátzcuaro areas. Archaeological finds also point to Central Mexican influences.

MAP 2   THE MODERN TARASCAN AREA

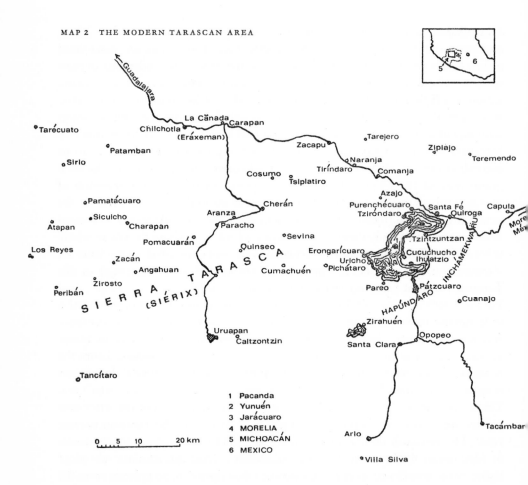

1 Pacanda
2 Yunuén
3 Jarácuaro
4 MORELIA
5 MICHOACÁN
6 MEXICO

0   5   10   20 km

Outside the Tarascan nuclear area, shown in map 2, there were only small
isolated Tarascan settlements, consisting of military garrisons, groups of
government officials and some Wakúxecha landowners and their families. The
few Tarascans in these settlements dominated several, sometimes locally
important, population groups: in the east the Matlatzincas and Otomíes, in
the north Otomíes and Chichimec tribes, in the west the mysterious Tekos,
Wetamas and other Chichimec or unidentifiable tribes, and in the south

Nawatlakas, Kwitlatekas, Eskamoecha, a tribe only mentioned in the Relación, and other small now extinct groups.[8] All these different ethnic groupings, which already belonged to one state before the arrival of the Spaniards, and were thus members of the same political-administrative and religious organisation, must no doubt have influenced each other in many ways.

It is very important at this stage to go more deeply into the developments which took place in the Lake Pátzcuaro area, where at the end of the 13th century the struggle for power began, which was eventually to result in the formation of the Tarascan state. In those days the area showed the following ethnic panaroma: On the islands in the lake, and probably also in some places on the southern and western shores, lived the descendants of 'Chichimec' tribes which had settled there a long time before. These people had largely been assimilated by and mixed with a more indigenous population probably speaking a Tarascan or Proto-Tarascan dialect, which was also adopted by the first immigrant Chichimecs. Very little is known about this original indigenous population, apart from the fact of their existence. Therefore the origin of the Tarascan tongue also remains a mystery. Attempts have been made by means of comparative linguistic studies to establish a southern as well as a northern origin of the autochthonic Tarascan-speaking population.[9] It is possible to assume that both southern and northern influences have been at work in Michoacán, but this does not permit us to draw definite conclusions as to their relative significance.

The dominant people on the eastern shore and in the south in those days were Náhuatl-speaking folk of possibly Toltec, i.e. Central and East Mexican origin. In the western mountainous area, too, there lived Náhuatl-speaking population groups, which had settled there together with Tekos, Chichimecs and more indigenous groupings. It is not known to what extent the Chichimecs formed an ethnic entity; probably the word is a collective name for various semi-nomadic and sedentary groups not belonging to the more highly developed cultures or assimilated by them only to a very limited extent. Considerable linguistic differences may have existed within the Chichimec group. According to Ixtlilxochitl the word 'Chichimeka' in the language of this 'nation' means eagles.[10] This is interesting because the Relación tells us that before the 13th century the members of a population group in the Tsacapu (Tsakapu) area, in the north of Central Michoacán, sometimes called themselves 'Chichimecas' and sometimes 'Wakúxecha'. It is interesting to know that in Tarascan the word wakux (plural: wakúxecha) means 'eagle'.

The following is a brief history of the tribe of the Wakúxecha as it is told in the Relación.

The Wakúxecha were divided into three groups:

1   the Wanakase, to whom belonged the lords of the tribe;
2   the Tsakapu-hireti, i.e. the people of Tsakapu;
3   the Eneani.

The Wakúxecha worshipped as their own special god Tirípeme-Kurikaweri, whose image they took with them on their war-expeditions and migrations. This god was apparently associated with the sun and with fire. Offerings of firewood were constantly brought to him and also deer-offerings, which were later replaced by human sacrifices. The Wakúxecha possessed qualities typical of a semi-nomadic Chichimec tribe, whose means of subsistence were hunting, collecting edible wild plants and incidentally agriculture. As they demanded excessive hunting rights in connection with their deer-offerings, they came into conflict with other, more acculturated Chichimec groups in the Tsacapu area. Consequently they were forced to migrate to Wayameo (now Santa Fé de la Laguna) on the northern shore of Lake Pátzcuaro. Here they came into contact with the Nahuatlacan inhabitants of Tzintzuntzan (or Witsitsillan), from whom they adopted the Xarátanga cult. Henceforth Xarátanga, the goddess of the moon, became the most important Tarascan deity next to Kurikaweri. In Wayameo the Wakúxecha, who still spoke a Chichimec dialect, divided into five different groups. According to the Relación de Michoacán four of these groups, each with its own god and its own ruler, established themselves successively in Kuríngwaro-achurin, Pichátaro, Irámuko and Pareo, that is to the southeast, west, east and south of the lake. Their gods were called 'the brothers of Kurikaweri'. This meant the almost complete disappearance of these groups from the 'official historical declaration', which was made at stated intervals by the Petámuti, the supreme high priest, in a long public speech and is found in the Relación de Michoacán. Henceforth the Relación only mentions the adventures, of the fifth group, which at first maintained its position in Wayameo, but was afterwards forced to migrate along the western lakeshore to Erongarícuaro. Here its members came into contact with the inhabitants of the island of Xarákwaro, who were said to speak a Chichimec dialect understood by them.

The lords of the Wakúxecha, the Wanakase, married important women of Xarákwaro, and acted as priests on the island. Of one of these marriages was born the first great Tarascan ruler, Taríakuri. Soon, however, the Wakúxecha began to quarrel with the inhabitants of Xarákwaro, which resulted in the expulsion of the former, who found safety on the southern lakeshore. The Relación contains an official statement saying that on this spot the Wakúxecha founded Pátzcuaro (Pátskwaro) around 1325. This 'foundation' should probably be understood as the establishment of one or more new village-wards attached to an existing village, some of the residents of which were Náhuatl-speaking people.[11] There the god of the underworld (the realm of the dead) presented the Wakúxecha with foundations for the temples of their principal gods. "It is true, our Gods say that this is called Tsakapu-Amúkutin-Pátskwaro ... and Kwiris-kwátaro in the higher part and Tarepu-uta-hopánskwaro in the lower part ... behold this stone should be called Sirita-cherengwe and this one Wakúsecha (perhaps Wakús-Acha, i.e. Lord of the Eagles), that is his elder brother, and this one Tingárata and this Miekwa-axewa. For behold, these gods are four in number".[12]

This at first sight slightly enigmatic passage is hardly commented upon in the Relación. Yet this enumeration of localities within the limits of Pátzcuaro, and similar statements in other indigenous Mexican sources, are likely to have been purposely inserted in the text and to be very significant. The 16th-century Tarascans probably completely understood the text. As the social organisation of the pre-Spanish Tarascans, especially as regards its structural principles, closely resembles that of the Aztecs, a comparison of the above passage with Aztec sources may supply a means of correct interpretation. It appears that the Aztec texts relating to the divisions and social organisation of the tribe of the Asteka'-Mexitin in Aztlan indeed suggest a plausible explanation of the passage concerning Pátzcuaro.

Aztlan consisted of two parts: the four calpollis (village-wards) of the Asteka', situated on an island, and the three calpollis of the Mexitin, situated on the southern shore of the water that surrounded the island. At first the group of four units ranked higher than that of three units. This difference in status corresponded with the ethnic difference between Toltecs (the four Aztec calpollis) and Chichimecs (the three calpollis of the Mexitin). There also existed differences in social functions between the two groupings. The three

Chichimec calpollis were mainly concerned with priestly and military, i.e. predominantly external, duties, the four Toltec calpollis with predominantly internal, administrative functions.[13]

This division of Aztlan suggests the following analogous division of Pátzcuaro: (The four sacred places found in Pátzcuaro and mentioned last in the relevant text of the Relación are known to have been in the higher part of the town, where the Basílica of Pátzcuaro stands today.)

I	KWIRISKWATARO (the higher part)	1	Sirita-cherengwe
		2	Wakúsecha (or Wakus-Acha)
		3	Tingárata
		4	Miekwa-axewa
II	TAREPUUTA-HOPANSKWARO (the lower part)	5	Tsakapu
		6	Amúkutin
		7	Pátskwaro

A striking fact is that of the above-mentioned seven parts of Pátzcuaro only one bore the name of 'Wakúxecha', while the name of the seventh group was given to the whole town. What actually happened after the expulsion of the Wakúxecha from Xarákwaro was probably that they took refuge with existing groups in Pátzcuaro, of which at least one was Náhuatl-speaking and therefore ethnically different. Many examples can be found in Mexican history of ethnically different groups combining to form one single village organisation.[14] Afterwards, when they had become powerful, this association of the Wakúxecha with the inhabitants of Pátzcuaro was represented in their 'official interpretation' of historic events as the 'foundation of Pátzcuaro'. Like the Aztec story of the foundation of Mexico-Tenochtitlan, this should not be taken too literally.

"In Pátzcuaro was the gate of heaven, through which the Gods descended and ascended. There were three temples and three fireplaces with three priests' houses".[15] This connection between tripartition and religious organisation was also found among the Asteka'-Mexitin. In Aztlan the three Chichimec units, which started with a distinctly lower status than the other four units, soon assumed the principal priestly offices.[16] A similar situation apparently existed in Michoacán, where the Wakúxecha were divided into three groups, and already performed priestly functions on Xarákwaro Island, when their status was still lower than that of the islanders. Therefore the Relación de Michoacán always mentions three priests as counsellors of the ruler.[17]

After their settlement in Pátzcuaro the Wakúxecha were forced by the Chichimecs of Kuríngwaro, a related tribe, to wage a ceremonial war ('war of flowers') against them. The ceremonial and restricted 'war of flowers' was alternated and sometimes accompanied with total ordinary wars against the islanders and against the Nahuatlacan rulers of Taríaran. The chief of the Wakúxecha, Taríakuri, who was born on Xarákwaro, fought with varying success. He succeeded in defeating the islanders and the ruler of Taríaran, but when afterwards he invited his cousins of an older lineage (FaBrSo), Sétako and Aramen, to eat from the maize in the storehouses of Kurikaweri, i.e. when he tried to persuade them to admit their dependence, they fled and settled outside the territory ruled by him. This weakened his position, and now Chánshori, the ruler of Kuríngwaro, in his turn tried to make him eat from the maize of his god Urendekwawékara, thus forcing Taríakuri himself to flee. With his followers he left Pátzcuaro, but managed temporarily to improve his position by marrying a daughter of Chánshori. Of this marriage was born Kurátame. Meanwhile at least five genuine Wakúxecha families[19] had come into conflict with Taríakuri, while afterwards he had also great trouble with his wife and their son Kurátame. She continued to be a political tool in the hands of her father while Kurátame, with the help of his grandfather, became ruler of Pátzcuaro. Nevertheless Taríakuri returned to the Pátzcuaro area, where after an initial period of ill luck he acquired great influence again.

In reading about all these deeds, which the Relación attributes to Taríakuri, we should bear in mind that his historicity is ambiguous. The picture is largely that of a legendary tribal chief, and events may have been attributed to him which in reality took place under more than one member of the dynasty. Moreover the Relación shows the setbacks of the dynasty in a special light. While the facts lead to the conclusion that until that time the chief of the Wakúxecha had been little more than a village-ward chief, who had repeatedly been deposed, the Relación always represents him as a great ruler.

Taríakuri retired to one of the wards of Pátzcuaro called Kutu and continued to intrigue against his son Kurátame. For instance, he tried to excel Kurátame by organizing a greater feast than the latter. Under the pressure of circumstances Taríakuri was forced to try and restore the unity of the Wakúxecha, which he achieved by appointing the sons of Sétako and Aramen, Hiripan and Tangax'wan respectively, and his own son Hikíngare, a half-brother of Kurátame, as governors. The Relación de Michoacán on that occasion ascribes to Taríakuri the following words: "You, Gentlemen, will be three rulers. Hiripan will rule over one part and Tanga'xwan over another, and my youngest son Hikíngare over a third part (And in those days Hikíngare was a priest in charge of sacrificial ceremonies)".[20] Now it becomes clear that the territory of the Wakúxecha had been divided into three parts, each with a ruler of its own. This marks the beginning of the great expansion of the Wakúxecha, and again it is remarkable to notice in Aztec historical documents that the beginning of the expansion of the Mexi'ka' is also marked by a tripartite division of the state. Taríakuri gave the three new lords a knife made of obsidian, which formed part of the god Kurikaweri. They took the knife 'across the water', that is to Ihuatzio (Hiwatsio) and "start building a temple and a priests' house and the house that is called 'the eagle's house' and for the knife that Taríakuri had given them they built a maize storehouse".[21] When Taríakuri heard that they had thus created a completely new religious centre he was furious, knowing that it had to be consecrated with human sacrifices and fearing an untimely conflict with the neighbouring tribes. Then Taríakuri drew the little island of Pakándani into a 'war of flowers', thus retrieving the difficult situation. Sixty persons were taken captive, forty of whom were sacrificed in Pátzcuaro. The temple in Ihuatzio was consecrated with the twenty other human sacrifices from Pakándani, and this temple, called Kerétaro, became the temporary abode of Hikíngare, the priest in charge of sacrificial ceremonies. Hiripan settled in a village-ward called Hiwatsi-harata and stationed his warriors at Siwango. At the same time Tanga'xwan settled in the village-ward of Hiwatsi-xanthakuyo. Apparently Ihuatzio was then already divided into two territorial parts; one chief of Hiwatsio, or Ihuatzio, ruled in the part called Hiwatsi-harata (hole, pit, or grave of the wolf), the other ruled in Hiwatsi-xanthakuyo(?), while the religious leader governed the ceremonial centre.

Shortly afterwards Tanga'xwan, at a feast, kills Kurátame, whom he had invited himself, after which Taríakuri became ruler of Pátzcuaro again. From the above-mentioned division of human sacrifices from Pakándani between

Name:

Address:

Country:

Will you please indicate in which subjects you are interested, by placing a cross in the appropriate square?

We shall then keep you informed of our latest publications in those fields.

☐ Sociology
☐ Medical subjects
☐ History
☐ Language and Literature
☐ Religion
☐ Philosophy
☐ Economics
☐ Mathematics
☐ Psychology
....
☐

☐ Criminology
☐ Psychiatry
☐ Politics
☐ Natural Science
☐ History of Law
☐ Genealogy
☐ Geology
☐ Veterinary Science
☐ School Publications
....
☐

How was your attention drawn to this book?

By means of:

☐ Review in: ....

☐ Bookshop: ....

☐ Radio programme of: ....

☐ Prospectus: ....

☐ Advertisement in: ....

☐ ....

ROYAL VANGORCUM LTD.
NETHERLANDS

ROYAL VANGORCUM LTD.
INDUSTRIEWEG 38
ASSEN
NETHERLANDS

Petatero (tule weaver), returning home from cutting tules in the mud flats of Chalpultepec.

Tules drying in the sun before the Katáhperakwaro.

Pátzcuaro and Ihuatzio, and from other passages in the Relación de Michoacán it appears that at the beginning of the Tarascan expansion Taríakuri, and Pátzcuaro with him, still held the most important leading functions. Yet even then Taríakuri was already in a critical position, as five of the six most important Chichimec 'Principales' of Hiripan and Tanga'xwan were the chiefs of the five Wakúxecha families who formerly rebelled against him. At that time Hiripan also succeeded in winning the support of at least some of the inhabitants of the islands, which appears from the following list of "Principals and braves of Hiripan and Tanga'xwan":[22]

Chichimecs:

1	Kwetse	
2	Katsimato	
3	Kiriki	(the first five men had been
4	Kwakángari	enemies of Taríakuri)
5	Angwasikwa	
6	Kupawaxansí	

Islanders:

7	Sapiwátame	
8	Tsangwata	(these four names probably
9	Chapata	indicate only two persons;
10	Atache-húkane	cf. p. 59).

After that time the inhabitants of the islands began to play an important part in the empire of the Wakúxecha, forming a kind of second estate in it. And it is from this time, in which the Tarascan dialect of the islands must have become the official language in the state, that this state can be justly called a Tarascan one.

When Taríakuri created three administrative centres in this Tarascan state he was evidently still its supreme ruler: "Therefore, Hiripan, there must be three governors. You will stay on this mountain, which lies in the middle, that is in the village of Kuy(uw)akan (i.e. Ihuatzio), and you Tanga'xwan will stay on this mountain, which is the village of Michwakan (i.e. Tzintzuntzan), and you Hikíngare will stay on this mountain, that is the village of Pátskwaro. Thus there will be three rulers".[23]

MAP 3   THE STATE OF MICHHUACAN IN 1520

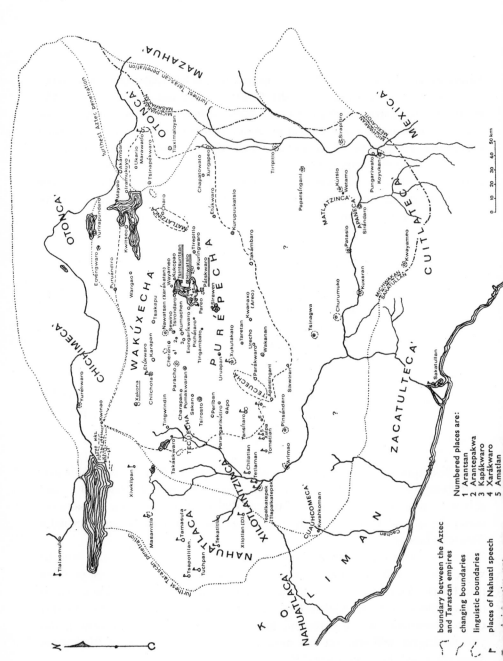

Now government in three parts had become a fact, and Pátzcuaro was still the most important administrative centre. Soon Taríaran was conquered, followed by a sacrificial offering of 400 persons, among whom was the ruler of that state, Híwacha. About this time Taríakuri died, whereupon Hiripan assumed the supreme leadership. Then it was Ihuatzio which became the most important of the three capital towns. Here were built the treasury store-houses of the state and here fields were cultivated on behalf of human sacrifices and their keepers. Soon afterwards the Tarascan high lands were conquered as also were the 'Tierra Caliente', the tropical lowlands of Michoacán to the south. The spoils of war and the considerable tributes received from the conquered territories made the Wakúxecha and the islanders more prosperous. Soon territorial expansion also took place to the north as far as the southern shore of Lake Chapala and the neighbourhood of the town of Querétaro (see map 3). Just as in the Aztec empire, the newly-conquered regions were divided into different administrative units; some were placed under war-chiefs from the islands and the rest under Wakúxecha chiefs. Sometimes Wakúxecha women were given a chieftainship. Territories under direct Wakúxecha control were divided between Ihuatzio, Pátzcuaro and Tzintzuntzan, so that each of the three administrative centres would have tributaries of their own. As was often done in the Aztec empire, here, too, some conquered territories may have been placed under joint control, the tributes being divided between two or more administrative centres according to certain rules, which need not always be the same in each case. It is likely that the indigenous rulers often retained their office as vassals of the conquerors; one cannot resist the impression, however, that the Tarascan regime was apt to be more centralizing than the Aztec system of government; this was as a matter of fact facilitated by the circumstance that its territory was much smaller and more concentrated. Furthermore it should be noted that the two systems of government had developed in entirely different ways, which is another explanation for the centralizing tendencies in the Tarascan state. Unlike the Aztec tripartite system of government, which could always function in peace notwithstanding the rivalry between the three parts, the Tarascan threefold throne witnessed from the first violent internal conflicts. When Hikíngare died, Hiripan ordered the former's sons to be killed,[24] so that there were no descendants of Taríakuri in the male line eligible for succession to the throne. This no doubt caused Pátzcuaro to lose much of its prestige, because henceforth it was ruled by war-lords or by men belonging to the lesser nobility. Thus Ihuatzio became the undisputed main capital and 'Kurikaweri's knife' was henceforth looked upon as the official representation of the tribal god. But Ihuatzio soon had to give up its powerful position. After the death of Hiripan his son Tikátame succeeded him, but his power was soon eclipsed by that of his second cousin TsʌtsʌspandáKware, son and successor to Tanga'xwan I of Tzintzuntzan. Tikátame retained his throne, but Kurikaweri's knife, "that stone which was said to be Kurikaweri himself" was removed to Tzintzuntzan together with the State treasures;[25] the assumption of power by the rulers of Tzintzuntzan was a fact. It is likely that the conflicts between the three capital towns made it impossible for the Tarascans to have within their state ritual wars of the same type as the Aztecs fought against Tlaxcallan, Huexotzinco, Cholullan and other towns. Kuríngwaro's government, which consisted of seven chiefs and at first fought ritual wars against Pátzcuaro, was destroyed by the Tarascans after they had accomplished the major part of their expansion.

Like the Aztec empire, the Tarascan state was divided into seven administrative units, three supreme central capital towns and four provinces each with a governor of its own. The original septempartition of the Aztlan type as it was found in Pátzcuaro seemed to have been turned inside out; the three units which in the original system were external appendages now held central positions. In the Tarascan state this was especially emphasized by the fact that the rulers of the four provinces were referred to as 'princes of the state boundaries', 'they who ruled at the four boundaries', etc.[26] These boundary princes were related to the Kasonsí,[27] the highest state functionary, whose position was similar to that of the Huey Tla'toani (Weyi Tla'toani) of the Aztec empire. The Kasonsí was always the most important of the three principal rulers; or rather ruler of the most important of the three administrative centres. During the Spanish conquest the Kasonsí was therefore ruler of Tzintzuntzan as well as the highest government official in the whole state. Six or seven decades before, however, it had been the ruler of Ihuatzio who occupied the highest office.

Unfortunately the scarcity of historical data makes it impossible to give an exact and detailed survey of the Tarascan system of government. As a matter of fact, the Relación de Michoacán leaves some important questions unanswered. It is certain that the seven above mentioned administrative units had seven different functionaries; these were in successive order of importance:

1   The Kasonsí, also called Kwangwa-pagwa (Brave chief) or Acha Irecha (Supreme prince); he was the chief of the Wakúxecha, and as such he was the highest person in rank in the empire. He arranged the external relations, he decided matters of war and peace, and was considered to be the representative on earth of the tribal god Kurikaweri. He was the supreme judge, although not all kinds of offences were submitted to him. He was ruler of the most important of the three administrative centres, the town where the main ceremonial centre was established, i.e. the main temple of Kurikaweri. Probably he was primarily at the same time the chief lord of the Wanakase, who where said to be the most important of the three groups into which the Wakúxecha were subdivided.

2   The rulers of the two other administrative centres. They bore the title of Irecha. We do not know if they were equal in rank; some passages in the Relación de Michoacán suggest that, when Tzintzuntzan had overshadowed the other capital towns, Ihuatzio became second in rank above Pátzcuaro.[28] It is quite possible, however, that Ihuatzio ranked higher than Pátzcuaro on certain occasions only, while in other situations their mutual relations were the reverse.

3   The four boundary princes with perhaps the title of Kamachakúhpeti.[29] The seat of only one of them is known with certainty. For, during the preparatory war ceremony it was the prince of Xakona, 'who ruled over one of the boundary provinces', who was the first to make a speech.[30] It may be that this prince of Xakona ranked a little higher than his three colleagues, because he ruled over the most original territory of the Wakúxecha within the state. Where his three colleagues lived is a guess, as there are no records mentioning their seats. Wakanan, Kurupuukatsio and Tsinapékwaro or Tlaximaloyan, however, are the most likely places to have been the three other 'boundary capitals'.

It is not quite clear whether the boundary princes were lords over the lower chiefs in each of the four provinces of the state, or only held the position of primus inter pares. As relatives of the Kasonsí they had of course a higher status, but no further conclusions can be made on this ground only. In any case the local chiefs (Karachakapacha) were not appointed by the boundary princes, but directly by the Kasonsí.[31]

From the foregoing it is clear that we know one functionary in each of the seven administrative units. We do not know, however, whether or not there were other leading administrative functionaries in the seven units. For the Relación mentions other high functionaries in the Tarascan state without any reference to their positions in these units. As second in rank after the Kasonsí, for instance, is mentioned the Angatákuri, which title is translated in the Spanish text as 'gobernador' (governor). His position and office seem to resemble that of the Mexican Cihuacoatl (Siwakóatl, i.e. 'Female Escort'), the second highest administrative functionary in the Aztec Empire.

Ranking equal with the Angatákuri was the supreme commander of the army. The Relación de Michoacán only mentions the Spanish title of 'Capitán General'; his indigenous title may have been Angawatángari or Urerukútsperi.[32] In the Tarascan state the offices of Angatákuri and supreme commander of the army were sometimes united in one person.[33] In the history of the Aztec empire the combination of the offices of Cihuacoatl and supreme commander occurred only once, in the case of Tlacayelel I. At the time of the Spanish conquest the office of supreme commander of the Tarascan army was held by Kwinierángari, whom the Spaniards, with whom he collaborated, called 'Don Pedro'. He was a descendant in the male line of the chiefs of the islanders who had joined the Wakúxecha during the rule of Hiripan of Ihuatzio. It is possible that when the islanders joined the regime of the Wakúxecha they were rewarded with the right to this high office in the new constitution of the state. The question arises whether the islanders formed a separate administrative unit or held a special position in one or more of the seven administrative units mentioned above. This question is partly answered by the opening words of one of the ceremonial speeches given in the Relación de Michoacán, where the High Priest says: "You, Chichimecs, you who are called Eneani and Tsakapu-ireti and (relatives) of the rulers, Wanakase, who as Chichimecs are not established in one single place – on the contrary, everywhere it is the Chichimecs who are found on the roads of this empire, working in behalf of Kurikaweri – listen to what I have to say to you: you, who pretend to be people of Michwakan (Tzintzuntzan), are not you 'visitors' (Purépecha!)? Where are more Chichimecs to come from? They all left their homes to conquer the border territories and therefore (compared with this) you are 'visitors' (parvenus); partly you belong to Tangachurani (a god of the islanders), you who pretend to be people of Michwakan, and (furthermore) you belong to the conquered peoples . . . . Oh you, lower people of Michwakan, now you are all Noble Ladies and Gentlemen, and your seats and thrones are carried after you and you all believe yourselves to be rulers, even those of you whose duty it is to count the inhabitants, the officials called Okámbecha".[34]

The Spanish translation that has been preserved of this originally Tarascan text evidently uses the word 'advenedizos' (those who have come from outside, parvenus) as a translation of the Tarascan word 'purépecha'. Even today this word is still used by the Tarascan-speaking population to refer to their own ethnic entity; a Tarascan will always prefer to call himself and other Tarascans purépecha instead of 'tarascos'. Asked about the literal meaning of the word purépecha, informants in Ihuatzio and Yunuén unanimously translated it as 'visitadores', 'los que visitan' (visitors). The Aztecs translated the word purépecha with their term macehualtin (masewaltin), by which in their own society were meant those members of the calpultin (ward communities) who are not of noble birth. It is interesting to see that the foregoing text clearly states the fact that the Wakúxecha continue to consider the purépecha as a lower class with a decidedly lower status than that of their own group, although together they dominated the peoples and tribes subjugated by them. The purépecha are reminded of the fact that they were originally a subject people, too, and that they had become 'Noble Ladies and Gentlemen' thanks only to the military achievements of the Wakúxecha. Evidently the purépecha were all the non-Wakúxecha members of the Tarascan people, that is of the nuclear population group of the state of Michoacán. It was the purépecha who best endured the Spanish conquest; therefore the word has survived to the present day. Several authors[35] have tried to explain the word 'purépecha' in the sense of 'visitors' on the ground of the foreign origin of the Tarascan rulers, who are thus said to have come to Michoacán as 'visitors'. Apart from the fact that conquerors are not likely to call themselves 'visitors', we have seen that as a matter of fact this word was not used to refer to the Chichimec rulers, who came last, but to the islanders and Mountain Tarascans, who had settled in Michoacán before the Wakúxecha. As the Tarascan regime is known to have demanded of the subordinate chiefs that they should visit the palace in Tzint-

zuntzan at stated intervals,[36] it seems to be more plausible to regard this fact
as the origin of the use of 'visitors' in the above speech.

In connection with the duty of the village chiefs and other functionaries to
visit the palace at regular intervals and to stay there for some time it seems
justifiable to presume that, just as in the Aztec empire,[37] many administrative
units had two supreme functionaries, one who remained in the village or in the
province, and another who stayed at the court most of the time. This would
reflect, at a lower level, the supreme government of the whole state, consisting
as we have seen, of the Kasonsí and the Angatákuri together.

The palace of the Kasonsí was also visited by another group of male dignitaries,
who bore the title of Acha (plural: Achaecha). They were the 'Principales',[38]
noblemen directly responsible to the Kasonsí. The supreme keeper of the
treasury and head of the tributary system was the Chuperipátsari, who was
also directly responsible to the Kasonsí. He was at the same time head of the
Okámbecha, a kind of ward chiefs. This information is found in one of the
many passages in the Relación de Michoacán where the absence of the original
Tarascan text is a great drawback. The Spaniards used the word 'barrio'
(city or village ward) to indicate a number of entirely different indigenous
units of organisation. When the Spanish text, speaking about the Okámbecha
(singular Okámbeti), says that 'each of these (functionaries) was in charge of a
barrio',[39] we do not know whether they governed village wards, i.e. real
territorial units into which village communities were divided, or subdivisions
of such units. There is a passage, however, telling us that during the reign of
Don Pedro Kwinierángari, who collaborated with the Spaniards and was
appointed 'Governor' by them, the Okámbecha were in charge of the fiscal
administration of 25 houses.[40] This justifies the supposition that they were
chiefs of the subdivisions of the wards, the smallest administrative units in the
state. So they may be considered as the equivalent of the Aztec Centecpanpix-
que' (Sentekpanpixke'),[41] the more so as they also had the task of enumerating
the people and assembling them to carry out public works.[42] As a reward for
their work the Okámbecha received their robes of office and firewood, while a
small piece of land was cultivated on their behalf.[43]

So far some points of resemblance between Tarascan and Aztec forms of
organisation and offices have been dealt with, but there were also differences.
Now that we know the Okámbeti to be the equivalent of the Centecpanpixqui,

the question arises what is the Tarascan equivalent of the Calpullec, the chief of a ward or comparable social unit in the Aztec state. Is it the Karachakapati? This does not seem likely; it is more plausible to regard the Karachakapacha as chiefs of entire village communities, because they, the 'chiefs who were appointed in the villages', are mentioned immediately after the four boundary princes. The theoretical possibility that the Tarascan regime was the only one in the region of Mexican culture to do away with the office of village chief seems highly improbable. Moreover it is sufficiently known that this office did exist in Michoacán. Kurátame of Pátzcuaro, the village chief of Pacándani and many other village chiefs are mentioned in the Relación de Michoacán. But which office-holders could be compared with the Aztec Calpullequê? This is one of the fundamental problems in Tarascan ethno-history. In the first place it should be observed that none of the sources contains an indication that the Tarascans knew anything like the calpulli of the Aztec state. The Aztec calpulli is a territorial unit inhabited by a group of people having the same calpulco (local temple) as their ceremonial centre and possessing land in communal ownership.[44] The calpulli has been particularly described for its territorial aspects, for instance with regard to the management of landed property. Now, according to an emphatic statement made by Zurita, the situation in Michoacán differs in this respect from that in the Aztec state: "Michoacán had a tradition different from that in Mexico and its provinces, because everybody, chiefs as well as agricultural workers, possesses land in private ownership, and there are also communal lands which they cultivate for their ruler and communal lands cultivated for the lower chiefs and for the temples".[45] The head of the calpulli allocated to the Aztec 'free farmers' (macehualtin) a piece of land, a part of the collective calpulli grounds, to provide food for themselves and for dependent relatives; but they were not the owners of those allotments. Evidently the purépecha, the ordinary subjects in the Tarascan state, owned their lands and there was no equivalent of the Aztec calpullali (i.e. calpulli-land). Probably the Tarascans had communal village grounds too, for these still exist today. Just as in the Aztec state they will mainly have consisted of forests and waste land. Further the Tarascans also had land belonging to the state or to a temple; these were cultivated by compulsory service. Tarascan village communities were also subdivided into smaller social and territorial units. The smallest subdivision was one governed by an Okámbeti. A unit between the village community as a whole and these smallest units was the village-ward.

The function of the Aztec calpulli and its chief as a body regulating the use of land was a very important one and since the Tarascan wards lacked this function they are not comparable with the calpulli in all respects. Among the Tarascans the organisation of occupational groups was much more important than among the Aztecs. Furthermore the Tarascan wards had a marriage-regulating function, which most of the Aztec calpullis had not. The Tarascan wards were endogamous[46] and occupations (ambekwárekwa) were hereditary, descending from father to son.[47] So an occupational group was at the same time one lineage or a combination of lineages, and the members of one occupational group evidently lived in the same ward.[48] The heads of the occupational groups may have been ward chiefs at the same time, which might account for the fact that ward chiefs are not mentioned separately. The Relación de Michoacán gives the following list of heads of occupational groups at the court of the Kasonsí:[49]

1 Kwahta-uri or Wekskuti, head of the more than 2.000 house-builders and the 1.000 temple-builders in Tzintzuntzan.
2 Kakari, head of the kakacha, the masons.
3 Kwaníkoti (i.e. archer), head of the Kwanikocha, the hunters and makers of bows and arrows (kwanikokwaucha).
4 Kuru-hapindi, head of the bird-hunters.
5 Waruri (i.e. fisherman), head of the men fishing with nets.
6 Tarama (i.e. he or she who puts a stick into the water), head of the anglers.
7 Ehpuspati or Kwipuakuri, head of the honey-collectors, beekeepers as well as makers of maize honey.
8 Atari, head of the makers of pulque (pulque is agave wine).
9 Kutusuri, head of the tanners (kutsucha).
10 Uskwarekuri, Uskwarekwa-uri, head of the feather-mosaic workers (uskwarekucha).
11 Pukurikwari, head of the foresters and gamekeepers (pukurikwacha).
12 Kwirínguri (i.e. owner of a wooden drum) head of the drum-makers.
13 Tekari, head of the carpenters (tekacha).
14 Cherénguekwa-uri, head of the makers of cotton warshirts. This occupational group also had 'principales', noblemen, among its members.

15 Icháruta-wandari (i.e. ruler of boats), head of the boat-builders.

16 Xuríhkakaheri or Tsʌnapeti, head of the healers or curers.

17 Urani-atari (i.e. decorator of cups), head of the painters of cups.

18 Xunicha, deputy head of the painters (karacha).

19 Hukátsikwa-uri, head of the makers of vessels of food (bowls, plates, etc.).

20 Tsʌtsʌkikanakwa-uri, head of the weavers of flower-chains.

21 Mayapeti, head of the merchants (mayapecha), particularly traders in gold, feathers and precious stones.

22 Kwatas-uri, head of the makers of trunks and the tule-weavers.

23 Akawekwa-uri, head of the sandal-makers.

24 Kwinguingata-uri or tayakata punitati, head of the silversmiths.

25 Tsinahpu-uri, head of the makers of obsidian knives.

The two drawings accompanying the texts in question in the Relación de Michoacán give three more occupational groups of which the texts give no further indication, so there were twenty-eight occupational groups in all in the capital city. Of course, these groups were not equally large; the builders' group, which was probably the largest, was the only one said to have had more than 3.000 members. We may assume that for instance the group of the curers was a much smaller one, as were those of the drum-makers, decorators of cups and weavers of flower-chains. Therefore many wards probably contained more than one occupational group. It is not easy to form a clear picture of the whole social significance of these occupational groups in the pre-Spanish Tarascan society. Did they resemble castes, or European medieval guilds? Or were they less closed groups, and could one and the same person belong to various occupational groups, which would mean that 'occupations' were not full-time jobs? Now we should be careful not to make false comparisons. The Tarascans themselves have given a list of the heads of occupational groups, interspersed with functionaries who are not, or perhaps not directly, connected with occupational groups:

1 Tareta-waxáteti (he or she who keeps the people in the fields), i.e. the overseer of compulsory labour on the State lands.

2 Pirúwakwa-wándari (ruler of threads), the supervisor and keeper of the state supply of blankets (a means of barter) and of the seats of functionaries.

3 Kawáspati (manager of pepper), the overseer of the State production of pepper, huauhtli (a cultivated amaranth)[50] and beans.

4   Kwaníkokwa-uri, head of the production of bows and arrows for use in war; these were made daily in the capital. He was also head of the arsenals.

5   Waxanoti, head of the messengers and runners in charge of the intelligence service (waxanocha).

6   Atápukwa-kwatari, head of the shield-makers and deputy head of the shield arsenals.

7   Kengue, keeper of the maize storehouses of the Kasonsí and of the regular supply of maize.

8   Erongkarikwa-wándari, head of the war-spies.

9   Ankskúkwapari, the chief ensign, keeper of the banners and head of the standard-bearers.

10   Wakuxeránguti, the keeper of the eagles, keeper of the birds of the Kasonsí

11   Ahpenstieránguti, the attendant of the wild animals of the Kasonsí.

12   Kahratati, kahrakasri, head of the cleaning staff in the palace.

13   Kwángariecha, the 'braves', the noble warriors at court, serving as body-guard of the Kasonsí. It is not clear if they were the same men as the Achaecha.

"All these offices were hereditary; when a functionary had died a son or a brother took his place and was appointed by the Kasonsí".[51]

Another important group of dignitaries was that of the priests. Among them the following offices can be distinguished:

I   *General ranks of priesthood:*

1   Petámuti, the Supreme High Priest, head of all the other priests. Unlike the Aztec high priests the Petámuti also had an important judiciary function. The Petámuti appears to have had a colleague, equal in rank, who resided outside the capital.[52] His title is not mentioned. This is another example of dual organisation, which was also a common phenomenon in Aztec society. Tarascan law, as well as the administration of justice could hardly be called refined or highly developed. According to the Relación lesser offences were punished by humiliating the offender in public, but a repetition of the same offence was followed by capital punishment or slavery, as were major offences.

2   The Kuritiecha, "they went into the country to order firewood (for the temple fires) to be collected. . . . Every temple had

3 (the Teruhtsikuri?), a high priest, appointed, like a bishop, to have authority over the other priests."[53]

4 the Kuracha "all lower priests were called kura, that is 'grandfather' and all were married men and their office was hereditary. They knew the histories of the gods and their feasts".[54]

II *Special ranks of priesthood:*
   (perhaps referring to functions performed on special occasions; 'double parts'):

5 the Kurisitacha, those who burned copal (a kind of fragrant resin) for the gods and brought the branches for some ceremonies (comparable to the Aztec Tlenamacaque').

6 the Kwirípecha, priests who executed the war ritual; their leader bore the title of Hirípati.

7 the Thiwimencha, priests who carried the images of gods on their backs and thus accompanied the army on their expeditions (the teomamaque' of the Aztecs).

8 the Áxamencha, priests in charge of sacrificial ceremonies; "the Kasonsí and the principals held this dignity and they were greatly respected".[55]

9 Hopitiecha, 'those who held the hands and feet' of the human sacrifices (the chachalmeca' of the Aztecs).

10 Patsariecha, 'the guards', keepers of the images of the gods, comparable to the Aztec teopixque'.

11 Atápacha, those who beat the drums.

12 Pungakucha, the hornblowers.

13 Hatápatiecha, the heralds, who chanted while walking in front of those who brought the war captives.

14 Antsikucha, 'those who drag along the human sacrifices'.

15 Kikiecha, priests whose duty it was to chant prayers and ritual formulas as the smoke rose from the burning andúmukwa, a kind of tobacco (Nicotiana rustica). This was done in the priests' houses at the edge of the ever-burning fires, when the Tarascans had to go to war.[56]

They probably had female priests, too, at least if women charged with religious ceremonial functions can be so called. No further particulars about them are to be found in the existing literature. Yet many data suggest that Tarascan women often occupied important positions. This was also the case in the Aztec empire, but the Tarascan system apparently differed from the Aztec with regard to the position of women in the administrative system. Almost the entire household of the Kasonsí, for instance, was managed by women. Another interesting peculiarity was the existence of an institution of public education for girls only. The young women were trained in a communal house, which was called Gwatapera. The Aztecs had institutions of public education for boys and girls from 7 to 20 years of age. It is not surprising that the Tarascans did not possess educational institutions for boys, since occupations were hereditary in the male line and boys received their training from their fathers or elder brothers. The girls in the Gwatapera were looked upon as 'wives' of Kurikaweri. In the capital they were under the direct authority of the Kasonsí; in a provincial Gwatapera they were under the immediate authority of the village chief. At the head of a Gwatapera was always an elderly woman, generally called 'old aunt' and bearing the title of Gwataperi. The girls or young women in a Gwatapera were referred to as Gwanancha.[57] Probably these institutions only admitted the daughters of aristocratic families, not the daughters of commoners. Membership of a Gwatapera terminated when the girls were asked in marriage by army officers. Entrance into a Gwatapera probably did not take place before puberty. Therefore these Tarascan institutions cannot be called the equivalent of the Aztec girls' schools.

The following list of titles and offices is given for the domestic staff of the Kasonsí:

1 Ireri, the female head of all female functionaries at the court. She was more closely related to the Kasonsí than the other women and was the ruler's official 'wife' with the highest status.

All the women under the authority of the Ireri were called 'wives' of Kurikaweri,[58] and as such they were also wives of the Kasonsí, who had many children by them. Most of the women were bloodrelations of the ruler. Some of them were given in marriage by the Kasonsí to principals and military officers.

Each son[59] of the Kasonsí had a house of his own from the time he was no longer a baby. Relatives of the child's mother came to work his fields and to give him blankets to be used as capes (= money), while he (the child) presented them with some of his male and female slaves, war captives who had not been sacrificed and were called teruparakwaewaecha (i.e. 'men or women servants subjected to forced labour').[60]

The fact that the women functionaries in the palace were considered to be the 'wives' of Kurikaweri and that the Kasonsí married some of them to high dignitaries proves that the women's quarters in the palace were a kind of Gwatapera. Probably it was the most important Gwatapera in the country and a unique one, the more so as it was the only one to maintain direct relations with the only representative of Kurikaweri on earth, the Kasonsí. Thus it may have been the only Gwatapera where children were born, although it is possible that a similar situation existed in all three Tarascan centres of administration.

After the death of the Kasonsí all the women passed to his successor,[61] except seven of them, who followed him into the grave. These seven women were very personal servants of the ruler and perhaps his favourite partners in life. They held the following offices at court:[62]

- keeper of the gold and turquoise lip-ornaments of the ruler,
- personal attendant (Xukutahpe),
- keeper of his turquoise necklaces,
- his cook (Thirekwa-uri),
- his winecup bearer (Atari),
- she who washed his hands and handed him his cup,
- keeper of his urinal.

Of his male personal attendants a good forty accompanied him into the grave; among them were his blanket-bearers, the weaver of clover flower-chains, his seat-bearer, his shade-bearer, his copper axe bearer, the keeper of his snuffboxes, an oarsman, a palace-sweeper, men of his own and his wives' body-guards, a feather worker, a gold-and-silversmith, a maker of arrows, a maker of bows, foresters, some of his healers, a story-teller and many more.[63]

The Ireri was not one of the seven women who accompanied the ruler to the realm of the dead; she passed to the successor of the deceased ruler, probably retaining her office. Therefore the Ireri will often have been an 'old aunt' or 'aunt' or sometimes even the mother of the new Kasonsí.[64] The Relación tells us that she, too, was related to the female functionaries under her authority. Of these the following are mentioned in the Relación:

2   the Chuperípati, head of the keepers of the ruler's jewels. The two jewel-keepers among the seven human sacrifices for the ruler's grave were under her authority;

3   the principal female attendant and her subordinates;

4   the keeper of the military tunics and the ruler's staterobes, which were ornamented with feather mosaic;

5   the ruler's chief cook and her subordinates. It is not known whether the ruler was followed into grave by his chief personal maid and his chief cook, or by a subordinate in each case.

6   the Atari, the cup-bearer for wine and chocolate; she is also one of the women to be sacrificed at the ruler's death;

7   the 'lady of the Table', who served the ruler's meals;

8   the Iyamati, who was in charge of the ruler's apartments;

9   the Sikwapu-uri, the keeper (and maker?) of his thin blankets;

10   the keeper of his bracelets (probably subordinate to the Chuperípati);

11   the Pasápeme, the head of all his female slaves;

12   the keeper of the Kasonsí's sowing seeds;

13   the keeper of his sandals;

14   she, to whom all the fish for the palace was delivered;

15   she, who cooked the ruler's maize gruel;

16   the Kwapímekwa-uri, the keeper of the ruler's large blankets used as offerings to the gods;

17   the Gwataperi, the head of the Gwatapera in its restricted meaning of women's quarters; the guard of the Kasonsí's wives. Probably she ranked next to the Ireri; and she, too, must have been closely related to the ruler. It is possible that the Ireri was always the most important wife of the ruling Kasonsí, and that the Gwataperi was his predecessor's Ireri, who received her new office after the death of her royal spouse. The existing records do not contain a decisive answer as to the exact relations between these two female functionaries.

18   the keeper of the ruler's supply of salt.

Besides the male personal attendants mentioned before, who followed the ruler into the grave, there were more people directly connected with him. There were the Ahtsípecha, farmers and their headmen, who worked the Kasonsí's pepper fields and bean fields, the irrigated maize fields as well as the early-maize fields and who supplied him with fruit. Probably these people had the same position as the Aztec tecpanpouhque' (tekpanpowke'). Male as well as female heads in the villages also had such dependent people to work their fields.[65] These serfs who were tied to the land, were descendants of war-slaves, or people working as slaves in settlement of a debt, or perhaps slaves bought by noblemen from merchants.[66] Furthermore the Kasonsí had in his service story-tellers and court-jesters, called wandonsikwarecha.

Finally there was one important official in the capital who knew the boundaries of all the plots in Tzintzuntzan, and knew exactly who was the owner of each plot of land. He settled all disputes with regard to land-titles.

Although in Michoacán as well as in Mexico as a whole the Kasonsí had to be elected by a number of high State dignitaries, some sources suggest that in the Tarascan state the supreme ruler could exercise a decisive influence on the election. When the Kasonsí felt that he was getting too old and infirm to continue his reign he could appoint one of his sons as his successor, who then acted as a kind of regent.[67] The election which took place after the Kasonsí's death can then have been little more than a purely formal ceremony. The rulers of Ihuatzio and Pátzcuaro, the four boundary-princes and all the local chiefs came to Tzintzuntzan to attend the funeral of their deceased supreme ruler and the election of his successor. A chief who did not make his appearance was considered a rebel.

The lords of Ihuatzio and Pátzcuaro together with the four boundary princes, the Wakúxecha Elders and the Kwangariecha (the Braves) formed the College of Electors, whose duty it was to name the new Kasonsí and induct him to his office. The discussions held by the College of Electors usually lasted five days. On that occasion the following considerations were put forward: "What are we to do, my Lords? Is this house (the palace) to remain empty? Is it to remain wrapped in darkness and mists? Shall nobody enter or leave it any more? . . . Who is to say the ritual formulas over the firewood of the mother Kwerawáhperi? and of the Gods of heaven, the creating Gods, and of the Gods of the four parts of the universe and of the God of the realm of the dead (the underworld) and of the Gods who assemble from all parts and of our God Kurikaweri and the Goddess Xarátanga and of the firstborn Gods?".[68] Then the most eligible son of the deceased Kasonsí said that his uncle or one of his brothers was to be his father's successor. The uncle then answered that he was too old. When in 1521 Tanga'xwan Tsintsicha was to be elected as successor of his father Tsʌwanga, who had died from smallpox, he said: "Do not say that you will elect me, oh Elders! Let it be my younger brothers and I shall be a father to them or let it be the lord of Kuyuakan (Ihuatzio), he whose name is Pakingata".[69] Shortly after he had taken up his office this same ruler ordered all his younger brothers to be killed, in case they should drive him from the throne!

After long formal discussions between the members of the electoral college the candidate named by the majority of electors says at last: "Princes and lords, thou who art assembled here, as thou hast with judgment decided that it is desirable that I should undertake this 'cargo' (i.e. burden, task), I ask thee to take care not to leave me and rebel against me. I shall try to bear this 'cargo'. If I should prove to be unable to rule over thee, I beseech thee not to kill me, but peacefully to dismiss me from my office and to remove my headgear, which is the symbol of my authority as thy supreme ruler".[70]

Five days after the election of the Kasonsí the Petámuti (the Supreme high Priest) accompanied by the high dignitaries and lords went to the house of the new Kasonsí and addressed him with the title of Kwanga-pagwa. Then the new ruler joined the procession. At the head of the procession went the Petá-muti with ten high priests, then came the Kasonsí and the high State dignitaries, followed by the provincial local chiefs. In the ceremonial centre they joined the other priests, the lesser functionaries and the people of the capital. There seven kuritiecha received five captives handed to them by three high military officers and two standard-bearers, who probably represented the three ad-ministrative centres and the islands respectively. Then the Petámuti began his speech: "Well, you lords, who have come here from all parts of the empire, let us not leave him (the new Kasonsí). Let us assist him by performing our individual 'cargos' (i.e. tasks). In your villages wait for his orders, to supply firewood for the temples of the mother Kwerawáperi and those of the heavenly Gods, the Creators, and those of the Gods of the right hand (i.e. the north) and of the Gods of the left hand (i.e. the south) and of all other Gods, among whom the God of the underworld, for our new ruler has to fulfil his duty of pronouncing the ritual formulas over the firewood on behalf of Kurikaweri and his brothers and the Goddess Xarátanga . . . And you, lords of Michuacán (= Tzintzuntzan) and of Cuyacan (= Ihuatzio) and of Pátzcuaro, and you provincial chiefs, be prepared to obey and now return to your homes".[72]

After the Petámuti it was the Angatákuri who addressed the people present and then followed the speeches of the rulers of Ihuatzio and Pátzcuaro and the princes of Xacona and the three other boundary capital towns. Then gifts were presented to the Kasonsí. Then the people went into the woods for ten days under the supervision of the kuritiecha to collect firewood. Three days later the Hirípati started the war ceremonies. The Kasonsí called up his warriors and met all the real Wakúxecha chiefs in the house of the Eagle, which was dedicated to Kurikaweri. At the same time messengers were sent out to proclaim the state of war "at all the frontiers bordering on enemy territory".[73] The Kasonsí remained in the capital for two days and then said that he would go out hunting "and so everybody thought that he was going to hunt in the mountains".[74] Meanwhile the army gathered in Ihuatzio to attend the war ceremonies. Now the Kasonsí set forth accompanied by the kurisitacha (the copal-burners) and the others who had remained in the town. He also took trumpets with him to pretend that he was going hunting, but actually he went straight to a nearby frontier-village, Cuinao, upon which he made a quick raid, returning to his capital with a hundred or a hundred and twenty captives, before his army had actually started its campaign. Later the army commanders and all the chiefs came back with their war captives to sacrifice them. This then was how the reign of each new Kasonsí began.

The description of the Tarascan system of government has given repeated evidence that kinship and membership of certain groups were decisive factors in appointment to various offices. Evidently social mobility in Tarascan society was low, in any case lower than among the Aztecs.

To give a more or less complete picture of pre-Spanish Tarascan society we shall now have to discuss marriage as a social institution. For in societies where occupations and most of the offices are hereditary, marriage is a matter of great social significance. We have already seen that the Tarascan villages were divided into wards, and that the residents of the wards formed endogamous groups. There are several references in the Relación de Michoacán stating that for a boy and a girl to be married they had to belong to the same 'barrio'.[75] So there was a rule prescribing territorial endogamy. The social group living within such a territorial unit will mostly have consisted of members of several lineages, so that endogamy within a barrio did not exclude marriage outside one's own lineage. Among aristocratic families, i.e. among the Wakúxecha or perhaps more particularly the Wanakase, there was a rule prescribing marriage with a blood-relation: "they married women of the lineage they belonged to themselves and lineages did not mix, just as with the Jews".[76] Thus there were two important criteria for the arrangement of marriages: the territorial unit to which one belonged (hayákwaro) and one's lineage (sΛrukwa). To ordinary people the territorial principle was probably the more important one, while to the nobility, the Wakúxecha, who lived in various parts of the country, kinship was probably the only criterion. These were standards or 'rules' and rules are apt to be broken. We have seen that after the division of Wayámeo the lords of the Wakúxecha neglected both criteria when they married women from Xarákwaro. Yet the ruler Taríakuri was born of such an exogamous marriage. And Taríakuri himself married a lady from Kuríngwaro, of which marriage Kurátame was born. The reproaches exchanged between Taríakuri and this son during a quarrel over the lordship of Pátzcuaro prove, however, that the Tarascans considered such exogamous unions as abnormal. Kurátame scorned Taríakuri for being an islander and not a genuine Wakux, because he was born on Xarákwaro Island and therefore he could not be a real ruler of Pátzcuaro. Taríakuri replied that Kurátame did not come from Pátzcuaro either, but was born in Kuríngwaro and owned only part of the god Tangachuran (a god of the islanders). According to Taríakuri the true rulers were the genuine Wakúxecha chiefs Hiripan and Tanga'xwan.[77]

Some authors, among whom are Seler and Aguirre Beltrán[78] are of the opinion that the arguments produced in this dispute indicate that the pre-Spanish Tarascans had a matrilineal descent system. In the author's opinion, however, this text alone should not be taken as such an indication; for in Taríakuri's case as well as in Kurátame's the territorial criterion was the main argument and their mutual reproaches may very well have been based only on this criterion and not on the social positions of their respective mothers. Neither may we conclude from the above-quoted text that the quarrelling parties considered each other to belong to the mother's social group, for again it is quite possible for either of the two men to reckon the other to be a member of the group belonging to the territory of his birth.

Marriage preparations among the nobility were accompanied by many ceremonies. The father of a marriageable young man sent a messenger, often a priest, to the parents of the girl that he had chosen usually in consultation with his son. The girl's father asked the messenger: "Well, sir what is it, what have you come for?" Then the messenger answered, saying "Acha so and so, Mr. so and so, who holds an office in such and such a place, has sent me to ask for your daughter". Then the girl's father spoke again, saying: "You are welcome, your principal's request will be granted, it is sufficient that you have told me so". Then a present was handed to the girl's father. The middleman then said: "Sir, do you say that you will part with your daughter and give her to his son?" And the father of the girl answered: "The request will be granted as you say. For a long time I have intended to give her to him, for I am of that lineage and of the same descent and a resident of that ward; you are welcome, I shall send somebody to bring her, tell him that". Then the girl's father discussed the matter with his wives, who left the decision to him after which he said to them: "Let it be as you say, for do not we have our fields there?"[79] (The last passage might be an indication that noble ladies possessed land-titles just as the men).

Then the girl's family started collecting the dowry; the young woman was dressed as a bride, and blankets and shirts were brought for the groom, and axes to cut the firewood for the temples, and also mats which they laid upside down, and the mecapal (a sling) to carry the firewood. The other women of the bride's family also dressed up and made up their faces. They collected the bride's most valuable household goods, her mats, the cotton spun by her, and together with the bride and one or more priests they went to the house of the groom. The latter was already waiting in a special room, ready to receive them and with them to partake of the wedding-dish, consisting of bean tamales.[80] The family of the groom had also collected and stored his share in the new household: jars, casks, other kitchen utensils, blankets, maize, pepper, seed beans, wawtli-seed (amaranth seed), as well as a set of skirts and other articles of dress for his wife. The bride sat down in the middle of the room and the two families gathered there, the priest was greeted, after which the latter performed the actual wedding-ceremony concluding with a ceremonial speech. The priest admonished them to be good and faithful to each other; he spoke special words to the woman, saying: "Be what you are expected to be. I have been chosen to show you the site that you will have here and the house (or household) that you have to establish".[81] Further he told the husband not to use force in punishing his wife for adultery committed by her, but to send her back to her parents.

After the priest, the groom's father delivered a speech in which he mentioned the ancestors who in the past had lived in his grounds, where the young couple would also set up their home (patrilocal residence). Then there was a meal, after which the groom's father showed the guests over the fields that he gave to the newly married couple. Finally the presents were handed to the priest and to the women had accompanied the bride. These women were also given presents for the father of the bride.

During the first four days after the wedding the bridegroom had to collect firewood for the altars of the gods, while his wife swept the floor of their house and the path leading to it "to ensure a good path of life for herself and her husband".[82] Only after these ceremonies had been completed did the first sexual contact take place. Among members of the lower classes, however, these four days were often reduced to two or three. After the completion of all the obligatory religious ceremonies the noble lady requested her servants to cover her together with her husband; a lower-class woman would ask her husband to do this. This act completed the wedding ceremonial.

According to the Relación the common people knew various forms of marriage:[83]

1   THE TRADITIONAL PATRILOCAL MARRIAGE as described above for the nobility. The wedding ceremony itself, however, was not performed by a priest, but by relatives of the groom;
2   CHILD MARRIAGE, which was arranged by the parents when the marriage partners were mere children;
3   THE LOVE MATCH. Often a boy and a girl were associating without the knowledge of their parents. By having sexual relations or by a pretence of bride-capture they confronted the girl's parents with an accomplished fact, and usually the latter accepted the situation, except when the lovers belonged to different barrios (wapátsekwa);
4   MARRIAGE TO A WOMAN AND HER DAUGHTER. Sometimes a man married a woman with a young daughter. When the latter had reached womanhood she took her mother's place;
5   LEVIRATE MARRIAGES were common;
6   SORORATE MARRIAGES also occurred.

As may be expected in communities with a strong endogamous tendency, the number of incest taboos was relatively small. Marriages between primary relatives were not tolerated. A mother and her son could not marry, neither could a father and his daughter. Full brothers and sisters could not marry, neither could half-brothers and half-sisters by the same father (patrilineal half-brothers and half-sisters).[84] Further the Relación de Michoacán remarks that: "it is quite possible for the 'uncle' to marry his 'niece', but not for the 'nephew' to marry his 'aunt'.[85] This statement is interpreted by Aguirre Beltrán as another indication of a matrilineal organisation among the Tarascans.[86] Evidently Beltrán, a Mexican anthropologist, understood the sentence in the Relación to have this meaning: "It is quite possible for a man to marry a brother's daughter, but not his mother's sister".

If it should be possible thus to interpret the bad Spanish translation of the original Tarascan text, it would indeed refer to a matrilineal descent system. However, this interpretation is not confirmed by any of the other available data and should be entirely discounted. The existence of an incest taboo between patrilineal half-brothers and half-sisters (apparently not between matrilineal half-brothers and half-sisters) definitely conflicts with such an interpretation.

If the original text had been preserved, we should have known if the term 'uncle' was to be understood as awita (= father's brother), tatá (= father or father's brother), or papa (= mother's brother). Then we should know if the term 'aunt' was used for tsitsʌ (= mother's sister), naná (= mother as well as mother's sister), or wawá (= father's sister). As long as we do not know, the sentence in question does not contain any indication, for it is in the way in which the Spanish terms are replaced by indigenous ones that decides whether the sentence refers to a matrilineal or a patrilineal descent system. However, sexual intercourse between a man and his half-sister by the same father is described as an incestuous union, whereas such intercourse between a man and his half-sister by the same mother is not referred to as incestuous and may therefore not have been considered as such. Consequently we must conclude that the statement on the uncle-niece and nephew-aunt relations should not be interpreted as Aguirre Beltrán has done. In any case the great significance of the patrilineal descent is evident. But we do not like to run the risk of committing a similar error by taking it for granted that the Tarascans only recognised patrilineal descent. The only kinship system, however, that should be considered as out of the question on the grounds of available data is the purely matrilineal descent system. Finally we should like to point out that the statement on the uncle-niece and nephew-aunt relations may have nothing to do with kinship, but may only refer to differences in generation.

Succession to headship, to all kinds of offices and many occupations is known to be hereditary in the patrilineal way. Land-ownership too, was often thus inherited, but descent of property and offices to daughters may sometimes have been matrilineal. There were also female chiefs, although they were considered unusual and undesirable by the Tarascan functionaries in Tzintzuntzan; for they attributed the phenomenon to urgent measures to be taken when the speedy conquest of large territories necessitated the creation of more chiefships than there were adult Wakúxecha men to hold them.[87] However, it seems justifiable to assume that the social status of Tarascan women was fairly high. They were in sole or joint control of matters in several social fields in both their immediate and their extended families. In this connection it is interesting to note that the only legendary hero from the time of the Spanish conquest still known to every Tarascan today is the noble lady Eréndira, who was the daughter of Thimas or Thimaxe, the chief of a barrio in Pátzcuaro, called the 'barrio fuerte' (the strong or fortified barrio) to this day.

Some important questions in regard to the social divisions of the Tarascan people remain unanswered. It is not clear whether a non-aristocratic woman was reckoned in every respect to be a member of her husband's lineage and thus to be a member of the corresponding social units, or whether she continued to belong to her father's or her mother's lineage. Neither do the available data yield any clear insight into the relationships between the principle of territoriality and kinship within the social institutions. In what way did territorial groupings and kinship intermingle and to what extent did they overlap?

Let us begin with the smallest units, the administrative units of the Okámbecha. Were they territorial units, or kin groups, or both? What were the relationships between village wards on the one hand and kinship groups on the other? As will appear in later sections of this book the study of the present indigenous forms of social organisation in Ihuatzio has yielded a partial solution of some of these problems (cf. chapter VIII).

We can now consider some specific conditions prevailing in Ihuatzio before the Spanish conquest. From the Relación de Michoacán it appears that the village (or town) had nine chiefs during the rule of Hiripan. These were the three highest functionaries – the war-chiefs Hiripan and Tanga'xwan and the high priest Hikíngare – and the six other Wakúxecha chiefs: Kwetse, Katsimato, Kiriki, Kwakángari, Angwasikwa and Kupawaxansi.[88] According to village folk-lore the population in those early days was, just as today, divided into nine groups, each with a territory of its own. It seems reasonable to assume that the said nine chiefs were the respective chiefs of these various groups. Each of these groups, however, is said to have been made up of a number of patrilineages. But if this is true, the above-mentioned chiefs could not have represented nine, but only seven groups at most, for Hiripan, Tanga'-xwan and Hikíngare belonged to the same patrilineage; for the first two men had the same grandfather (FaFa), while all three had the same greatgrandfather (FaFaFa).

There are two slightly different versions on the folklore with regard to the nine original wards of Ihuatzio. They agree as to the location of the nine social and territorial units of the village; it is only in the names of these nine groupings that they differ. The Medina manuscript[89] contains names and their interpretations, which differ from the present almost universally accepted traditions with regard to the ancient ruined city, situated north of the present village a little higher on the mountain-slope. Map 4 shows the nine barrios located around the ceremonial centre. The names mentioned in the Medina manuscript are given in brackets.

Around the temples of Tatá Huriata (Father Sun) and Naná Kutsi (Mother Moon) lay four barrios:

1 ERECHOO ('where people live')
2 WEKAMITIO ('sunken place')
3 THOROO ('the Leap')
4 GWATARI ('Nut-bearing Tree' or Nogal) or according to the tradition of the Medina manuscript: MARITARU ('Maize storehouse').

The arrangement of these four barrios apparently agreed with that of the four 'real Aztec' calpollis in Aztlan.[90] South of these four barrios lay:

5 TSIRISEKWA or TSIRISEKWARU ('Place of the Acacia')
6 GHANDSU ('The hidden Place') or UMIRU ('Place of the Bones') and
7 TSAPAKWÁRU ('Place of flowering')

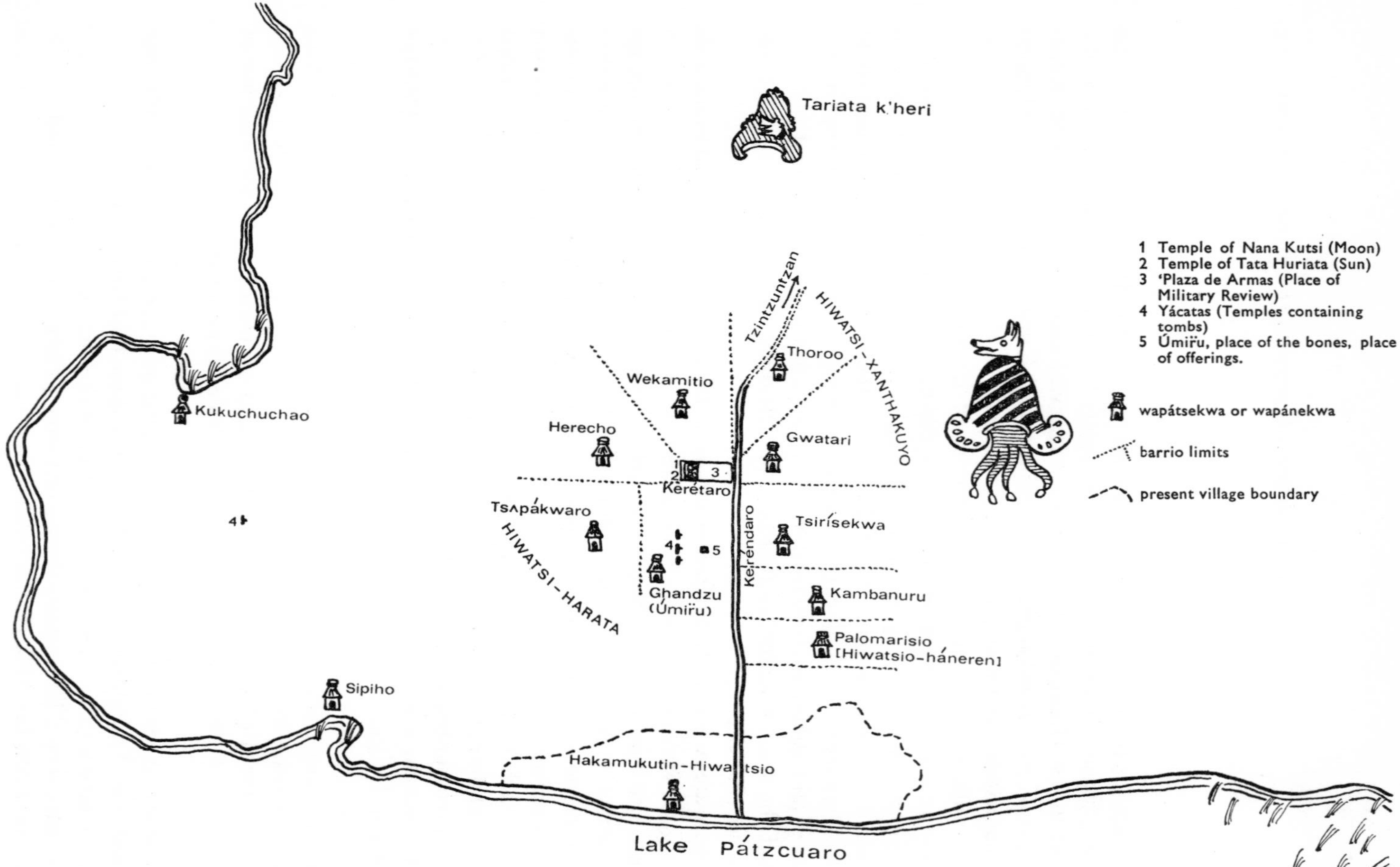

1 Temple of Nana Kutsi (Moon)
2 Temple of Tata Huriata (Sun)
3 'Plaza de Armas (Place of Military Review)
4 Yácatas (Temples containing tombs)
5 Úmiru, place of the bones, place of offerings.

wapátsekwa or wapánekwa

barrio limits

present village boundary

Tariata k'heri

HIWATSI – XANTHAKUYO

Tzintzuntzan

Thoroo

Gwatari

Tsirísekwa

Kambanuru

Palomarisio [Hiwatsio-háneren]

Kerendaro

Wekamitio

Herecho

3
2 1
Kerétaro

5

4
Ghandzu (Úmiru)

Tsapákwaro

HIWATSI – HARATA

Hakamukutin–Hiwatsio

Lake Pátzcuaro

Sipiho

Kukuchuchao

4

MAP 4   ANCIENT IHUATZIO, HIWATSIO, OR KUYUWAKAN

These three barrios show the same arrangement as the three calpollis of the Mexitin in Aztlan.[91]

Finally southeast of the three last mentioned barrios, near the present village, lay two more, which in accordance with a more popular tradition were called by Tarascan corruptions of Spanish names:

8   KAMBANORO ('Place of the Bell')

9   PALOMARISIO ('Place of the Pigeonhouse').

The Medina manuscript calls the last barrio Hiwatsio-Háneren ('Jewel of the Wolf'). It is worth noting that only these two most outlying barrios are indicated by Spanish (that is: foreign) names. Two possible explanations suggest themselves:

a Ihuatzio originally consisted of seven barrios ruled by the above mentioned nine chiefs, and the last two barrios were added to the village after the Spanish conquest, when bishop Don Vasco de Quiroga reorganized the whole region.

b The village already had nine barrios before the Spanish domination, but two of them were inhabited by a non-Chichimec population, strangers in the eyes of the Wakúxecha rulers. They were probably the islanders who had joined Hiripan's followers and whose chiefs are recorded under four names.[92] Elsewhere, however, we find an indication that the four names stand for two persons only, each bearing a double name.[93]

The explanation under *b* seems to be more plausible, especially since the Medina manuscript gives an old Tarascan name for one of the two southeastern barrios.[94]

At the beginning of this chapter mention was made of the considerable Aztec and, more generally, Nahuatlacan influence in Tarascan society. Not only the Tarascans themselves, but also the Aztecs, were aware of this fact, and several Aztec historical writings contain evidence of it. The Historia de los Mexicanos por sus Pinturas, for instance, recounts that during the migration of the Asteká-Mexîkâ the Chichimecs of Michoacán maintained contact with them and that the Chichimec lords, the Wanakase, married Mexican women, so that all the subsequent Tarascan rulers had Mexican blood in their veins.[95] Durán, Tezozomoc, Chimalpahin and others tell the legend that originally the Asteká-Mexîkâ and the Wakúxecha migrated together and together arrived on the shores of Lake Pátzcuaro.[96] Once, when the Wakúxecha were bathing in the lake, the Aztecs took their clothes and ran away with them. The Wakúxecha, angry at being thus deceived, changed their language.[97]

It is very doubtful if these Aztec accounts contain any data of historical relevance. It is noteworthy, however, that the name of the dominant group among the Wakúxecha, the Wanakase, has no meaning in the Tarascan language, whereas it much resembles the Nahuatl word Weinakastin, meaning 'People with big ears' or 'Plantain leaves'. Even more remarkable is the first line of a hymn in honour of the dead, which the Wakúxecha sang at the death of the Kasonsí and which does not contain a single word of Tarascan: "Utayne uze yoca zinatayo maco, etc.".[98] This line in the original language of the Wakúxecha, which is the only text in this language known to have been preserved, may, like the texts of the Lienzo de Jucutacato, be considered as a corrupted Nahua dialect. The reconstrued text could then read: "Tuta in teuktsi itokatsin yan teyomako, etc.", which is good Náhuatl for: "Our father the king, his noble name was given him by the God(s)". Therefore, if we assume first that the dominant group, that of the Wakúxecha, or perhaps more particularly the Wanakase, was of Nahuatlacan origin, and second that the governmental centres of Michoacán were entirely or partly inhabited by Nahuatlacas even before the formation of the Tarascan state, we may expect a relatively great Nahuatlacan influence especially in the administrative centres. Then we should not be surprised to find that in some respects there is more resemblance in social organisation between a Tarascan town such as Ihuatzio and an Aztec or Toltec town, than between the Tarascan administrative centres and, for instance, the island communities or the Sierra Tarasca villages.

Finally attention is drawn to the interesting description that Sahagún's Aztec informants gave of pre-Spanish Tarascan society:

'the Michwake' (owners of fish), the Kwaochpanme' (close cropped people) (the singular names being Michwa', Kwaochpan).

"These people were called 'Owners of fish', because there (in their country) many fish are found. And they were called 'Swept heads' or 'Close cropped people' because no one in their country wore long hair; they all shaved their heads as smooth as gourds, men as well as women; even old women; nobody wore any kind of headdress.

"Their country has an abundance of means of subsistence: cultivated maize, amaranth, beans, pepper, gourds and fruit in general.

"They dressed in the following way: the men wore long shirts and always carried their bows in their hands and a quiver of arrows on their backs. Other articles of dress were the skins of jaguars, ocelots, wolves, squirrels, foxes and deer. Their headgear consisted of a round yellow device fixed to a band made of the skin of squirrels, and on their backs they wore a device ornamented with feathers of the ayocuan.[99] Their houses were beautiful, although they were only made of straw; it was in such houses that they lived. They were excellent craftsmen, good feather-mosaic workers, carpenters, joiners, and woodcarvers; also good painters and workers in precious stones. The women of Michoacán were good at needlework and they were good weavers of the many-coloured materials. Their designs were beautiful and they made the so-called double mantles. The men were makers of very good quality sandals. They prepare their meals in the following way: they cook enough food for two or three days or even a week at one time, they do not prepare it daily. Here follow the shortcomings of the people of Michoacán: They do not wear a loincloth, but they leave their genitals uncovered. The only thing with which they cover their bodies is their long shirt, which is called 'sikwilli', and this garment much resembles a woman's shirt. They had big holes in their lips and ears; their lip-ornaments were very large. The women only wore skirts, without anything like a shirt. Their skirts were neither long nor wide, and only reached down to their knees. Women and men did not eat their meals together.

"These people had a God called 'Taras', wherefore they are now called Tarascans. This god Taras is the same God that in Nahuatl is called Mixcoatl (Snake of the Clouds); it is the God of the Chichimecs. They brought him offerings of snakes, birds and rabbits; they did not make human sacrifices.[100] Their war captives were simply left alive, serving them as their slaves.

"He, who was their ruler, had all their devotion, they greatly worshipped their king, everywhere in the land his commands were strictly obeyed. All the chiefs of all the villages gave him tributes and paid due regard to him; they put him on an equal footing with the king of Mexico".[101]

It is interesting to note that this Aztec text gives an explanation of the term 'Tarascans' which differs substantially from the explanation usually found.

Nearly all other literature explains the term tarasco as deriving from the indigenous word taraskwe, meaning father-in-law, mother-in-law or son-in-law. The last meaning is said originally to have been a nickname for the Spanish conquerors who violated Indian women. It is said that the Spaniards did not understand this and came to use the term for the Purépecha themselves. It is a fact that today the Purépecha consider the term 'tarascos' as a slightly depreciatory one. The god 'Taras', mentioned in the Aztec text, is not found in Tarascan sources. It is true that there was a god called Thares-Úpeme,[102] but he resembled the Aztec god Coyolxauhqui (Koyolxawki) and like the latter was a god of the Moon and consequently not the equivalent of Mixcoatl. Hence it is more likely for the term 'Taras' to be connected with the Tarascan word 'Thares', which had the general meaning of 'image of a god'. Even today it is a wellknown concept in Ihuatzio and according to Lumholtz the Sierra Tarascans in the nineteenth century still used the word Taré, plural Tares, to refer to the idols found in that area.[103]

The main elements of the Tarascan religion were the same as those of the Aztec religion. Until the time of the Spanish Conquest, however, the Tarascan religion had laid much more stress on the worship of fire, and therefore burnt offerings were much more important than they were in the Aztec ritual. A general survey of the available data on the pre-Spanish Tarascan religion is given by Corona Núñez.[104]

The conquest and subjugation of the country by the Spaniards caused a great shock; most of the Tarascan institutions of government were destroyed, as was almost their entire religious organisation. Their economy, too, was seriously affected. The country was looted in a most senseless way, without any attempt to preserve at least the people's means of production. The Wakúxecha soon lost their high social status and their powerful economic position. The authority of the Tarascans over the tropical regions once conquered by them was eliminated by the colonial rulers; thus they were henceforth deprived of the tributes, which before the coming of the Spaniards had enabled them as the ruling class to be consumers of luxury articles and to devote themselves to military and religious offices. The nobility and the clergy were eliminated or merged into the masses of the people, the Purépecha. This process was so thorough that the term Wakús as a member of the ruling class was absolutely lost to the Tarascans. Only the lower chiefs were at first retained as subordinate officials in the colonial regime. The population groups that used to produce luxury articles for the aristocracy naturally felt the consequences of the disappearance of the upper classes. If their services were of no use to the new colonial rulers, they were also bound to disappear. Thus it was not long before the art of feather-mosaic work vanished. Tarascan merchants travelling to the tropical lowlands were no longer protected by their own army units, while Tarascan garrisons and settlements in those regions had also gone; the Tarascan population retreated to the small area whence they had originally come. Serious damage was done to the foundations of the Tarascan economy. The surpluses which used to accrue from the spoils of war and the taxes, were now things of the past and trade with their former subjects could only be continued on a footing of equality, not, as before the Conquest, by intimidation. When during the reign of terror of Nuño de Guzmán the last Kasonsí Tanga'xwan II Tsintsicha had been tortured and killed in a most horrible way,[105] a large part of the population fled into the mountains. Some villages were completely abandoned; others retained only a fraction of their former populations. Meanwhile contagious diseases which had spread by Spanish contact and some of which had not existed in America in pre-Columbian days, such as smallpox, also took an alarmingly heavy toll. The death-rate in the whole territory of New Spain between 1520 and 1560 was terribly high. Recent investigations have revealed that here one of the greatest catastrophes in the history of mankind took place in that period.[106] In the Tarascan area the disaster was comparatively limited, serious though it was. In the course of the sixteenth century the population of the Tarascan highlands was reduced to about 30 per cent. of its pre-Spanish figure. The chaos was almost complete in the tropical lowlands, where the population was reduced to 7 per cent of its pre-Spanish figure. The said epidemics are only partly responsible for these enormous decreases in population. They are mainly due to the colonial regime, more specifically to the following aspects of it:

1   The system of encomiendas, by which the Spanish crown assigned villages and sometimes even whole areas to the conquerors and their descendants. This system gave the comendero almost unlimited power over the inhabitants of the encomienda assigned to him as well as over their labour and property. Abuse of power became commonplace.

2   Work in the mines caused the death of a great many tributary labourers

who were not used to this form of hard labour and mostly lived so far away from their families and places of origin that they were deprived of even the most elementary forms of care.

3   The very extensive use the Spanish conquerors made of the land. They imported a lot of cattle, goats and sheep, which were allowed to graze freely, thus accelerating the erosion of the soil, owing to which once fertile areas rapidly became desert-like.[108]

4   The introduction of compulsory military service for indigenous young men. Many indios from Central Mexico were forced to help the conquerors subjugate regions in western and northern Mexico as well as in Central America.

Eleven years after the arrival of the first Spanish rulers, the disorganisation of the Tarascan state and its people, who had abandoned their former homes, was very great. These were the conditions in Michoacán, when Don Vasco de Quiroga arrived there in 1533. This Spanish official was then sixty years of age and an exceptional man; in Mexico-Tlaltelolco he had been appalled at seeing desperate young Aztec mothers killing their new-born babies to save them from the bleak prospect of life under Spanish domination. From that moment it had been his conviction that he was called to bring back order to the country and act as the saviour of the indigenous people. He undertook this mission with great fervour. In 1538 he was appointed bishop of Michoacán and could begin to put his social ideas into practice in this region. For a short period he had already had an opportunity to do so elsewhere in Mexico, when he founded his first 'hospital' in the neighbourhood of the capital city. He owed most of his ideas to Thomas More. His 'hospitales' were to be the social centres of Utopian village communities, whose members had to devote themselves to all kinds of social activities as well as to the care of the sick. The second 'hospital' was established in Michoacán on the site of the old village of Wayameo, and was named Santa Fé de la Laguna. Often Don Vasco personally visited the groups of Tarascan refugees and in many cases he succeeded in persuading them to return to their original habitations or to come to the villages planned by him. His considerable success is due not only to his personal devotion and great persuasive power, but especially to his willingness to respect traditional indigenous forms of organisation. In practice his 'hospitales' became a transformed continuation of the old gwataperas, and the Tarascans therefore continued to call the institution by the old name. Don Vasco took the traditional occupational organisation of the Tarascans as a starting point for the economic reorganisation of the country, thereby maintaining a kind of division of labour between the various communities.

Although Don Vasco is now almost universally considered as a benefactor of the country, even by the Tarascans themselves, who remember him as 'Tata Vasco' (Father Vasco), his great zeal often brought him into conflict not only with the Spanish colonists, but with the Indians themselves.[109] He often demanded of the indigenous people heavy collective labour to build churches and 'hospitales', often causing the Tarascan people to demonstrate their protest against it. Moreover he was as devoted as the other Spaniards in his attempts to destroy the material expressions of the indigenous religion. But he differed from most of the other Spanish authorities by his important contributions to the restoration of the Tarascan socio-economic system. Much Tarascan resistance against Spanish attempts to concentrate the population made before the coming of Don Vasco was mainly due to the fact that early colonial authorities had ignored the traditional structure of occupational organisations, and of the village wards. Don Vasco took the autochthonous social structure more seriously into account, which was undoubtedly one of the reasons why he could accomplish more than his predecessors.

At the end of the sixteenth century more beneficial effects of Spanish rule gradually began to make themselves felt. The importation of useful domestic animals such as chickens, pigs, sheep, cattle, donkeys and horses enriched the indigenous communities.

Sources from colonial times, such as the Municipal Records in Pátzcuaro, proved to contain only the following incidental data, often of little interest, on Ihuatzio. In 1522 Ihuatzio was officially placed under Spanish rule without struggle, and the local chiefs were soon converted to Christianity. The statement contained in the "Titulo de Tierras de Chéran Hatzícurin" of 1539 that 'the son of the prince Guzmán has built the yácatas (temples containing tombs) of Ihuatzio"[110] is difficult to account for. The author, Pedro Qhamondange, was the son of a Tarascan nobleman of Tzintzuntzan, who had been converted to the Roman Catholic religion as early as 1522. At the beginning of the colonial period the village was given the name of San Francisco Ihuatzio and the saint of that name as its 'patrón', its patron saint. To the Indians St.

Francis was a new god taking the place of Kurikaweri. With Cucuchucho, Ucasanástacua and other villages Ihuatzio came to belong to the 'Doctrina de Tzintzuntzan'. Just as in other villages, the old Gwatapera of Ihuatzio assumed the new form designed by Don Vasco, but inside things remained much as they were. The original ceremonial centre, however, was soon abandoned and the village removed nearer to the lake shore. In 1580 there were inhabitants of Ihuatzio who paid individual taxes to the colonial authorities, a phenomenon very rare and unusual in those days.[111]

During the seventeenth century peace was often broken in this area by Tarascan attacks on convents and churches.

In spite of sometimes fierce antagonism and the power of autochthonous traditions the Roman Catholic clergy in Ihuatzio and other villages succeeded in exercising a permanent social influence. Sometimes they successfully adapted traditional forms of organisation, sometimes they created entirely new ones. Thus the cofradías were introduced, groupings responsible for certain branches of the new religious cult, such as the worship of a saint, of the Virgin Mary, etc. Spanish influence also changed the position of women in society; probably their status decreased. In many places the rules regulating marriage were changed. Polygamous unions were prohibited and incest taboos were extended. Unfortunately population figures referring to Ihuatzio in early colonial times are not available. The village may simply have been considered as a part of Tzintzuntzan. If mentioned separately at all, it was called Coyuca, which makes it very difficult, in the absence of further indications, to distinguish it from Coyuca de Catalán, Gue. The first population figure unambiguously referring to Ihuatzio dates back to 1746, when the village had 70 familias, that is about 400 inhabitants.[112] As in pre-Conquest days Ihuatzio contributed 40 banners to the state army,[113] which number probably corresponded with 40 Okámbecha, i.e. about 40 times 25 family-heads or 4000 inhabitants, we may assume the village population to have decreased in the last century of colonial rule to around 10 per cent. of its original figure.

The war of independence caused a great upheaval in the area; many engagements took place in Pátzcuaro and around Janítzio, but between 1810 and 1821 they did not lead to a social revolution, for which Mexico was to wait another century and Ihuatzio even longer. It was not until the end of the 19th century that president Benito Juárez's land-reform laws began to be applied in Ihuatzio.

Traditional communal land-ownership in the indigenous communities was abolished on paper and a Representante de la Comunidad Indígena (Representative of the Indigenous Community) was appointed in the village to settle affairs. In the last century Ihuatzio's population had slowly increased to about a thousand inhabitants.

During the Great Revolution (1910-1920) the majority of the population of Ihuatzio showed little interest in the struggle, although small minority groups and individual members of the community did join various rebel armies. Some of the men joined the Zapatistas, others the Constitutionalists. Some of them were killed, others did not return to Ihuatzio, but settled outside Michoacán. On the other hand refugees from other villages came to Ihuatzio, some settling there.

During the nineteen-thirties the social revolution at last spread among the Tarascans. Throughout the Tarascan area groups of modernists were formed, who called themselves 'agraristas' and whose main concern was to promote the execution of the government's projects of land-reform and the establishment of ejidos (see appendix 2). They encountered serious resistance on the part of the traditional leaders and their followers. Some of the traditional, conservative groups at first combined as Cristeros, fanatic rebels, who between 1927 and 1932 waged a bloody civil war against the anti-clerical national government, but later mostly adopted Sinarquismo, a Mexican form of Fascism. Now the most remarkable fact in this political upheaval in Michoacán is the survival of the tradition of village self-government. This was the reason why the political struggle was not fought on a national scale, but continued to be scattered over as many battle-fields as there were villages and their communal lands. This situation made it possible for neighbouring villages to have entirely different forms of government, according as it was the agraristas, the supporters of the national government, who won the struggle, or the traditionalists; and once the struggle had been settled the population recognized the new situation and accepted it. In Tzurumútaro, for instance, the agraristas won the fight, while in Ihuatzio they were defeated. This matter will be reverted to in later sections. The revolutionary ideas of the progressive-minded mestizos, who won the victory on a national scale, were at least for the time being defeated in the Indian village community of Ihuatzio. The existing forms of local government remained, the old temples, the yácatas, the church and the traditional organisation of feasts continued to function, thereby preventing the establishment of a museum[114] and a library, the execution of land reforms and the increase of the influence of the state school. But this traditional system did not survive unharmed, and during the deteriorating economic conditions it was faced with great problems, enhanced by an increasing number of inhabitants finding employment elsewhere, especially in the United States of America, a tendency which increased until 1960 and introduced entirely new influences into the village.

NOTES TO CHAPTER II

[1] Mateos Higuera, 1948.
[2] León, 1904.
[3] Seler, 1908.
[4] Borah and Cook, 1960; Cook and Borah, 1960.
[5] Villa Señor, 1748 II 35, 75, 78, 92, 103; Relación de Tancítaro, 214.
[6] Relación de Michoacán, 42, 151.
[7] Durán, 1951, 21-23; Tezozomoc, 1949, 27-28.
[8] Relación de Michoacán, 248.
[9] Ruiz, 1935, Swadesh, 1957.
[10] Ixtlilxochitl, 1952, II, 37.
[11] Relación de Michoacán, 42.
[12] Idem, 34.
[13] Van Zantwijk, 1963 b.
[14] cf. Aztlan (Van Zantwijk, 1963 b); Amaquemecan (Chimalpahin, 1949, 1950, 1952); Tulantzinco (Carrasco, 1963); Tezcoco (Ixtlilxochitl, 1952 I, 295; II 73-75; Pomar, 1941, 7); Cuauhchinanco (Torquemada 1723, I, 261).
[15] Relación de Michoacán, 35.
[16] Van Zantwijk, 1963 b.
[17] Relación de Michoacán, 39, 43, 63, etc.
[18] Van Zantwijk, 1962. The war of flowers (Aztec: Xochiyaoyotl) is a ritual war between warriors from different, but usually ethnically the same or closely related communities. These ritual engagements took place periodically on battlefields appointed for the purpose and were intended to enable the two parties to return with war captives, who could be offered as human sacrifices to the gods of the communities concerned.
[19] Relación de Michoacán, 99.

[20] Idem, 107.
[21] Idem, 126.
[22] Idem, 146.
[23] Idem, 148.
[24] Idem, 166.
[25] Idem, 166.
[26] Idem, 156, 173.
[27] Idem, 224.
[28] Idem, 224: here only the ruler of Koyuakan (Ihuatzio) is mentioned among the electors of the new Kasonsí, not the ruler of Pátzcuaro.
195: after the declaration of war it is the ruler of Ihuatzio, not the ruler of Pátzcuaro, who is the first to speak.
[29] Gilberti, 1559.
[30] Relación de Michoacán, 195.
[31] Idem, 173.
[32] Gilberti, 1559.
[33] Relación de Michoacán, 13.
[34] Idem, 155-156.
[35] Ruiz, 1935; León, 1904; Orozco y Berra, 1960.
[36] Relación de Michoacán, 173, 224.
[37] Van Zantwijk, 1963b: The Relación de Michoacán, p. 13, clearly indicates the dual authority of the priests. When the Petámuti has heard the offenders and criminals he administers justice "together with another priest who resided elsewhere". The same Relación, p. 191, suggests a dual chiefship of barrios: "Each of those brave men was given the charge of a barrio, which was like a war-chiefship, and each barrio was given a Principal, who kept a record of the numbers in his barrio, and knew all the residents personally".
[38] Relación de Michoacán, 173.
[39] Idem, 173.
[40] Idem, 173-174: "and these houses are not counted according to the number of fire-places, or families, but according to the number of persons of which each family consists; one house may be inhabited by two or three family-heads, and some may be inhabited by one man and one woman only, others by a mother and son, etc."
[41] Van Zantwijk, 1963b.
[42] Relación de Michoacán, 173.
[43] Idem, 174.
[44] Carrasco, 1961; Caso, 1956; Nutini, 1961; Zurita, 1941; Van Zantwijk, 1963b.
[45] Zurita, 1941 (1584), 152.
[46] Relación de Michoacán, 216.
[47] Idem, 177.
[48] cf. Gilberti, 1559: tekachao wapátsekwa = carpenters' barrio.
[49] Relación de Michoacán, 171-178; see also: Gilberti, 1559.
[50] Tarascan: ahpariepes; Aztec: huauhtli (wawtli), a plant of the Quenopodiacea family.

[51] Relación de Michoacán, 177.

[52] Idem, 13.

[53] Idem, 181.

[54] Idem, 181.

[55] Idem, 181.

[56] Idem, 182.

[57] Aguirre Beltrán, 1953; 172-174.

[58] Relación de Michoacán, 182-183.

[59] The Spanish texts do not afford a clue to the question of whether 'sons' or 'children' are meant; the former seems to be the more likely explanation.

[60] Relación de Michoacán, 184.

[61] Idem 229.

[62] Idem 220.

[63] Idem, 220-221.

[64] Both mother and mother's sister are in the Tarascan language addressed as 'naná'.

[65] Relación de Michoacán, 184.

[66] Idem, 184-185.

[67] Mendieta, 1945; I, 181.

[68] Relación de Michoacán, 224.

[69] Idem, 246.

[70] Idem, 224; for a detailed exposition of the concept of cargo the reader is referred to chapters III and IV.

[71] When the Tarascan army prepared to defend the country against the Spaniards the high command also consisted of three Wakúxecha generals and two generals from the islands (Relación de Michoacán, 248).

[72] Idem, 227.

[73] Idem, 229.

[74] Idem, 229.

[75] Idem, 211, 216.

[76] Idem, 213.

[77] Idem, 102.

[78] Aguirre Beltrán, 1953; 172.

[79] Relación de Michoacán, 211.

[80] Etamalli = dish made from maize flour and ground brown beans.

[81] Gómez de Orozco, 1954; 14.

[82] Idem, 16.

[83] Relación de Michoacán, 214.

[84] Idem, 218.

[85] Idem, 218.

[86] Aguirre Beltrán, 1953; 172.

[87] Relación de Michoacán, 154.

[88] Idem, 146.

[89] A manuscript written by Ramón Medina, entitled: "Sapichu Wandántskwa Hiwatse Eréteri", which records some traditions and folk tales of his wapánekwa ('clan') 'Kapitan'.

[90] Van Zantwijk, 1963b.

[91] Idem.

[92] Relación de Michoacán, 146.

[93] Idem, 154.

[94] Ixtlilxochitl tells us that the chiefships in the Aztec empire were distributed over the three administrative centres as follows:
Mexico: 9 chiefships, i.e. $7 + 2 \times 7 = 21$ units.
Tezcoco: 14 chiefships or rather 8, i.e. $7 + 1 \times 7 = 14$ units. Ixtlilxochitl, intent on proving the superiority of his own town of Tezcoco, purposely applies different standards to give the impression that his town had more chiefships.
Tlacopan: 7 chiefships (7 units).
We have already seen that Pátzcuaro probably had 7 chiefships and could therefore be considered as equivalent to the Aztec town of Tlacopan. Ihuatzio may, like Mexico, have had 7 'original' chiefships and two septempartite alien chiefships, while Tzintzuntzan would, like Tezcoco, have had eight, i.e. seven original and one septempartite alien chiefships.
Ixtlilxochitl, 1952; II, 165 ff.

[95] Zurita y Pomar, 1941, 222.

[96] Durán, 1951; I, 21-22; Tezozomoc, 1949, 27-28.

[97] Durán, 1951; I, 23.

[98] Relación de Michoacán, 221.

[99] ayocuan = a tropical bird with rich plumage.

[100] N.B. Aztec informants mentioned this ill-founded accusation among the "shortcomings of the people of Michoacán". They strongly emphasize the so-called Chichimec elements in the Tarascan culture, hence the statement that the Michwake' did not bring human sacrifices. As a general statement, however, this is not true at all, although it seems likely that originally the Wakúxecha did not bring human sacrifices.

[101] See for the Aztec text: Seler, 1927; 430-432. This translation was done by the present author and is based on the original text, not on Seler's German translation.

[102] Seler, 1908; 146-147.

[103] Lumholtz, 1903; 371.

[104] Corona Núñez, 1957.

[105] Gómez de Orozco, 1940; 23-28.

[106] Cook and Borah, 1960; Borah and Cook, 1960.

[107] Aguirre Beltrán, 1952; 71. Account should be taken of the return of Tarascan military men, officials and colonists to the high lands.

[108] cf. Zurita, 1941.

[109] Archivos de la Ciudad de Pátzcuaro.

[110] "Hieni wahpa eska, irecha Gusmán, híteki uka yákata Hiwatsio ka hieni wahpa eska irecha Ghamondange, etc." (Título de Tierras de Cherán Hatzícurin, 1539).

[111] Archivos de la Ciudad de Pátzcuaro.

[112] Villa-Señor y Sánchez, 1748; II, 16.
[113] Relación de Michoacán, 192.
[114] An attempt made twenty years ago by the National Institute of Anthropology and History (I.N.A.H.) to continue the excavation and restoration of the temple ruins of Ihuatzio failed due to the violent resistance of the inhabitants of the village.

III

outline of the social structure of the present community

All those who are considered to be members of the indigenous community of Ihuatzio – they include all the inhabitants of the village today, except the Roman-Catholic priest, the teachers, and the staff of the development brigade – are connected in one way or another with five different kinds of social groupings: the conjugal family, the extended family, the lineage, the wapánekwa and the barrio. Furthermore there are also groupings of a less general character.

1 The household

From the Tarascan terms referring to the conjugal family, and the household in general, namely *ma kwahta hánguekwa* (those living in one house) or *hingun hánguekwa* (those living together), it appears that the Tarascan conception of the term stresses the fact of the members living together, not their mutual relationships resulting from marriage and kinship. In a Tarascan community all persons living together in one house are regarded as members of one family, and in external matters they are represented by one family-head only. As is the custom in Western Europe, a Tarascan household may consist of parents and their children or of combinations of blood-relations belonging to three or even four generations. It may, however, also consist of a group of persons not all of whom are blood-relations, but who, for various reasons, live in the same house.

The Tarascan household is the smallest socio-economic unit in the community. In Ihuatzio it has a dual management, usually consisting of the oldest male, who acts on behalf of all the members in their external social relations within the community, and his wife, who keeps house and has control of the finances as well as of the movable property. This division of responsibilities is clearly manifested in their dealings with strangers. When in Ihuatzio our work within the development programme required us to visit people in their homes, it was always the husband who came to meet us. If he was not in, the door was only half opened by his wife, and we were promptly told that her husband was not at home, and any further contact was cut off as quickly as possible. Only when we knew our informants well, and were more or less looked upon as friends, did the women sometimes ask us to come in when their husbands were not at home. On the other hand when we did our shopping at the market at Pátzcuaro, and approached traders from Ihuatzio to buy something, the man remained in the background and it was the woman who came forward. Even when we tried to buy tule woven articles or agricultural implements in Ihuatzio itself, the men had to consult their wives about the prices. The wife determines the prices and receives the money paid. Even when we purposely asked only the husband, as we sometimes did, about the sale of his hoe (coa), he first went home to consult his wife, in spite of the fact that Tarascan men are well aware that the mestizos ridicule them for it.

Hence we may conclude that there exists a clear division of responsibility between the male head of the household and his wife, although it would be difficult to distinguish in all cases and circumstances what were the limits of their individual responsabilities. To a great extent it is the personal character of husband or wife that decides who exercises the greatest authority. Within the family the father will in the first place exert authority over his sons and the mother over her daughters and her daughters-in-law, if there are any in her household.

The normal pattern is for the newly-married couple to settle in the neighbourhood of the husband's father, in a house standing on his plot, which makes the man the representative of a separate household. Only if they lack the means to set up a household for themselves, will the young bride usually join her father-in-law's household, thus placing herself under the direct authority of her mother-in-law. In such cases relations between the two women are often strained, partly because the young woman has in many cases no control of the movable property. As has been mentioned virilocal residence is a rule, although exceptions are not rare. In the first place houselots and lands in private ownership may be scattered all over the Ihuatzio area, so it often happens that a man, on his son's marriage, gives him a piece of land far from the parental house, sometimes even in the other ward of the village. When the young couple settles on such a site, it may be considered as an instance of (viri-)neo-local residence. Sometimes a young man buys a piece of land for himself and his wife to live on, in which case there is no question of virilocal residence at all. There were also three cases in this village of a son-in-law settling in the grounds of his father-in-law, thereby placing himself under the latter's authority. It has already been said that even the smallest unit, the household, has the same dual organisation as prevails at all levels of the social order. Normally the household has a dual management. When the husband dies, however, the wife may feel obliged to take over his responsibilities. She will generally do so for as long as she has no adult sons. She can usually rely on the assistance of one or more adult male relatives, although the acceptance of their help will often imply some influence of these relatives on the members of her household. In any case the widow remains the undisputed head of the household and is admitted into the wapánekwa of her deceased husband (see later).

There is a sharp line dividing the male and female ways of life, even within the household. By the age of four children reveal differences in behaviour according to sex. Boys and girls have their own games at this age, children also start doing minor household jobs. There is usually a very clear division of male and female labour. The man cultivates the land, or goes fishing. The woman prepares the meals, makes maize-cakes (tortillas) and goes to the market at Pátzcuaro. The man cuts the bigger pieces of wood in the communal village-grounds, the woman gathers firewood. The man makes fishing-nets; the woman sews and embroiders the clothes. Some activities are shared by men and women; although it is the man who cuts the tule-reeds, both husband and wife make tule-mats and baskets. Decorative tule objects, however, are exclusively the work of men. Males and females also share the care of some domestic animals: pigs, chickens and turkeys for example.

Only men can perform official and traditional ceremonial functions in the village community. Also, except in special circumstances, a man is the exclusive representative of his household in the larger social units of the community.

2   Lineage

Tarascans have always referred to *lineage* by the terms *sarukwa* ('runner of a plant', line of descent) and *mayóhtsikwa* (mayóhtsani or mayohtsʌkuni = to succeed with regard to function or place). The entire population of Ihuatzio today is divided into more than fifty patrilineages. All members of one and the same patrilineage bear the same family-name. On September 1st, 1962, there were in Ihuatzio 437 household heads: 407 married men, 16 widowers, 10 widows and 4 bachelors. These 437 heads were distributed over the following 51 family-names (the number of household heads to each name is given in brackets):

1	Morales	(56)	18	Meza	(9)	35	Juan	(3)
2	Reyes	(31)	19	Santiago	(9)	36	Cortés	(3)
3	Joaquín	(22)	20	Fraga	(9)	37	Mariano	(3)
4	Baldovinos	(19)	21	Martínez	(9)	38	Villanueva	(2)
5	García	(18)	22	Lucas	(8)	39	Gabriel	(2)
6	Quiroz	(17)	23	Gaona	(8)	40	Abarca	(2)
7	Hilario	(17)	24	Rafael	(8)	41	Miguel	(2)
8	Ramírez	(16)	25	Rivera	(7)	42	Marcelo	(1)
9	Alcántar	(15)	26	Nambo	(7)	43	Jerónimo	(1)
10	Urbina	(14)	27	Trinidad	(5)	44	Nicolás	(1)
11	Hernández	(14)	28	Francisco	(5)	45	Contreras	(1)
12	Campos	(13)	29	Silva	(5)	46	Rendón	(1)
13	Rodríguez	(11)	30	Medina	(4)	47	Herrera	(1)
14	Rojas	(10)	31	Méndez	(4)	48	de Jesús	(1)
15	Marcelino	(10)	32	Ignacio	(4)	49	Damián	(1)
16	Flores	(10)	33	Domínguez	(3)	50	Barriga	(1)
17	Pedro	(10)	34	Soto	(3)	51	Sanabria	(1)

The ten widows in this list have been mentioned under their father's family-name according to the custom in Ihuatzio.

Further there are in Ihuatzio some women possessing surnames which in the village are extinct in the male line, such as Ramos (2), Matías (1), Agustín (1), and Magdaleno (1); other women bear surnames that have, like themselves, derived from outside Ihuatzio, such as Guillén (1), Torres (1), Mendoza (1; from the nearby hacienda of Tecolote), and Salgad (1; from Pátzcuaro).

It is noteworthy that the names are very unevenly distributed. One quarter of the total number of household heads possesses one of the three first mentioned names, while the ten last-mentioned names are each represented by one household head only.

On a closer examination the list is seen to contain only one genuinely Tarascan name: Nambo. The other names are of Spanish or Arabic origin. This is not surprising at all, as it is a generally known fact that in colonial times a great many Indians used to be given Christian names by the Spanish rulers, which came afterwards to be looked upon as surnames. Sometimes natives received common Spanish surnames, such as Morales, or Gracía, or even a name introduced into Spain by the Moors, such as Medina. Often, however, the names were only Spanish Christian names in origin. This list therefore contains rather a great number of Spanish Christian names: Joaquín, Hilario, Marcelino, Pedro, Santiago, Lucas, Rafael, Trinidad, Francisco, Ignacio, Juan, Mariano, Gabriel, Miguel, Marcelo, Jerónimo, and Nicolás, seventeen names in all, which, as a matter of fact, can be considered as traditionally Tarascan surnames like Nambo, because they hardly ever occur as surnames among Spaniards and their patrilineal descendants.

More data on the nature of these surnames are obtained from a comparison of the names occurring in Ihuatzio with those in neighbouring places, and with names found in the colonial civil registers of births, marriages and deaths, which distinguished between 'indios' and mestizos, mulattos, negroes and white people. From this comparison it appears that the following names are also 'typically Indian' ones: Baldovinos, Campos, de Jesús, Meza, Martínez, Rivera and Silva. Other 'Indian names which were, however, also found among negroes and mulattos, were: Morales, Reyes, García, Ramírez, Hernández and Gaona.

Rodríguez was a common name among 'indios' and negroes, as well as among Spanish colonial families. The names of Fraga, Barriga, Damián, Herrera, and Sanabria belong to typical, racially predominantly white 'rancheros', i.e. Spanish and mestizo stockfarmers. The last-mentioned names, except Fraga, are represented in Ihuatzio by one household head only. Therefore these families may be considered with certainty to have settled in the village in fairly recent times. The Fraga family hails from the hamlet of Santiago Sipiho, just west of Ihuatzio. Although many members of this family are decidedly fair-haired and fair-skinned, physical characteristics probably due to West Gothic or Basque ancestors (the name is Basque or Navarrese in origin), the family has been connected with Ihuatzio from time immemorial, and has therefore been incorporated into the Indian community of the village. All the Fragas speak Tarascan and participate in the community life of Ihuatzio. In this respect they differ from the Mendoza family, the owners of the hacienda of Tecolote east of Ihuatzio. This mestizo family has long maintained economic relations with the residents of the village, without having been incorporated into the village community.

The other twelve names offer few clues as to their ethnic connotations. Alcántar and Medina are Arabic in origin, but in Michoacán the former is often indicative of purely Indian, the latter of mestizo descent. Urbina, Domínguez and Rendón are quite common names in Tzintzuntzan, and have their origin in this place.[1] Rojas, Villanueva, and Méndez are also found in other places, amongst others in Quiroga; the last name was also borne by mulattos in colonial times.[2] The names of Soto and Cortés may have been introduced into this area by Aztecs accompanying the Spaniards, or they may derive from later intrusions. No further data were found on the names of Abarca and Contreras. A simple calculation made with the above data will show that at least 80 per cent. of the household heads in Ihuatzio possess 'indigenous', that is not specifically 'white' or mestizo, family-names.

The most prominent social significance of patrilineage in Ihuatzio is its marriage-regulating function. The norm is for patrilineage to be exogamous. Consequently one could expect a marriage taboo for people possessing the same family-name. In Ihuatzio, however, some such marriages may take place without the persons concerned being considered to violate the norm. First it should be noted that in Ihuatzio the number of recognized patrilineages is larger than that of family-names. For instance, the persons bearing the name of Morales are considered never to have belonged to one and the same lineage, but always to have been members of three different lineages. Likewise the surnames of Reyes, García and Marcelino are considered always to have belonged to two different lineages. To put it another way from time immemorial there have been some lineages in Ihuatzio with the same family-name as one or two other lineages in the village. This was explained to us by our informants, when in a test sample of 105 marriages we found two married couples where both husband and wife had the name of Morales, and two other couples where each partner possessed the name of Reyes. These marriages were not considered as unions between members of the same lineage, but between people who happened to bear the same family-name. Later we shall see, however, that in Ihuatzio marriages may take place between persons who, in our opinion, are members of the same lineage, but are not considered as such by the villagers. The author will explain this after describing the wapáne-kwecha.

The Tarascans of Ihuatzio attach much value to bilateral kinship relations as a marriage-regulating factor, which may or may not be due to Spanish influence. They have fairly strict incest taboos, particularly strict in comparison with the nearby Tarascan communities on the islands. It happened at the end of 1960 that the whole village condemned the marriage between a certain Daniel Fraga and his father's sister's daughter's daughter (FaSiDaDa), a relative in the fourth degree. In this connection it is noteworthy that for instance on the island of Yunuén (175 inhabitants), which is 10 km from Ihuatzio, marriages between relatives in the third degree are common, while even marriage with a brother's daughter is allowed there. In Ihuatzio, however, the incest taboo terminates with relationships in the fifth degree. Therefore every inhabitant of the village belongs to a lineage as well as to a family in a wider sense of the word, a family consisting of a number of bilateral relations.[3]

3. *Ceremonial kinship relations*

As in many other Mexican village communities the compadrazgo, i.e. the ceremonial relationship, is an important factor in social relationships. Ceremonial relationships arise from baptism, confirmation, marriage, or a given pledge, and their degree of importance depends on the grounds on which they are formed.

When a child is baptized, the parents seek a married couple with one or more children, as a rule outside the group of their own blood-relations but mostly from the circle of their friends, to act as compadres or kumbeecha ('godparents'; literally 'co-parents'). After the ceremony the four parents will henceforth address each other as compadre or comadre (in the case of a woman). The compadrazgo de bautismo (or pila), i.e. the godparentship of baptism (or the baptismal font), is the most important form with the greatest number of consequences. It is, as it were, a safeguard to the baptized child, for if he should be orphaned, his 'co-parents' will be obliged to take care of him. On the occasion of a confirmation or a marriage 'co-parents' are also sought, but their obligations are restricted to the duration of the ceremony itself. Like the compadres de bautismo they contribute towards the cost.

A special form occurring in Ihuatzio is the compadrazgo of pledge. If somebody is ill, meets, or fears that he will meet adversity, he will sometimes make a pledge to a saint to bring an offering for the solution of his difficulties or averting the expected adversity. A pledge is for instance taken to ensure timely rains, to remedy a pest in the crops, or to prevent hailstorms and thunderstorms which might destroy the crop. Sometimes the person taking the pledge seeks a friend to act as 'compadre'. If the saint grants their prayer, the two persons bring a joint offering.

The compadre system in Ihuatzio is very far-reaching, for it is the custom to include the close relatives of the compadres. In this way a person will soon be ceremonially related to a great many people in the village.[4]

More complete information on the compadre system is to be found in Beals' description of the same situation in Cherán, and in Foster's detailed account of it in Tzintzuntzan.[5]

4 *Age-groupings*

Ihuatzio of today distinguishes between five age-groupings. The following table gives the terminology today as well as the pre-Spanish terms for the sake of comparison:

age	Ihuatzio 1962		Old Tarascan[6]	
	male	female	male	female
0-4 years	charaku	charaku	charaku	charaku
4-12 years	hosetu	marïkwa	watsi	maneti
12-20 years	tumbi	yuritsk'eri	tumpskati	yuritsk'eri
married	acha(tatá)	wari (naná)	acha (tembuchati)	wari (tembungati)
aged	tharé'peti	kutsʌ'meti	tharé'peti	kutsʌ'meti

Tule weavers (petateros) at work.

Woman shaping and baking tortillas (maize cakes).

The term *hosetu*, now commonly used in Ihuatzio for boys from 4 to 12 years old, differs from the pre-Spanish term, which is commonly used by the modern Tarascans of the nearby islands of Yunuén and Pacanda: *watsi* or *watse*. Instead of *marikwa* people on the islands use the term *marikwa sapichu* ('little marikwa'), because with them the word marikwa refers to a marriageable girl (12 to 20 years old). The term *yuritsk'eri*, which has survived in Ihuatzio, is no longer used on the islands; neither are the terms *tharé'peti* and *kutsa'meti*.

Our informants were not agreed as to the age limits for the *charaku*. Some call only nurseling babies by this name, others continue to use the term as long as the children are carried on the women's backs (up to the age of three), others again use the world until an actual social distinction is made between boys and girls (4-5 years). As the last criterion is socially the most important, the author has given preference to it in the above table. The sharp social division between the sexes begins actually to be observed when the children are four. They have separate games, the girls beginning to join their elder sisters, while the boys play together, or if possible, occasionally join an elder brother.

Although from the age of seven or eight a child is entrusted with more and more domestic and economic activities, he is not required to perform any public service until he is twelve years old. From this age the child begins to take a place of his own in the village community, and with it to acquire a social status of his own.

Bachelorhood and spinsterhood may last until the age of twenty, after which it is considered fitting for it to be terminated. A wedding is a socially very important event, because it is then that a man is actually introduced into the barrio- and wapánekwa-organisations (see below).

Entrance into the group of village elders (over 60 years of age) is also of great significance in connection with the gerontocratic aspects of the village administration (see next chapter).

5 *The wapánekwa*

Every household head in Ihuatzio belongs to a social institution which in Tarascan is called *wapánekwa* (= place where one puts wood on the fire, fireplace, place of offering), and which the Spanish-speaking inhabitants call 'barrio' (= village ward). The Spanish term may at first confuse outsiders, because, as we shall see later, the term barrio, as it is applied in Ihuatzio, may mean something quite different from a wapánekwa. Therefore the author will not use the term barrio in the latter sense, but use the term wapánekwa, (plural wapánekwecha).

During the first six months of our study it was impossible to gain much insight into the nature of the wapánekwa organisation. It appeared to be cloaked in secrecy, and informants were very reticent on this subject. Even the term wapánekwa was at first kept secret; we received only incidental and apparently contradictory information on the division of the village into, according to some informants, two or, according to others, nine barrios or village wards. The villagers evidently also used the Spanish term 'barrio' to refer to the two large territorial units into which the village is divided. One informant during that early period of our study was more explicit by once speaking about nine 'barrios ceremoniales' (ceremonial wards). What he referred to were the wapánekwecha, which he thus described as 'ceremonial' units to distinguish them from the two large 'barrios'. Even after the existence of the wapánekwecha had been revealed, and the informants could be confronted with the indigenous name for these groupings, it remained difficult to gain a deeper insight into the nature and the functions of the groups. When after a period of nearly three years the time came for our investigations to be terminated, there were still several questions that remained unanswered.

A wapánekwa consists of a number of conjugal families or houses, and every married man in the village is a member of one of the nine wapánekwecha. Even eighteen months after we had started our investigation there were still some household heads who denied their membership of a wapánekwa, but later they also admitted the fact. This did not happen, however, before the Prioste, the head of all the wapánekwecha together, had given us in August, 1962 a complete list kept by him of the members of the nine groups.

All twenty-two people who were prepared to supply further particulars about the wapánekwa system mentioned as its most important aspects the weekly terms of duty in the church, and the collective labour for the community. The duty periods consist of cleaning the front court of the church, making preparations for the divine services, and rendering personal services to the Prioste and the Roman-Catholic priest. Each wapánekwa is entrusted with these services for one week, beginning and ending on Saturdays, so that it has its turn once in nine weeks. The year of service for the wapánekwecha lasts from December 12th (the feast of St. Mary of Guadalupe) till December 12th of the next year. The first duty period in the year is from December 12th till the next Saturday. The wapánekwecha take their turns for the duties in a fixed order. All informants gave the same order, although there were differences in starting-point; most informants began with the wapánekwa of Rivera, but most members of Kapitan started the order with their own wapánekwa.

The same order applies to the execution of public works, such as building new roads, paving roads, building a new fence around the church-court, building houses belonging to the community, laying water-conduits, etc. This collective work is divided into nine equal parts, and each wapánekwa performs its own part, rivalry encouraging them to expedite the work and do it well.

A list now follows of the nine wapánekwecha in the order in which they have to enter upon their duties. The number after the name of each wapánekwa refers to the number of its real members. Then follow the surnames occurring in the wapánekwa with the number of members bearing the name. The numbers are derived from the census taken by the Prioste and his assistants in August, 1962.

wapánekwecha	total	married	unmarried	widower	widow	lineages:	
						1 Alcántar	15
						2 Morales	3
						3 Baldovinos	11
						4 Rivera	5
						5 Ramírez	2
I Rivera, Riveras or Rivérecha	48	46	2	–	–	6 Reyes	2
						7 Meza	1
						8 Martínez	1
						9 Mariano	2
						10 Nambo	4
						11 Miguel	1
						12 Hernández	1

wapánekwecha	total	married	unmarried	widower	widow	lineages:	
II Juan Cruz, Hwankrúsecha	48	47	–	–	1	1 Joaquín 2 Reyes 3 Urbina 4 Domínguez 5 Contreras 6 Hernández 7 Martínez 8 Rojas 9 Morales 10 Meza 11 Marcelo	22 8 2 3 1 1 2 1 4 2 1
III Kapitan, Kapítanicha	39	39	–	–	–	1 Quiroz 2 Martínez 3 Hernández 4 Méndez 5 Lucas 6 Pedro 7 Medina 8 Nambo 9 Rojas 10 Santiago 11 Morales 12 Campos 13 García	6 4 1 2 7 2 4 3 5 1 1 2 1
IV Luis Miguel Migueles Miguélecha	42	38	–	2	2	1 Morales 2 Reyes 3 Marcelino 4 Quiroz 5 García 6 Ramírez 7 Soto 8 Méndez 9 Flores 10 Trinidad	4 13 6 4 3 3 3 2 1 1

wapánekwecha	total	married	unmarried	widower	widow	lineages:	
V Tsʌtsʌ'ki TsʌtsʌʼkichA	60	56	–	3	1	1 Hilario 2 Juan 3 García 4 Francisco 5 Morales 6 Quiroz 7 Reyes 8 Urbina 9 Rodríguez 10 Trinidad 11 Marcelino 12 Pedro 13 Baldovinos 14 Ignacio 15 Jerónimo 16 Hernández 17 Flores	8 3 7 5 11 5 2 2 3 4 2 1 1 1 1 1 1
VI Melchor Melchores or Meřchórecha	63	58	–	4	1	1 Gaona 2 Urbina 3 Flores 4 Morales 5 Hernández 6 Campos 7 Reyes 8 Meza 9 Silva 10 Hilario 11 Santiago 12 García 13 Baldovinos 14 Pedro 15 Herrera 16 Marcelino 17 Nicolás	8 5 2 13 2 2 2 3 5 7 4 4 1 1 1 2 1

wapánekwecha	total	married	unmarried	widower	widow	lineages:	
VII Úskuti, Úskutich'	41	37	1	3	–	1 Santiago	3
						2 Rodríguez	7
						3 Rivera	2
						4 Ramírez	4
						5 Hernández	5
						6 Gabriel	2
						7 Morales	8
						8 Campos	3
						9 Villanueva	2
						10 Ignacio	2
						11 Sanabria	1
						12 Reyes	1
						13 Lucas	1
VIII Sánduri, Sándurich'	53	45	–	3	5	1 García	3
						2 Rafael	8
						3 Urbina	4
						4 Baldovinos	5
						5 Cortés	3
						6 Morales	6
						7 Meza	2
						8 Flores	5
						9 Hernández	1
						10 Rojas	4
						11 Martínez	1
						12 de Jesús	1
						13 Damián	1
						14 Barriga	1
						15 Santiago	1
						16 Mariano	1
						17 Hilario	1

wapánekwecha	total	married	unmarried	widower	widow	lineages:	
						1 Abarca	2
						2 Campos	5
						3 Ramírez	7
						4 Pedro	5
						5 Morales	6
						6 Reyes	3
IX San Gabriel,	43	41	1	1	–	7 Fraga	9
Gabrieles or						8 Flores	1
Gabriélecha						9 Meza	1
						10 Miguel	1
						11 Rendón	1
						12 Hernández	1
						13 Baldovinos	1
Total: 9 wapánekwecha	437	407	4	16	10		

The family-names in each wapánekwa have been given in the same order as they appeared in the records of the Prioste in 1962. The lineage of the Ureti, i.e. the external wapánekwa-chief (see the next chapter), is always mentioned first. The two names for each wapánekwa are the name of the group as a whole and the plural form referring to the individual members; the latter is often given in both the Spanish and Tarascan forms.

Long before the complete list of wapánekwecha and their household heads was known to us, our informants were asked the requirements for admission as a member of a wapánekwa, the composition of the wapánekwecha, who were members and who were not. The twenty informants who were prepared to answer these questions gave the same information: a man belonged to his father's wapánekwa. Normally a young man began to participate in the activities of his father's wapánekwa when he had reached marriageable age (15-18 years) or sometimes before that time (as early as twelve). 'Voting rights' – strictly speaking these consisted of no more than a right to join the discussions at a meeting – in the wapánekwa are given to a man only after he has moved into a house of his own (normally on marriage). Women are required to participate in some of the ceremonies and activities within the framework of the wapánekwa, but normally they are not real members. Only widows with young sons of non-marriageable age are regarded as heads of family and have 'voting rights' in the wapánekwa. These data seemed to justify the supposition that each wapánekwa consisted of a number of household heads and a number of adult males, belonging to certain patrilineages. Thus the 56 lineages in the village might be expected to be divided into nine groups, each embracing a certain number of undivided lineages. A superficial examination of the above list will readily show that the actual situation deviates considerably from this supposition.

It is true that all the members of such large lineages as Joaquín and Alcántar belong to the same wapánekwecha, but the persons with the name of Baldovinos on the other hand are found in no less than five different wapánekwecha. Hernández, a not very large lineage, has members in eight of the nine wapánekwecha. If the Morales (occurring in all 9 wapánekwecha), Reyes (in 7), García (in 5), and Marcelino (in 3) are left out of consideration because, as we have already seen, these names are borne by several lineages, the twenty other large lineages show the following picture:

The name of Joaquín with 22 household heads is only found in the wapánekwa of Juan Cruz.

Baldovinos	(22 family heads) is represented in 5,		
Quiroz	(16),	,, ,, ,, 3,	
Hilario	(16),	,, ,, ,, 3,	
Ramírez	(16),	,, ,, ,, 4 wapánekwecha.	
Alcántar	(15), belongs to Rivera.		
Urbina	(15),	is represented in 5,	
Hernández	(13),	,, ,, ,, 8,	
Campos	(12),	,, ,, ,, 4,	
Rodríguez	(10),	,, ,, ,, 2,	
Rojas	(10 family heads) is represented in 3 wapánekwecha.		
Flores	(10),	,, ,, ,, 5 ,,	
Fraga	(10),	belongs entirely to San Gabriel.	
Santiago	(9),	is represented in 4,	
Meza	(9),	,, ,, ,, 5,	
Martínez	(8),	,, ,, ,, 4 wapánekwecha.	

Gaona   (8) belongs entirely to Melchor.
Rafael   (8) belongs entirely to Sánduri.
Lucas   (8) is represented in 2, and
Rivera   (7) is also represented in 3 wapánekwecha.[7]

Of these twenty names five are borne by numbers of household heads belonging to one single wapánekwa each. In eight cases half or more than half the number of household heads bearing the same name belong to one wapánekwa, in the other seven cases less than half the number of household heads bearing the same surname belong to one wapánekwa.

This shows that there are a great many exceptions to what informants called the 'normal situation'. The sum of the largest concentrations of household heads in the various wapánekwecha shows that out of 243 household heads 149 reflect the 'normal situation', which is only 61 per cent. It is of little use to examine the other, less widely distributed, names, because the chance of the household heads of these names belonging to two or more wapánekwecha decreases as their numbers decrease.

Even before the above data had been collected, it had become clear to us that there were many exceptions to the rule mentioned by our informants. The exceptions were laid before the most reliable informants with a request to account for them. They all stated that these were only apparent deviations caused by different lineages bearing the same name. Some, however, admitted that under certain circumstances a change of wapánekwa-membership could take place. As an example they mentioned the possibility of a newly-married man establishing himself on the lot of his father-in-law, who has no sons. When the father-in-law admits him into his own household, and makes him his heir, then it may happen that on inheritance the son-in-law transfers to the wapánekwa of his wife's father. In this way a new name could be added to a wapánekwa. But our informants said emphatically that such changes are rare, and that the apparent exceptions to the rule were much more likely to have been caused by people from outside having settled in Ihuatzio during and after the time of the Revolution. Many of these immigrants possessed names which already exsisted in Ihuatzio; but they were admitted to a wapánekwa with which they happened to have the most contacts, or of which they happened to know some prominent members. This was how our informants explained the present confusing state of affairs, and they added that people of the same surname who belong to different wapánekwecha are hardly ever related to each other.

All the information supplied emphasised kinship relations and sometimes other social relations as the basis of the wapánekwa system. At first the explanation given by our informants sounded plausible and reliable as regards the main points. However, it did not solve one question. The information supplied by several informants on a former occasion, namely that only the names of Morales, Reyes, García and Marcelino were distributed over different lineages was inconsistent with the statement now made that people with the same family-name but belonging to different wapánekwecha are hardly ever related. Our informants always avoided giving a straight answer to our questions concerning this inconsistency, or remarked that they could not possibly be expected to know the exact explanation of past events, but that they knew for certain that every lineage used to belong to one wapánekwa only.

It was not until November 1962 that our insight into the wapánekwa system was considerably enhanced. It so happened that at the time two disputes over wapánekwa-membership came to light one shortly after the other. The first was one between one of the Kapítanich' and the leaders of Juan Cruz. A Kapitan had bought a piece of land in the village from a member of Juan Cruz. With his wife and his mother he had moved into a house standing upon the plot. Some time later the leaders of Juan Cruz came to see him. They sat down in the roofed verandah of the house and started a friendly conversation about unimportant things. At last they explained what they had come for; one of the visitors spoke, saying: "Well, compadre, Acha B. J. and we, too, have seen that you have moved into this house, and we welcome you on Juan Cruz soil, for this lot has belonged to our wapánekwa from time immemorial. Now that you have moved into a house on this lot, we hope that you will help relieve the tasks that we, Hwankrúsecha, have to perform; we expect to see you in the house of the Ureti[8] A.J.". To this the Kapitan replied: "I thank you, that you have been so kind as to pay me a visit, and I shall be pleased to help you, if I can. However, I would like to remind you of the fact that I did not acquire this land by inheritance, but by purchase. Therefore I consider it as belonging to Kapitan, and I shall continue to serve the Kapítanich', for there is nothing to bind me to the wapánekwa of Juan Cruz".[9]

The Hwankrúsecha once more tried to persuade the Kapitan, but when their efforts failed they left him, and never made another attempt.

Not long afterwards there was a similar dispute between the heads of Tsʌtsʌ'ki and a Rivera. Now the issue was slightly different: the Rivera household head had moved into a house on the lot of his father-in-law, who belonged to TsʌtsʌAƛ'ki. So the Rivera lived on a lot acquired through marriage, not by purchase. Like the heads of Juan Cruz in the above case, the TsʌtsʌAƛ'ki heads wanted the new inhabitant of their territory to join their wapánekwa. But the Rivera also refused to change over to the other wapánekwa, and in spite of their repeated and urgent requests the TsʌtsʌAƛ'kich' failed.

But the consequences of the two disputes were different. In the first case there were no indications of the Kapitan being blamed by people other than the Hwankrúsecha, who refused to accept the loss of a house and land which had traditionally belonged to their wapánekwa. His refusal to comply with their request was considered a normal thing to do, not only by the other Kapitanich', but by members of other wapánekwecha as well. In the second case, however, public opinion clearly turned against the Rivera, who consequently suffered a loss in prestige. He was only supported by his fellow Riveras. So if the Rivera in question had changed over to TsʌtsʌAƛ'ki, his act would generally have been considered as normal in the circumstances.

These incidents revealed an important new aspect of the matter. Previously there had been no indications of a territorial basis for the wapánekwecha. It is true that the use of the Spanish term 'barrio' suggested the existence of such a basis, but out informants continued to deny that today the wapánekwecha were still based on territorial criteria. They did admit that in olden times, in the old ruined city, each wapánekwa had had a territory of its own, but this was no longer the case, and people could live anywhere in the village. The latter information was certainly true, and implied confidence in the informants. The members of each wapánekwa lived in various parts of the village. Investigations were made to establish to which wapánekwa each house and houselot in Ihuatzio belong. This information was obtained in almost all cases and the results are set out in map 5, which clearly shows that the houses belonging to each wapánekwa lie scattered over nearly the whole village. There are, indeed, a few striking concentrations of houselots belonging to one and the same wapánekwa, such as the Melchores in the extreme west, the Riveras just north of the centre of the village, and the Tsʌtsʌ'kich' between Benito Juarez Street and Vasco de Quiroga Street, but these data are not sufficient to reconstruct former joint territories of the wapánekwecha, if such territories actually existed. In our opinion such joint wapánekwa territories are not likely to have existed on the site of present-day Ihuatzio, although some people in Ihuatzio say that the large wooden crosses now found in some places by the side of village streets used to be much more numerous, and "marked the boundaries of the wapánekwecha". Other informants told us that these crosses marked places with a ritual significance; each wapánekwa possessed several such crosses scattered all over the village, like the members of a wapánekwa today. The Gwatapera (see appendix 2) of Ihuatzio was said to have been surrounded by nine crosses, each representing one of the wapánekwecha.

Only the old male members of Kapitan were able or willing to give information on the positions of the wapánekwecha in the distant past. In the second chapter the names were given of the nine 'barrios' into which Old Ihuatzio was divided (see map 4). We do not know whether these nine areas formed closed residential quarters or village wards, or whether they were ceremonial centres of nine population groups living scattered around the sites of their temples. The common traditional pattern of settlement of the indigenous population of Mexico would suggest that the latter possibility is the most likely one for Old Ihuatzio, too. It was the old members of Kapitan who at the end of 1962 told us the traditional story which explains the development of the old 'barrios' into the present wapánekwecha.

"In olden times our ancestors used to live where the ruins are now. They lived in areas around the temples higher up the mountain-slope, and there were nine places each with its own name. Those were the places where the first inhabitants lived. The nine places are found around the yákatas (temples containing tombs): Wekamitio (Place that fell into the water), Erechoo (Place where they lived), Tsʌpákwaro (Place of Flowering), Kambanuru (Place of the Bell), Úmiru (Place of the Bones), Tsirísekwaru (Place of the Acacias), Hiwatsio-háneren (Jewel of the Wolf), Marítaru (Place of the Maize storehouse), and Thoró (Place of the Leap). As there were nine places, so there were nine groups of people, who today form the nine wapánekwecha: Kapitan, Luis Miguel, Tsʌtsv'ki, Melchor, Úskuti, Sánduri, Gabriel, Rivera, and Juan Cruz. Each of the present-day groups, or wapánekwecha, now bears the name of one

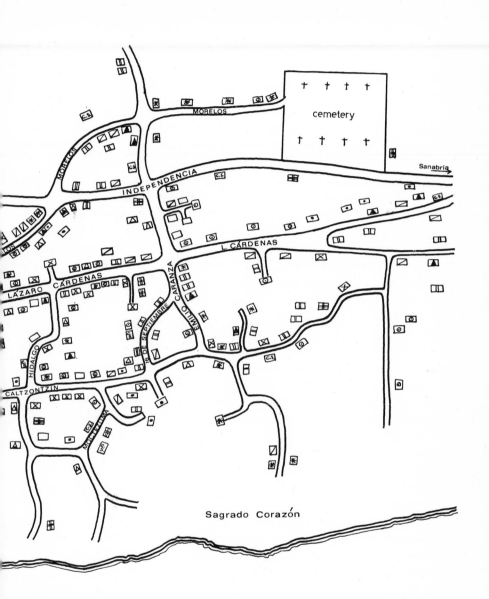

cemetery

Sanabria

MORELOS

INDEPENDENCIA

L. CÁRDENAS

CÁRDENAS

LÁZARO

HIDALGO

CALTZONTZIN

16 DE SEPTIEMBRE

EMILIO CARRANZA

MOCTEZUMA

Sagrado Corazón

of the original chiefs,[10] elderly and respectable persons with names or family-names after which the wapánekwecha were called".

"In those days there was a fisherman of Wekamitio whose name was Alejo, and his wife was Emengwa ('Early Maize'). Every day this fisherman came down the hill to go to his work in order to provide for his daily subsistence, for on the hillslope there was a constant lack of water. This man Alejo was the Kapitan. Other groups from the dwelling-places mentioned before came down the hill, and this was how the wapánekwecha were formed, for before that time they had not existed (in their later form?). The fisherman built a small hut for himself and his wife Emengwa, and no sooner did the other people see that he lived a more comfortable life than they also came down to settle near him, and the fisherman was called 'captain', and his followers were consequently called Kapítanich'. Thus ended Wekamitio. And the wapánekwa which came next was Luis Miguel from Erechoo, and then TsʌtsʌA'ki from Tsʌpákwaro, followed by Melchor from Kambanuru, after which came Úskuti from Úmiru, Sánduri from Tsirísekwa, Gabriel from Hiwatsio-háneren, Rivera from Marítaru, and finally Juan Cruz from Thoró. These groups occupied various sites on which they built their huts, until at last they had all established themselves at the foot of the hill; and thus organised, they continued to live on the shore of the lake".

This tradition is especially interesting in that it connects the territorial plan of the old ceremonial centres with the wapánekwecha today. In the second chapter it was pointed out that the nine parts of Old Ihuatzio were arranged in three groups, four units lying in the neighbourhood of the temples of the Sun and the Moon, three units south of them and surrounding the yákatas, and two groups in the southeast, just north of the present barrio Sagrado Corazón. It is noteworthy that this tradition associates the names of the *social units* today with those of the *dwelling places* of the ancient social units. The group-names of the original wapárekwecha are unknown.

A grouping of the nine wapánekwecha today according to the ancient units (see chapter II, p. 57), from which the Kapitan tradition believes them to have originated, yields the following picture:

1st group: 1   Rivera   (family-name)
                2   Juan Cruz   (family-name)

3	Kapitan	('captain')
4	Luis Miguel	(family-name)

2nd group:

5	Tsʌtsʌ'ki	(Flower)
6	Úskuti	(featherworker)
7	Sánduri	(winemaker)

3rd group:

8	Melchor	(one of the Three Kings)
9	San Gabriel	(the archangel)

This arrangement is also reflected in the names of the wapánekwecha. The first group contains a military rank and three family-names, the second group contains occupational names (Flower may be an abbreviation of Flowerchain-maker, or Flowergrower), while the third group consists of two wapánekwecha with the names of a saint and the archangel. The last two names may have replaced those of pre-Spanish gods. The question arises if it is possible that the social structural organisation of Ihuatzio as an administrative centre was originally based upon three strata: military men, craftsmen, and priests? If this is the case, the fact that only three of the nine wapánekwecha possess Tarascan names might also be explained. For the occupational names will not have had unpleasant associations for the Spaniards, in contrast perhaps to those of the noble families and high military officers, and no doubt to those of the autochthonous gods. Thus it would not be surprising for the six original wapánekwa-names to have been replaced by Spanish ones.

Do present-day conditions contain any suggestions which might support the opinion expressed above? For a long time nothing seemed to justify this. Most informants at first maintained that all the wapánekwecha were equal in rank, but that they just happened to have a fixed order for the performance of communal services, which had nothing to do with differences in status between the wapánekwecha. It is true that the order of responsibility for the performance of services does not quite agree with the arrangement of the three groups of wapánekwecha; for Melchor is the sixth wapánekwa to start the services, and has therefore been placed between Tsʌtsʌ'ki and Úskuti. But it does agree with the order in which the wapánekwecha settled on the site of the present village as it happened according to the above Kapitan tradition. But now another difference arises, namely the difference in starting-point of the cycle of obligatory services. All informants from wapánekwecha other than Kapitan mention December 12th as the beginning of the cycle, with Rivera as the first wapánekwa. The Kapitanich' now also admit that the Riveras start on December 12th, when the new functionaries have been appointed (see the next chapter), but in their opinion the new religious-ceremonial year begins on the second Saturday after December 12th, when Kapitan has to start its services. The Medina manuscript, which has its origin in the wapánekwa of Kapitan, gives a picture of this system which also deviates from that given by our present informants. It tells that (formerly?) "on December 12th an Ureti of the wapánekwa which happened to be first on the list for that year, takes up his duties together with the Prioste". This passage suggests a continuous cyclical system of succession, according to which each year a different wapánekwa starts its first period of service on December 12th. This view was not supported by our informants, and we shall describe the system as it has been explained by them. It should be noted that, however incredible it may seem, we were never able to witness the moment of a wapánekwa taking up its duties, as it was always carefully kept secret. Neither was the Prioste prepared to say which wapánekwa performed the services in any particular week. Watching the people at work did not yield any certain evidence either, because among these people were female relatives and sometimes also male compadres (ceremonial relatives) of the Ureti, people who might belong to a wapánekwa other than the one charged with the week's services. Naturally in matters like these, the author's investigations were always hampered by his inevitable periods of absence. If it had been possible to watch the proceedings uninterruptedly, the situation might have become perfectly clear to us. The atmosphere of secrecy surrounding this particular aspect of the system is all the more remarkable because some informants, including village-principals, revealed to us many other, more intricate, matters.

The three versions agree in the order of responsibility. Duty periods of a wapánekwa are always from Saturday to the next Saturday, except around December 12th. In years when December 12th also happens to be a Saturday, the first period of duty as well as the last of the preceding ceremonial year, which began on December 5th, lasts a full week. In years when December 12th is another day of the week, the last period of duty of the preceding year is from the Saturday preceding December 12th until December 12th; the first service of Rivera after the installation of the new functionaries (see the next chapter) is reckoned to last from December 12th till the next Saturday. This system has some striking consequences, which are best illustrated by some practical examples. December 12th, 1960, was a Monday. On that day the Riveras began the first service of the new ceremonial year. This duty period lasted till Saturday, December 17th, when Juan Cruz took over to be relieved by Kapitan on Saturday, 24th December. Luis Miguel followed on December 31st, TsΛtsΛ'ki on January 7th, 1961. On January 14th it was the turn of the Melchores to take up their duties, etc. The following table sets out the order of the services over the period from October, 1960 to February, 1964:

			Mo.						Tue.						Wedn.						Thu.
I	Rivera	22	12	11	15	17	19	21	12	10	14	16	18	20	12	9	13	15	17	19	12
II	Juan Cruz	29	17	18	22	24	26	28	16	17	21	23	25	27	15	16	20	22	24	26	14
III	Kapitan	5	24	25	29	1	2	4	23	24	28	30	1	3	22	23	27	29	31	2	21
IV	Luis Miguel	12	31	4	6	8	9	11	30	3	5	7	8	10	29	2	4	6	7	9	28
V	TsΛtsΛ'ki	19	7	11	13	15	16	18	6	10	12	14	15	17	5	9	11	13	14	16	4
VI	Melchor	26	14	18	20	22	23	25	13	17	19	2	22	24	12	16	18	20	21	23	11
VII	Úskuti	3	21	25	27	29	30	2	20	24	26	28	29	1	19	23	25	27	28	30	18
VIII	Sánduri	10	28	1	3	5	7	9	27	31	2	4	6	8	26	30	1	3	5	7	25
IX	San Gabriel	x	4	8	10	12	14	x	3	7	9	11	13	x	2	6	8	10	12	x	1
		Oct., Nov., Dec.	Dec., Jan., Febr.	Febr., Mar., Apr.	Apr., May, June	June, July, Aug.	Aug., Sept., Oct.	Oct., Nov., Dec.	Dec., Jan., Febr.	Febr., Mar., Apr.	Apr., May, June	June, July, Aug.	Aug., Sept., Oct.	Oct., Nov., Dec.	Dec., Jan., Febr.	Febr., Mar., Apr.	Apr., May, June	June, July, Aug.	Aug., Sept., Oct.	Oct., Nov., Dec.	Dec., Jan., Febr.
		1960	1961						1962						1963						1964

All the dates in the table are Saturdays, excepting 12 December, 1960 (Monday), 1961 (Tuesday), 1962 (Wednesday), and 1963 (Thursday).

Vasco de Quiroga Street in Ihuatzio, with women carrying water.

Old woman, with a load of dead wood, returning from the communal village grounds.

The table shows that each of the first eight wapánekwecha has six duty weeks a year, but the Gabrieles only five. This is the logical consequence of the system, in which the special significance of December 12th causes each year to be divided into 53 periods, i.e. $8 \times 6 + 1 \times 5$. Even a year with December 12th being a Saturday would not bring any change for the Gabrieles. In such a year Sánduri begins on December 5th, immediately followed again by Rivera on the 12th. Between 1900 and 1963 there were nine years when December 12th was a Saturday, viz. 1903, 1908, 1914, 1925, 1931, 1936, 1942, 1953, and 1959. In 1964 it happened again. Only in such years do the last period of the preceding ceremonial year with Sánduri on duty and the first period of the new ceremonial year with Rivera on duty each last a full week. In all other years the last period of Sánduri and the first period of Rivera together last one week. Like the Gabrieles, the Sándurich' and the Riveras in most years are on duty for a total length of time slightly shorter than that of the other wapánekwecha.

The above system of taking turns for the duty weeks especially affects the Kapítanich' in that each year they start the first of their six periods of service on the second Saturday after December 12th. When December 12th is a Saturday or a Sunday, the first period of duty of Kapitan includes Christmas as well as New Year's Eve and New Year's Day, the celebrations of which lay a heavy burden on the members of that wapánekwa. Between 1900 and 1960 this happened seventeen times. The members of Kapitan sometimes use this as an argument, in addition to the above told tradition, to claim the highest status among the wapánekwecha. When after two years of research we had at last to some extent won the confidence of about twenty informants, some jealousy between the wapánekwecha came to light. The Kapítanich' expressed their claim to the highest status, after which the Riveras did the same by arguing that it was they who opened the ceremonial year and headed the list. The members of the other wapánekwecha generally stuck to their opinion that the nine wapánekwecha were equal in status, but a number of Tsʌtsʌ'ki-members formed an interesting exception. They maintained that their wapánekwa was more important than the others, because it supplied most of the principals (cf. the next chapter, p. 133). Then there were quite a few members of wapánekwecha other than San Gabriel who called the Gabrieles 'lazy people', who did little for the community, whereas the Melchores were mostly praised for their diligence. Later on it appeared that status differences were more significant than they had at first seemed to be. They may have been much more important in the past, but today they are slowly dying out. In any case there are evidently three wapánekwecha with a relatively high status, viz. Kapitan, Tsʌtsʌ'ki and Melchor, and one with a relatively low status, San Gabriel. The Riveras lay claim to a special position and a higher status, but their claims find little or no support from other wapánekwecha. It is noteworthy that one of the three most prominent wapánekwecha is in each of the above-mentioned groups.

Some of our informants, especially the older ones, expressed the opinion that the four 'central' wapánekwecha (Rivera, Juan Cruz, Kapitan, and Luis Miguel) as a group rank higher than the other five wapánekwecha, that is to say higher in that they are more autochthonic. These informants also mentioned a differentiation for the other five wapánekwecha, dividing them into Tsʌtsʌʌʼʌʼʌʼʌ'ki, Úskuti and Sánduri on the one hand, and Melchor and Gabriel on the other. The latter two appear to be considered as the least related, the most alien population groups in the village community.

In speaking about the above differentiations in status, our informants seemed to consider them as final and a direct consequence of the position occupied by each wapánekwa in the existing system. On some occasions, however, temporary differences in prestige may arise between the wapánekwecha. When the members of a particular wapánekwa excel in making preparations for a festival and in conducting the festivities, or when they are superior to and quicker than members of other wapánekwecha in executing their part in a communal project, their group will for some time enjoy a higher prestige in the community. It will not be possible to give more details concerning the respective positions of the wapánekwecha within the community's social system before the hierarchy of functions has been described (see the next chapter).

Before giving a more detailed description of the functions fulfilled by the wapánekwecha in the life of the community, which the author will do in the next chapter, attention should be paid to the question of the relationship between non-wapánekwa-members and these groups. As we have said, only household heads are real members of the wapánekwecha.

From the age of twelve to the age of fourteen boys and girls should be increasingly involved in the activities of their father's wapánekwa. The boys become members as soon as they are married, but they do not actually have a say in things before they live in a house and on a lot of their own. Yet today it is not uncommon even for a young man to fulfil his first function in the service of the wapánekwa before he is married. In this case he also participates in the meetings and ceremonies.

A more difficult problem is the relationship between married women and the wapánekwecha, and whether wapánekwecha have any marriage-regulating functions? To this question all informants answered that the wapánekwa does not exercise any regulating influence in regard to marriage. It is possible for any man to marry the daughter of a member of his father's wapánekwa, but he is also free to marry the daughter of a member of another wapánekwa. This information was checked by examining 56 marriages for the purpose of establishing the wapánekwa of the wife's father. In 51 cases he appeared to belong to a wapánekwa other than that of the husband, in the other five cases to the same wapánekwa. Therefore the information received from the local people is probably correct. This shows that almost every woman in Ihuatzio is connected with two different wapánekwecha: that of her husband, and that of her father. On certain occasions a woman executes tasks for the husband's wapánekwa, for instance preparing the meals for ceremonial celebrations, and waiting on the visitors in the case of her husband fulfilling a ceremonial function. Sometimes a woman's father or brother may call upon her to assist in the execution of tasks which these relatives have to perform in their wapánekwa. In this way married women usually act as the binding element in the social structure of the wapánekwa system. This organisation is interconnected in more ways, for instance by the compadrazgo, which often connects members of different wapánekwecha.

In spite of the fact that the wapánekwa system lacks a clear marriage-regulating function, it has an interesting indirect influence in this respect. As the villagers associate membership of a wapánekwa with membership of a certain lineage – wrongly, as we have seen – and membership of another wapánekwa with the absence of kinship relations, they usually do not object to marriages between persons with the same family-name but belonging to different wapánekwecha. In some cases this implies an actual infringement of the rule of lineage-exogamy, without the villagers themselves considering it as such.

6   *The barrios or village wards*

As it was before the Spanish conquest, Ihuatzio today is divided into two large wards or barrios. This division of the village into one part east of the village church, which is called Sagrado Corazón (Sacred Heart), and another part west of the church, which is called Ascensión (Ascension), has several social implications. The two parts are separated by a street called Taríacuri, which in the north continues as the old Keréndaro highway, running right through the pre-Spanish ceremonial centre, formerly as far as Tzintzuntzan. The two parts are almost equally large, but Sagrado Corazón has more inhabitants and more houses. Of the 391 dwelling-houses in the village in 1963, 213 were in Sagrado Corazón and 178 in Ascensión. The latter number does not include the residences of the Roman Catholic priest and the Prioste; with the church they are found in Ascensión. They are ceremonial buildings with a special position and are not reckoned to belong to the wapánekwecha. The following table is a general survey of the distribution of 359 houses over the wapánekwecha and the two barrios (see also map 5):

wapánekwecha 6	household heads	Barrio Ascensión	Barrio Sagrado Corazón	Total
1 Rivera	48	8	28	36
2 Juan Cruz	48	21	23	44
3 Kapitan	39	21	14	35
4 Luis Miguel	42	8	21	29
5 TsʌtsʌʼkI	60	22	27	49
6 Melchor	63	37	28	65
7 Úskuti	41	7	30	37
8 Sánduri	53	22	12	34
9 San Gabriel	43	19	11	30
sub-total wapán.	437	165	194	359
uninhabited		11	10	21
unknown		2	9	11
Total		178	213	391

The table calls for some remarks. The relative ownership of houses of the wapánekwecha varies from a little less than 7 houses to 10 household-heads in Luis Miguel to a little more than 10 houses to 10 household-heads in Melchor. What has been said about the *number* of houses is also true for the *number* of houselots, but of course these data do not give much information on the extent of the wapánekwa possessions, because they do not give the sizes and values of the houses and lots. Members of all the wapánekwecha live distributed over the two barrios, but in different ways.

Rivera, Luis Miguel and Úskuti are much better represented in Sagrado Corazón than in Ascensión; it is the other way about for Kapitan, Sánduri and San Gabriel; the other three are fairly evenly distributed over the two barrios. A more significant fact in our opinion is that Rivera, Juan Cruz, Kapitan and Luis Miguel are mainly concentrated in the middle of the village, while the houselots of Melchor, San Gabriel, Úskuti and Sánduri are chiefly situated at the two extreme ends of the village. The TsΛtsΛ'kich' live partly in the Ascensión part of the village centre, and for the rest are distributed over the whole area of Sagrado Corazón.

There does not appear to be a direct connection between barrios and wapánekwecha. We must therefore consider the part played by the barrios in the social life of Ihuatzio.

Each barrio forms an unbroken territorial unit, and the people living in it are organised in various ways. In the next chapter we shall see that the barrio-system is related to the religious-ceremonial organisation, but first one of the most important aspects of the barrios must be described, namely their marriage-regulating function. Soon it appeared to us that in Ihuatzio there was a strong tendency towards barrio-endogamy. Although the villagers maintained that the 'prohibition' to marry a person from the other barrio was a thing of the past, and that everybody was allowed to marry anybody else, a test sample of 62 marriages yielded 60 cases where husband and wife came from the same barrio. The two exceptions had great social problems. Moreover one of the two couples was slightly unusual in that the husband and the father of the woman belonged to the same wapánekwa. When our informants noticed that we were acquainted with the high percentage of barrio-endogamy, they gradually supplied interesting information. For instance, we soon heard that there was a strong sense of antagonism in many fields between Sagrado Corazón and Ascensión. Until about 1940 unmarried men and boys of Ascensión were not permitted to pass through the barrio of Sagrado Corazón. Consequently they could only get to Pátzcuaro by crossing the lake in a canoe. On the other hand, those of Sagrado Corazón could not enter Ascensión, but to them this was not a great handicap, as Ascensión is only traversed by the unimportant road to Cucuchucho, and this only partly.

A larger sample of 105 marriages (i.e. nearly 26 per cent. of the total number of 408 married couples in the village at the time) yielded the following results:

a   barrio-endogamy in 94 cases (= 89%)
b   marriages between members of two different barrios: 7 (= 7%)
c   marriages to women from outside Ihuatzio: 3 (= 3%)
d   one marriage of a man from Sagrado Corazón and a woman from the rancho of 'El Tecolote' (= 1%).

So the endogamous tendency is very strong in both barrios.

Several informants told us that until a few years ago, when a boy from one barrio married a girl from the other barrio, the marriageable boys from the latter barrio would gather on one of the nights following the wedding to capture a girl from the former barrio (i.e. that of the bridetaker). It should be observed, however, that we must also assume the first inter-barrio marriage to have been contracted after the capture of the bride. For inter-barrio marriages would never, certainly not in the past, have received the necessary parental consent, if the families concerned had not been confronted with an accomplished fact by means of the 'bride-capture'.

Socially the two barrios do not rank equally. Yet this fact alone does not mean that one barrio ranks higher than the other in every respect; it depends on the particular social situation under consideration. In worldly matters Sagrado Corazón generally ranks higher in the public estimation than Ascensión. Sagrado Corazón is often said "to have residents who are better organised". Ascensión, however, is highly respected in ritual and ceremonial matters.

Some elderly informants associated Sagrado Corazón with the male sex, and Ascensión with the female. In this connection it is interesting to note that in nearly all ceremonies men and women are separated, the women always facing west (the direction of Ascensión) or south, the men facing east (the direction of Sagrado Corazón) or north.

The barrios do not possess a real executive committee such as the wapánekwecha have. But they do form the framework in which the occupational groups (see below) are organised, and in other respects, too, they are connected with certain functionaries (see the next chapter).

7 *Occupational groups*

There are still occupational groups in Ihuatzio, but according to our informants they have lost most of their significance with regard to the social order of the village. During our stay in the area we witnessed only sporadic and minor manifestations of these groups; so we agree that they must have suffered a great loss of function, considering their importance in pre-Spanish times and later under Vasco de Quiroga.

In Ihuatzio occupations are generally referred to by the term 'destino' (destiny, lot). The use of this term seems to point to the rigid structure the Tarascan occupational groups originally had, when fathers were succeeded by their sons. Men of the same 'destino' form one group. Today there are three such occupational groups left in the village:

1   the fishermen (warúrich' or warucha),
2   the tule-weavers (petateros),
3   the peasants (tarérich' or tarecha).

The fishermen, no more than 5 per cent. of the total occupational population, form a special group within the community of Ihuatzio. In some respects they are part of the larger community of inhabitants of the lake district, the islanders and the Tarascans of some lakeshore villages, whose predominant occupation is fishing. During the night of 1st to 2nd November they join the islanders and other lakeside Tarascans in the ceremonial duck-hunting parties, using the pre-Spanish spearthrower, the tsʌpakhi (Aztec: atlatl). Besides ceremonial relations they also maintain other social as well as economic relations with the real Lake Tarascans, in which respect they differ from the other inhabitants of Ihuatzio. Formerly, when the tule-weavers of Ihuatzio used to cut reeds in Lake Pátzcuaro, their contacts with the islanders were probably more frequent, but now that the tule-beds in the lake are exhausted, and the tule-weavers have to go to the swamps near Chapultepec to obtain their material, the fishermen are the only important link with the other Lake Tarascans. Moreover the Ihuatzio fishermen are the group with the largest number of external kinship relations. Nine or ten fishermen's daughters from Ihuatzio are married to men from the islands of Pacanda, Yunuén and Janitzio, and have thus deviated from the fairly common practice of endogamy as it exists in the village.

Originally economic relationships between the fishermen of Ihuatzio and those of the other lake villages cannot have been very extensive, and must have been confined to the trade in dugouts and hats from Jarácuaro. Some of the Ihuatzio fishermen, however, have begun to apply themselves to the manufacture of fishing-nets, which they sell to fishermen from other villages, especially those from Janitzio. This industry was started when the fishing-grounds which have from ancient times belonged to the fishermen of Ihuatzio began to be affected, more than other fishinggrounds, by the falling water-level of the lake, because they were located in the shallowest parts.

As a population group the fishermen of Ihuatzio are socially not ranked very high by the other inhabitants, although in the other fishing-villages, especially on the islands, they are held in high respect, as we observed.

During the three years of our study we witnessed only one public celebration of the occupational group of fishermen in Ihuatzio. This was on Sunday, June 16th, 1963, when the fishermen celebrated the traditional festival of their group – according to our informants this had not taken place for the past eight years – with the performance of dances for the gods and the principals. Such dances represent the fishermen's daily work. A more detailed description of this festival and the ceremonies attending it will be given in chapter V. The fact that this festival had not been celebrated for the past eight years is an indication of the decline of the occupational groups. Early in June, 1963, however, the most important fishermen of Sagrado Corazón combined to organise the festival, whereupon those of Ascensión were obliged to follow suit. On this occasion the organisers and leaders were fishermen who ranked highest in the general occupational hierarchy of the village (see the next chapter). There was nothing to suggest an independent administrative organisation of this occupational group. It is noteworthy that the festival was organised within the framework of the respective barrios, but the situation today may differ from what it originally was in these and other respects.

The tule-weavers or 'petateros' are not a close unit either, and between 1960 and 1963 they did not perform any of the traditional ceremonies of their occupational group. The feast of the tule-weavers had not been celebrated since 1958.

During the time of our study they twice acted collectively; the first time they successfully tried to come to an agreement with the inhabitants of Chapultepec regarding the exploitation of the tule marshes in that place; their second collective action was an unsuccessful attempt to change the too low prices paid by the mestizo middlemen, who sell their products in the markets in the tourist centres and the large cities. Both actions were organised by men enjoying a high status in the village community as a whole, so that they, too, should not be considered as the specific heads of this occupational group. The tule-weavers are the largest of the three groups, comprising a good 50 per cent. of the occupational population.

The last of the three groups, the peasants (tarerich'), embraces less than 35 per cent. of the occupational population. More than half of them are land-owning farmers, the others are farm labourers. The latter generally own a houselot, some even possess small pieces of land away from their houselot, but these are not big enough to provide food for themselves and the members of their household. The organisation of this group is closely connected with that of the entire village community. Hence the heads of this group are again difficult to distinguish from the principals of the village as a whole.

In contrast to the two other occupational groups, the group of the peasants has a recognised status within the official Mexican administrative organisation, and is referred to as the 'Comunidad Indígena' (Indigenous Community). This fact gives the group a more or less legalised title to the traditionally communal village-grounds on the slopes of mount Tariatak'heri.[11] The main function of this group consists of regulating the exploitation and defence of the communal lands. The practical importance of this title will be discussed in the next chapter.

The peasants contribute in their own specific way to the traditional festivals by performing ceremonial imitations of their daily work. The annual ceremonies consist of ploughing with a yoke of oxen, planting maize and beans, scaring birds, and invoking rainfall.

We could not discover any connection between occupational groups and wapánekwecha. It is possible for one person to participate in the activities of more than one occupational group. A closer study of this aspect was impossible owing to the rarity of group-activities of the occupational groups.

8   *Religious women's organisations*

Ihuatzio has four groupings of women performing service for the local church, the priest and the Prioste:

1   La Vela Perpétua ('The Perpetual Watch'),
2   Cabezas de Día ('Heads of the Day'),
3   Santo Depósito,
4   Sagrado Viático.

The members of the Vela Perpétua keep the inside of the church clean. There are thirty-one of them, so that each day of the month requires a different member of the group to take her share in the common task. In months of thirty days the last day is divided into two parts, the last two women on the list each working half a day. The members are married women and a few marriageable girls.

The 'Cabezas de Día' in turn keep watch over the Holy Sacrament, every day from sunrise till sunset.

The women of the 'Santo Depósito' guard the possessions and revenues of the church and act as housekeeper to the Roman-Catholic priest.

The members of the 'Sagrado Viático' attend upon the priest when he administers the last sacraments to a dying person, and help him to guard the ceremonial objects. Unfortunately it appeared to be hardly possible for male investigators to obtain information about these women's organisations. The little information given above was largely collected by one of the female Crefal students.

9   *Political groups*

At the time of our study about forty per cent. of the household heads in Ihuatzio proved to be interested in one or other of the Mexican political parties. The majority of the population showed little or no political interest and hardly felt themselves involved in the struggle between the political parties.

By far the greater part of the politically-interested household heads, namely more than 30 per cent. of all household heads, were adherents of the Sinarquista movement, which is a Mexican party of the fascist type and is very popular among the traditionalist peasants in the states of Guanajuato, Jalisco and Michoacán. It flourished greatly in the late nineteen-thirties, but since 1942 its popularity has gradually decreased. The Sinarquistas oppose the present Government's policy of land-reform, particularly the expropriation of the landed property of the church. Many local priests and some bishops avowedly or secretly support the movement. Until about 1948 Sinarquismo was very strong in Ihuatzio, with at least 80 per cent. of the household heads supporting it. But then large parts of the lake fell dry and the leaders of the Sinarquistas tried illegally and without consideration for the village traditions to appropriate these fertile dry lakeside grounds. The movement lost the confidence of many of its adherents, among whom were influential traditional principals, and within a short time the number of Sinarquistas was reduced to the figure mentioned above. The local priest sympathizes with the Sinarquista movement; this partly accounts for the comparatively large number of adherents, although the other leaders of the movement and the party members from outside Ihuatzio exercise very little influence (cf. chapter II, p. 67). An interesting fact is that Sinarquismo has many followers not only among the Roman-Catholic clergy but also among farmers with little or no landed property in the above mentioned districts. The spread of Sinarquismo has been strongly promoted by the radical government policy, which was felt as a menace to the traditional forms of organisation. The ejido-system and the land-reform it implied were important parts of the radical government programme, and were consequently also looked upon as threats to the indigenous communities, in spite of the fact that the ejido-system is based on autochthonous Mexican foundations.

The party in office, the P.R.I. (Partido Revolucionario Institucional), is supported by about 5 per cent. of the household heads. They are men with little prestige in the village community, or even almost outsiders, because they purposely endeavour to win a position in the greater national community. They consider themselves Mexicans rather than Tarascans, and can therefore be looked upon as 'transitional people', people in process of transition to another culture, and of social adjustment. Their contribution to the village community life is small, for the very reason that their interests are directed to the greater national society, and they often leave Ihuatzio after a while.

A third political grouping is formed by the Agraristas, which group embraces about 3 per cent. of the household heads. Originally, in the late nineteen-twenties and thereafter, up to and including the administration of General Lázaro Cárdenas, the Agraristas were ardent supporters of the leftish regime of the then federal government. In Ihuatzio so far they have vainly advocated the creation of an ejido (a piece of land in the common ownership of a number of farmers, formed according to the official national project of general land-reform). Being a minority group, their demand was never complied with, which caused them to leave the P.R.I. Although some twenty or thirty years ago they caused a lot of trouble in Ihuatzio, they are now no longer taken seriously by the majority of the villagers, and the group is likely to disappear after the death of its leader, the only leader it has had during the three decades of its activity.

There are other groups in Ihuatzio, such as the co-operative societies of chicken-farmers and of beekeepers, a women's sewing-club, a parents' society of the State school, a group of unqualified nurses and midwives in training, etc. All these groups have been formed at the instigation of outside bodies, mainly through the activities of Crefal, and recently of the Brigade for the Development of the Indigenous Population. All these societies, even the co-operative ones, give a slight impression of being artificial products forced upon the people from outside, and if at this moment the aid given from outside were to be terminated, these groups would be likely to vanish within a short time.

Notes to Chapter III

[1]   Cf. Forster, 1948; 232-233.
[2]   Brand, 1951; 85-97.
[3]   The pre-Spanish Tarascan kinship terminology is only partly in use in Ihuatzio. The autochthonic kinship system and its original social implications apparently changed considerably during the Spanish domination. Little genealogical research could be done. The data on kinship relations collected for this study therefore lack an adequate background. The following chart of words now in use in Ihuatzio is given for comparison with the kinship terms collected by Beals in Cherán (See Beals, 1946):

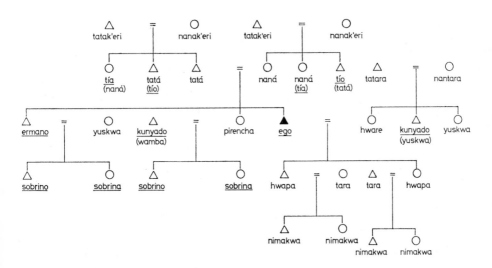

Female usage differs in some respects from the male:

In comparing the nomenclature as it exists today with the pre-Spanish kinship terms known from literature, it is interesting to note that, apart from the replacement of original Tarascan terms by Spanish ones, more indigenous terms have now been added to the list. The Spanish terms now in common use are: tío, tía (MoBr, FaBr, MoSi, FaSi), ermano (hermano = brother), kunyado, kunyada (cuñado, cuñada = SiHu; BrWi), and sobrino, sobrina (BrSo, SiSo, BrDa, SiDa).

The following modern Tarascan words differ from the corresponding pre-Spanish ones: tatak'eri (FaFa; formerly kura), nanak'eri (FaMo; formerly kukú), pirencha (Si; formerly pipi), nimakwa (SoSo, SoDa; formerly nimátekwa); further Gilberti gives the term tuwiskwe for 'cuñada de mujer' (wife's sister-in-law), whereas in Ihuatzio today a female calls her brother's wife hingóneskwa and her husband's sister yuskwa. Gilberti does not mention the word wamba, but it is quite possible that in those days sister's husband also used to be referred to by a different name from husband's or wife's brother.

The change of kura into tatak'eri and of kukú into nanak'eri is remarkable. Tatak'eri means literally 'great father'. The Spanish terms abuelo, abuela entirely lack this agreement with our words grandfather and grandmother. Modern speech in Michoacán, however, does associate the terms 'great' and 'old'. The elimination of the kinship term kura may be explained by the fact that it happens to be identical with the Spanish word for a Roman-Catholic priest. Other important pre-Spanish kinship terms have disappeared completely, for instance awita (FaBr),papa (MoBr), wawa (FaSi), tsitsi (MoSi), tsiwandihpensti (Fa FaFa), chuwindihpensri (FaFaFaFa), tsiwándinskwa (SoSoSo), and angándinskwa (SoSoSoSo); (cf. Gilberti, 1559).

[4]   In Ihuatzio there seemed to be a preference for finding compadres in the wapánekwa of the wife or in that of the mother. Unfortunately we had no opportunity to make an adequate study of this aspect. Another problem still awaiting complete solution is the acceptance of a request to be compadre or comadre. Such an invitation can be declined. Sometimes a refusal may result in loss of prestige, though not always.

[5]   Beals 1946, 102-104; Foster, 1961, especially pp. 1182-1183.

[6]   Gilberti, 1559.

[7]   Of course, widows have not been included.

[8]   Ureti = 'First', the external chief of a wapánekwa (see the next chapter).

[9]   This is an approximately correct brief summary of what was actually said.

[10]   This is not correct (see the following note).

[11]   In the second half of the last century the federal government, by introducing land-reform laws, tried to do away with traditional communal land-ownership in villages with aboriginal communities by dividing the communal land into small private holdings. During the 'period of transition' a so-called 'Representante de la Comunidad Indígena' (Representative of the Indigenous Community) was appointed in every Indian village with lands in communal ownership. After the failures of this policy of land reform the office of R.C.I. was continued in several places, for instance in Ihuatzio (cf. Brand, 1951; 53-55).

IV   *commissioners and principals*

1 *Commissions and leadership*

Traditional leadership or chieftainship in Ihuatzio as in Indian Mexico as a whole is characterised by the acceptance of commissions (cargos), by prestige and the enjoyment of its benefits rather than by responsibility, power and the exercise of it. In Ihuatzio chieftainship is considered not so much as a goal in itself, but as a means to acquire prestige. Leadership is looked upon as a burden, and not everybody is fit to bear it. Its acceptance brings prestige on the one hand, it demands sacrifices on the other. Another characteristic feature of the organisation of the traditional chieftainship is the sharp distinction made between internal leading offices (within the group) and external representative ones.

The concept of leadership as a burden, as a troublesome task performed on behalf of the community, is manifested in the cargo system, the system of commissions, which is the basis of indigenous authority. The tasks performed by individuals for the benefit of the village community are called cargos (i.e. 'burdens'). There are major and minor cargos, and their respective magnitudes decide their places in a system which might be called the cargo-hierarchy. It is a scale of values for individual commissions undertaken in the service of the community. It is closely connected and partly identical with the hierarchy of the village executives. For in Ihuatzio a man cannot be called upon to hold an executive function before he has completed a traditionally fixed number of commissions necessary for the assumption of the office. Chieftainship as a commission is considered by the Tarascans of Ihuatzio as comparable with any other commission which the community can impose upon one of its members.

ACHA REPRESENTANTE

highest 'external' authority
'elected' for seven years

ACHA ALKANDE

highest 'internal' authority
'elected' for 2 years;
head of the
genuine commissioners

Pasados

HURÁMUTICH (Principals)

about 25 elder pasados;
village elders, among whom
    9 Urétspecha (Jefes)
    chiefs of the
    wapánekwecha
    (indefinite period
    of office)

PRIOSTE
one year; head of
the substitute
commissioners

ROMA
CATHOⅠ
PRIES
(indefinite p

ACHA HEFE

Head of the
police;
holds office
for one year;
subordinate to the
Acha Repr.
 1 *Suplente*
 1 *Secretario*
 10 *Katáhpecha*
   (guards;
   assistant
   policemen)

'genuine' commissioners (cargueros)   major   minor

Mesa de Campo   Mesa de Campo

1 SOLDADO CAPITÁN   2 MORO CAPITÁN
    Alférez   Alférez
    Sargento   Sargento

Tiputádox
- 3 Capitán de Guadalupe
- 4 Capitán de San Nicolás
- 5 Capitán de la Virgen de Soledad
- 6 Capitán de San Antonio
- 7 Capitán de la Virgen del Tránsito
- 8 Capitán de Nuestro Amo
- 9 Capitán de la Madre Mayor

+ their Ayudantes

WANDÁR

'priest
'speake
(indefinite p

'substitute' cargueros

Urecha or *Urétich'* (singular: Ureti)

hold office for one year; 'external' chiefs
of the nine wapánekwecha

Kénich'   for one year ⎱ assistants of the
Wakérox for one year ⎰ the Prioste

A Chirémekwa-fisherman.

Pátzcuaro harbour with dug-out canoes.

It appears that in former times the concept of cargo used to be interpreted in a more restricted sense. In the course of time it has been extended to tasks which were originally not connected with it. This may explain why many people in Ihuatzio distinguish between 'genuine' cargos and 'substitute' cargos. The genuine cargos are divided into major and minor ones. The following sections will describe the two hierarchies, that of the cargos and that of the executive functions in the village, and their relationships. As this chapter is a continuation of the preceding one, it has occasionally been necessary to deviate from the hierarchic order, because the executive functions must be described on the basis of the social units mentioned in the preceding chapter. A description of the relationship between offices and social units is particularly useful in the light of the general purpose of this study.

The chart on p. 112, representing the two hierarchies, may serve as a guide for the relations between cargos and executive functions.

2 *The management of a wapánekwa*

The management of a wapánekwa includes the lowest and the second highest ranks in the hierarchy of offices. On the one hand a wapánekwa has an Ureti or Oreti, literally 'the First One', who is also called Semanero 'He who acts for a week' (the 'man of the weekly term of duty'), on the other hand it has an Urétspeti or Orétspeti, whose Spanish title is 'Jefe' (Chief). According to nearly all informants the Ureti's task is the first cargo; some added that, properly speaking, it was not a genuine cargo, but a condition which had to be fulfilled before a man could assume a real cargo.

Most Uretich' are newly-married young men, ambitious enough to be desirous of promotion in the cargo hierarchy, or rather to gain social prestige. Yet the ambition of a young married member of a wapánekwa is not the only, and in some cases not even the most important, reason for striving after the office of Ureti. His parents and other relatives within his wapánekwa may exercise considerable influence on his social 'career'. Often a commission is undertaken on the initiative of older relatives occupying more or less high social positions themselves. Every year, some time before December 12th, the old and distinguished men of the wapánekwa and other influential members meet to discuss who is to be their next Ureti. Small pressure-groups come into action, trying to persuade the really powerful men on the one hand, and the often reluctant candidates on the other. Then at last a newly-married man who has never performed a cargo is named, and on December 12th he is officially installed in office. If there is no suitable newly-married candidate, a single young man is often appointed, sometimes even a boy of twelve or thirteen; in practice this means that his nearest relatives perform the greater part of the commission, thus justifying his appointment at such an early age.

The Ureti is appointed for twelve months, and has to organise the weekly duties of his wapánekwa and to perform a considerable part of it himself. Until thirty years ago this meant that the Ureti and his wife went to live in the Gwatapera, where they looked after the sick, and in serious cases helped to take the patients to Pátzcuaro. In the Gwatapera they received and attended upon the persons who were the guests of the village, and offered atole (a maize beverage) to all the casual visitors at the community-hall. The present Roman-Catholic priest of the village, a Tarascan himself, disliked the Gwatapera and did not rest until the building was closed. Then he arranged for the private school which he had founded to be built on the site against the front of the old building, which was then soon reduced to ruins. These ruins were still visible behind the new school building until the beginning of 1963.

After the closure of the Gwatapera the Urétich' or Urecha (alternative plurals of Ureti) performed their duties partly at home, partly in the house of the Prioste, who is the head of all nine Urétich' and one of the village-chiefs (see a later section).

Today the Urétich' have the following duties:

a cleaning the front court of the church, and the passages in the priest's residence during the wapánekwa's weekly terms of duty;

b fetching water for the priest and the Prioste, and watering the plants in the garden of the priest's residence during the same periods;

c collecting and storing firewood for the priest and the Prioste during these weeks;

d looking after the priest's pigs and hens;

e receiving at their own homes members of their own wapánekwa for collective activities, for meetings and for certain ceremonies;

f passing on to their wapánekwecha the orders given by the highest village executives concerning public works to be carried out collectively.

The first four items call for little explanatory comment. It is a rule that a Ureti has to replenish the water supply at least ten times during his weekly term of duty, but this minimum is hardly ever complied with. Further it is noteworthy that as a rule the Urétich' themselves do the jobs around the buildings of the ceremonial centre and perhaps in the corridors and portals, while their wives and the members of the women's organisations do the jobs inside those buildings.

The items (*e*) and (*f*) refer to the executive tasks of the Urétich' within their respective wapánekwecha. This is a strange situation, which was at first hard to understand. Outsiders trying to get in touch with a wapánekwa are referred to the Ureti; he is presented as the 'chief' of the wapánekwa. During the first year of our study we were occasionally introduced to boys and young married men in the function of 'barrio chiefs' (i.e. wapánekwa chiefs). In view of their striking lack of prestige and their comparatively low status within the community we suspected them to be mere 'puppets'. Later it appeared, however, that they were real external chiefs, but that the external chieftainship of the wapánekwa was not considered a very influential position. Yet the office of Ureti is an important part of the daily management of the wapánekwa; he is above all an executive, not a man who takes decisions. The Ureti organises the wapánekwa meetings, but he has hardly any voting rights. He has little or no influence on the decisions taken at a meeting. From the village chiefs (see the section on the Hurámutich) he receives the instructions for his wapánekwa and passes them on. The wapánekwa assembly decides the way in which the instructions are to be carried out (or ignored). The nine Urétich or Urecha together form a local order in the service of St. Martha (Santa Marta), who is therefore their patron saint.

Now who are the people who do have the power of taking decisions in the wapánekwa? They are the village elders, men who have as a rule completed a major cargo and have thus become 'pasados ('those who have passed'); they have gone through the whole hierarchy of commissions. Every wapánekwa usually has two to four of such old men. They bear the Tarascan title of Orénaṙikwecha (Rulers, Principals), or they are referred to by the Spanish term of 'Principales' ('Principals' or 'Notable men'). One of them, usually the oldest

person and in any case a pasado, is elected as the internal head of the wapánekwa, in which capacity he bears the title of Urétspeti.[1] The Urétspeti has a
high social status and is a greatly respected man, both in his own wapánekwa
and in the village community as a whole. He supervises the Ureti, who will do
nothing without his consent, and he is the most powerful man in his wapánekwa, but he is not its external representative. The Orétspeti exercises his
authority and takes his decisions in close consultation with the other Orénaříkwecha. In most cases they will hear the opinions of the other household
heads in the wapánekwa and will to a certain extent take these opinions into
consideration. When at last their decision has been made known, it is final.
They are not responsible to the general meeting of members of the wapánekwa.
The decisions taken by the Orénaříkwecha are made known to the wapánekwa
assembly by the Urétspeti. The formulation of decisions taken at a meeting
as a result of discussions held on a certain issue always maintains the fiction that
it embodies the opinions heard and the arguments made, and that the decisions
have been taken unanimously. This fiction of unanimous decisions also exists
in other administrative units. Although to us, outsiders, this appears to be a
fiction, it must be said that this method of management is one that works. Any
issue involving differences of opinion between members with voting rights is
discussed at such length that in the end no difference of opinion remains, or
discussions are continued until the advocates of a viewpoint unacceptable to
the principals realize that their ideas have no chance of being carried through.
Within the wapánekwecha there is another, quite different, functionary, the
Wandari ('Speaker'). The Wandari is a kind of Master of Ceremonies, and
every wapánekwa has one or two wandarich'. They are men who are familiar
with the ritual addresses, orations and formulas in the Tarascan language that
have to be said during social and religious ceremonies and rites. The Medina
manuscript calls the Wandari the modern equivalent of the pre-Spanish
Petámuti (high priest).[2]   An interesting fact is that the Wandarich' are the
only male functionaries in the village, besides the Roman Catholic priest, who
are in no way connected with the cargo-hierarchy. They are elected solely on
the ground of their knowledge of the traditional orations and addresses and
for their fluency, irrespective of the number of commissions completed by
them. This function offers almost the only possibility outside the cargo-
hierarchy for male inhabitants to gain prestige and influence. A good Wandari

is indeed a highly respected man, who, especially through his oratory, may exercise considerable influence in his wapánekwa.

3   Other 'substitute' commissions besides that of the Ureti

Other 'substitute' commissions besides that of the Ureti are the tasks undertaken by the other assistants of the Prioste and by the 'ayudantes' of the 'Tiputádox' ('Deputies'), the bearers of the minor cargos.

In addition to the nine Urétich' the Prioste has four or five other assistants in his permanent service all the year round: two Kénich',[4] each of whom has the duty to supply the ceremonial centre with fruit and vegetables two or three times a week; two or three Wakérox[5] ('cowboys') or Itsukwatáhperangutich', who daily supply the priest and the Prioste with milk.

A Keni is usually a man who has not been a Ureti; his task is considered to be a substitute for that of the Ureti.

Wakérox are always widowers, who have never completed a genuine commission. Kénich' as well as Wakérox are appointed directly by the Prioste. Like him, they remain in office for one year. Another functionary under the supervision of the Prioste is the Sacristán (Thioseoampátsari or Misaharuwáhperi), the sacristan or sexton, who sees to the interior decoration of the church and assists in preparing the divine service. The sacristán is appointed for an indefinite period of time and is not a commissioner.

Much more closely connected with the cargo-hierarchy is the last type of substitute commissioner, the Ayudante or Anátakuri or Haruwáhperi (Helper). Until a few years ago it was a rule for a man to have been a Helper of one of the seven Tiputádox before he could be charged with a minor commission himself. We were told that in the last nine or ten years this rule has been disregarded, much to the annoyance of the Orénarikwecha and the pasados, who do not like a young man to become a real commissioner immediately after he has completed his twelve months' service as an Ureti. Of late years, however, it has appeared to be so difficult to find a sufficient number of commissioners that the Elders had in some cases to consent to exceptions being made to the rule.

The Helpers support their Tiputádox financially to help them fulfil the pledge made on December 12th preceding, to organise the feast in honour of one of the saints. They also participate in the organisation of the feast itself, and in all the ceremonies executed in the Tiputado's house before and around the image of the saint. Tiputádox personally invite the men they like to be their Helpers, after which the appointment is officially confirmed by the village chiefs. Like the Tiputado, the Helpers remain in service for one year. A Tiputado may have three Helpers, but often he cannot find more than two persons willing and able to act as such. The last few years have seen an increasingly slack application of the original rules, at least this is what older men, among whom were some Orénaříkwecha, told us. According to them a man should have been an Ureti or a Keni before he could become an Ayudante; and he must have been a Helper twice before he could be appointed as a Tiputado. This organisation implies that there should be 9 Urétich' and 2 Kénich', that is 11 candidates, every year for the office of Helper. As Helpers have to serve twice for a period of one year and the Urétich' and Kénich' only once, there are 22 candidates every year. If each of the seven Tiputádox takes three Helpers 21 will be needed every year. This system meant that each year the number of available candidates used to exceed the required number of Helpers by one at most. It is easy to understand that this part of the cargo system was bound to fail as soon as it became impossible to maintain a very strict discipline, or when migration and other causes temporarily or permanently reduced the number of candidates. As migration of seasonal workers to the United States from Michoacán has been a regular phenomenon since 1943 it has been impossible to insist on a strict application of the existing rules. At first some Tiputádox were content to have only two Helpers, but even then it proved to be difficult to find enough candidates. Then the often rather young Tiputádox supported by other young men of their wapánekwecha, appointed Helpers who had never been Uretich' or Kenich'. Some Orénaříkwecha, who even in 1963 were apt to fly into a passion when they mentioned these difficulties, told us that there were some older principals who did not realise the danger involved in the decline of tradition; consequently, they said, the situation went from bad to worse. For once the principle was accepted that it was possible for a man to be appointed as Ayudante straight away, it appeared to be more and more difficult to find Urétich'; so sometimes very young men had to be accepted for this office. Worse than this was the fact that the Ayudantes who had served as Urétich' refused to serve as Helpers a second time, and asked to be appointed as Tiputádox at once. It was not long then before this, too, was actually granted. This brought back the situation as it prevailed before the liberalisation of the cargo system. And it was just as difficult to find enough Helpers as it used to be. Today the full number of 21 Helpers is indeed never reached. Some Tiputádox are satisfied with two Helpers, so that every year there are between 15 and 18 young men acting as Helpers.

4 *The minor commissions*

There are eleven minor commissions (therúnchekwa sapichu), and these are considered as the first genuine cargos. Seven of them are connected with the ceremonies in honour of seven santos ('saints'), who play an important part in the religious ritual of the village.

Every year the village chiefs and the Orénarikwecha look out for men who have served as Urétich', Kénich', or Ayudantes, to give them the charge of the seven saints' images, that is each of them will have to see to the proper worship of one of the 'saints'. On December 12th they are appointed for one year; after taking their vow they receive the title of Tiputado or Capitán. The latter is usually connected with the name of the 'saint' in question, for instance: 'el capitán de San Antonio' (The captain of St. Anthony).

The seven minor commissions are connected with the following saints and their feasts:

1   La Virgen de la Soledad ('the Virgin of Solitude'), a variable feast in February;
2   La Madre Mayor ('the Elder or Supreme Mother'), a variable feast during Lent;
3   Nuestro Amo ('Our Lord or Master'), a variable feast in March or April (during the Semana Santa, the 'Holy Week');
4   San Antonio (St. Anthony), June 13th;
5   La Virgen del Tránsito (Assumption of the Virgin Mary), August 15th;
6   San Nicolás de Tolentino, September 10th;
7   La Virgen de Guadalupe (The Virgin of Guadalupe, or Tonantzin of Tepeyac used to be the patron saint of Mexico only, but has gradually been adopted by the whole American continent; it is the image of the Holy Virgin that is most worshipped by the Mexican Indians. The main temple

of this 'Mother of God' is located on the very spot where the temple of the Aztec goddess of the Earth used to be), December 12th.

The seven Tiputádox or Capitanes, who guard these seven saints' images and organise the feasts and ceremonies connected with them, do not rank equally in the hierarchy of offices. The Capitán de Guadalupe ranks unquestionably higher than the others. This is accounted for not only by the importance of the Virgin of Guadalupe, but also by the special day on which this commissioner celebrates his feast, December 12th, the day when the new functionaries in the village are installed.

The difference between the Capitán de Guadalupe and his colleagues is not the only one; there are other mutual differences. A closer examination of the list of the seven so-called santos or 'saints' reveals that it contains in fact four images of the Virgin Mary, two male saints and a form of the supreme god (Nuestro Amo). They are the four female and three male anthropomorphous gods in the religious system existing in Ihuatzio today.[6] The organisation of the cult of these saints is probably connected with the division of these seven deities or divine forms into four female and three male ones. Those of the commissioners in charge of the worship of the four forms of the Virgin Mary, whom we know personally, for instance the Capitán de la Madre Mayor in 1961 and the Capitán de la Virgen de Guadalupe in 1963, belonged to the village-ward of Ascensión, while the Capitanes of San Antonio, San Nicolás de Tolentino and Nuestro Amo came from Sagrado Corazón. Our informants, however, definitely refused to give us more information on this subject; this was probably due to their suspicion of Crefal and the Government on the one hand, and of the Roman Catholic church on the other.

As has been said before, the Capitán de Guadalupe ranks higher than the other six Tiputádox, which does not imply that these six are themselves equal in rank. The differences in rank are noticeable in some ceremonies which require the participants in the ritual to visit principals and commissioners. There is a strict traditional order of succession for these visits. First the executive village chiefs have to be called on (the Acha Representante, Acha Alkande, Prioste, Acha Hefe; see later), then the Capitanes de San Francisco (see later), followed by the Tiputádox in the following order:

1 Capitán de Guadalupe;
2 Capitán de San Nicolás;
3 Capitán de la Virgen de Soledad;
4 Capitán de San Antonio;
5 Capitán de la Virgen del Tránsito;
6 Capitán de Nuestro Amo, and
7 Capitán de la Madre Mayor.

As will be seen in the next chapter, this order is frequently deviated from. This made it impossible for us to check the above order of succession, which was supplied to us by two informants only. Yet we thought it worth while publishing though with reservations, because it may provide an interesting datum. It is noteworthy that female and male gods are mentioned alternately, as it were in pairs, the Virgin of Guadalupe being linked with the patron saint of the village, St. Francis. As has been mentioned, their 'capitanes' are the first Tiputádox to be visited. If there are differences in rank between the seven Tiputádox, such differences are less important than the difference between the Capitán de Guadalupe and the six others.

Four minor commissions remain to be mentioned. These we consider to be the tasks of the four Helpers of the Capitanes de San Francisco, although their exact positions are not quite clear to us. Some people call them substitute commissioners, like the Ayudantes of the Tiputádox, but ranking higher than the latter. Others maintain that the assistants of the Captains of St. Francis rank equally with the Capitán de Guadalupe, and have therefore a higher status than the other six Tiputádox. Three elderly men, all 'pasados', informed us that in former times a man must have been a Tiputado as well as a Helper of one of the Captains of St. Francis before he could be charged with the great commission. It is evident that this custom is now no longer applied, and what used to be two rungs of the hierarchical ladder have been reduced to one. This is the reason why the author has ranked the Helpers of the Captains of St. Francis equally with the seven Tiputádox. These four Helpers have two different titles: there are two Alféreces (Ensigns or men second in command) and two Sargentos ('Sergeants, subaltern officers'). Each of the two Captains of St. Francis is normally assisted by one Alférez and one Sargento. These assistants contribute to the high cost of the great feast of the patron saint of the village, which is celebrated in the week of October 4th, and with their Capitán they perform the ceremonial dances.

5 *The Acha Hefe and his assistants*

According to the hierarchical system in Ihuatzio every person who has completed a minor commission is eligible for the office of Jefe de Tenencia (Tarascan: Acha Hefe), the 'sheriff' of Ihuatzio. In the State of Michoacán this is an official post within a Municipalidad.[7] According to the Municipal Corporations Act in Mexico the general administration of villages and hamlets outside a municipal capital is in the hands of the Jefe de Tenencia for a dependency called a tenencia, and of the Encargado del Orden (Preserver of the peace) for a hamlet attached to a tenencia.[8] These officials act as liaison officers between their districts and the municipal authorities concerned; they are responsible for the maintenance of peace and order and have to perform some administrative duties, such as the detection, arrest and the taking into custody of delinquents, the collecting of some taxes, the application of municipal by-laws, and the supervision of the maintenance of public places and roads.[9] Considered in the light of the administrative system of the state of Michoacán, the Jefe de Tenencia is the highest administrative officer in Ihuatzio. But since the traditional chieftainship in the village, which is de facto recognised by the higher authorities, is so important, he is in fact subordinate to a number of leading functionaries who are nominally his subordinates. The Acha Hefe or Acha Katahpe, as the Tarascans of Ihuatzio call him, has very little real actual influence in the village; as a matter of fact, he does little more than execute decisions made by the traditional village chiefs concerning matters with regard to the municipal, state or federal administration. Therefore in practice he is often the representative of the traditional principals in their dealings with the municipal corporation, rather than the representative of this body in the village. From an official point of view, the situation in Ihuatzio, as in many other Indian villages in Mexico, is anomalous in that the official public authority has been made subordinate to the traditional authority. This irregularity is also manifested in the appointment of the Jefe de Tenencia. According to the Municipal Corporations Act he has to be appointed by the municipal corporation, and a plebiscite cannot be taken in the dependency concerned unless at least fifty inhabitants have openly opposed the appointment.[10] The municipal corporation of Tzintzuntzan, however, always waits for the traditional chiefs and principals to recommend a candidate, after which this nomination is legalised by an official appointment.

The influence of an Acha Hefe depends not only on the goodwill of the traditional chiefs or principals, but even more so on his own personality and social status. The Acha Hefe in 1962 was a man in his fifties, who had distinguished himself as a Tiputado. He was a conservative man, who was looked upon by the principals as one of themselves. He enjoyed a fairly high prestige, and occasionally exercised considerable influence. It was quite evident that this man was trying to oppose the influences of the municipal authorities and Crefal. The next year there was a younger Acha Hefe, a weak personality, who was inclined to mix with the turíxecha (the strangers). At a large meeting, for instance, he tried to arouse popular interest in a Crefal project to enlarge the state school. But he was silenced by the principals in a most direct way; he was pushed aside and in subsequent speeches he was ridiculed and treated like a child. Another deviation from the official pattern is the term of office of the Acha Hefe; in Ihuatzio it is one year, although it should be two according to the Municipal Corporations Act.[11]

The Acha Hefe has a Suplente (a deputy) and a Sekretario as his immediate subordinates. Furthermore the Acha Hefe of Ihuatzio has one assistant, officially called 'assistant policeman', to every forty houses in the village. The Tarascan name for these helpers or assistant policeman is Katáhpecha. Their office is not included in the cargo-hierarchy. The village has ten Katáhpecha, who form the 'armed force' of the Acha Hefe and have to arrest delinquents and imprison them in the Katáhperakwa, (the cell). This is a room with wooden bars within the Jefatura de Tenencia, the office building of the Acha Hefe, immediately southeast of the ceremonial centre, on the boundary between Ascensión and Sagrado Corazón, at the south side of the plaza. The Acha Hefe, however, is seldom called upon to exercise his power; in general the people try to correct breaches of the peace in other ways, within the framework of the wapánekwa. The Acha Hefe and his assistants have to act only in serious cases. During the three years of our study we never heard of anyone having been imprisoned in the Katáhperakwa. The Katáhpecha occasionally dealt with drunken behaviour.

6   *The Major commissions (k'eri therúnchekwa)*

Every year two men are in charge of the organisation and financing of the most important feast in the village, that of the patron saint St. Francis; they have to supervise the proper worship of the 'saint' and guard the 'saints' images. They both bear the title of Capitán de San Francisco[12] (Captain of St. Francis), and are the highest commissioners (cargueros) in the village. In addition to their general title, each has a personal title, which refers to each individual office. One is called Moro Capitán (Moorish Captain), the other Soldado Capitán (Soldier Captain). These two captains are ceremonial rivals during the feast of St. Francis, which is organised by them in open competition.

The present-day temple or church of Ihuatzio has two niches. One contains an image of St. Francis, which is about a metre high, the other has three images of the same 'saint', all three about twenty centimetres high and to the eye equally tall. The Moorish Captain is in charge of the biggest image and the Soldier Captain is the keeper of the three small ones. These three images, however, are considered to be 'greater' than the big one. Further a distinction is made between the three images, one being the 'tallest', one the 'middle' one, and the third the 'smallest'. "And", our informants used to add, "the smallest is by far the most dangerous".

In accordance with these views on the most important objects of religious worship in the village, the Soldier Captain is ranked slightly higher than the Moorish Captain. Normally each of the two captains is assisted by three Helpers, two of whom are the above mentioned Alférez and Sargento. The third man attending on each Capitán de San Francisco is one of the two captains of the previous year and is given the somewhat strange title of Mesa de Campo (= Table of the field, i.e. 'Leader of the Battle-field'). Unlike the Alférez and the Sargento the Mesa de Campo does not contribute to the cost of the feast proper, although he does pay for some of the ceremonial offerings and presents. It is noteworthy that the Soldier Captain's Mesa de Campo is always the Moorish Captain of the previous year, and the Moorish Captain's Mesa de Campo is always the previous Soldier Captain. Outsiders may find it difficult to understand why this should be so, especially since the task of a Mesa de Campo, who is an experienced and nearly 'passed' carguero, consists of leading his Captain in the ceremonial fights, dances and rituals. One would therefore expect a former Soldier Captain to instruct his own successor, instead of acting as the master of the next Moorish Captain.

Our informants were reticent on this point, while our own direct observations were restricted to the celebration of the feast of St. Francis in October, 1963, as this was the only opportunity for us to be present. Therefore in this question too, we have not been able to ascertain the actual facts and motives. Yet, though the information gained was scarce, it was sufficient to justify a few cautious conclusions. It appeared that the people associate the Captains of St. Francis in various ways with social units and religious conceptions. First the Soldier Captain and the Moorish Captain are associated with Christianity and paganism respectively, which probably corresponds with the wishes of the Roman Catholic priests in colonial times, who may have wanted to introduce a new interpretation of an indigenous ritual by explaining the ceremonial fight between the two Captains and their Helpers, which takes place annually in October, as the struggle between Spaniards (Christians) and Moors (Heathens). If this was the object the colonial Roman Catholic priests had in view, many inhabitants of Ihuatzio today hold a different opinion. Their interpretation reveals ideas of pre-Spanish origin. Many people interpret the contrast between the Spanish and Moorish Captains as the contrast between Spaniards and Tarascans. The Soldier Captain and his men are considered to represent the Christian Spanish conquerors, the Moorish Captain and his helpers the pagan indigenous Tarascans. The two captains are also particularly associated with the two village wards, the two barrios. In 1963 the 'Soldados' represented Sagrado Corazón, the 'Moros' Ascensión. The year before it had been the reverse, the Moorish Captain and his men representing Sagrado Corazón, the 'Soldados' Ascensión. Evidently the two groups change places annually in the social system of the village. This makes it more plausible for the Mesa de Campo to be attached to the successor of his ceremonial opponent instead of to his own successor, for it is the only way for him to retain his connection with the same barrio.

The festivities in honour of St. Francis in October, 1963 suggested to us that there were more associations in connection with the two Captains, their subordinates and the various images of St. Francis. The Soldier Captain, his assistants, and the three small images were associated with the sun, and bore golden symbols, while their relations with the barrio of Sagrado Corazón may be the reason why they were particularly considered to symbolise the male element in life. The Moors, on the other hand, carried silver moons as symbols; they were associated with the moon and their relations with Ascensión may have resulted in their being looked upon as representatives of the female element. From ancient times the opposition of sun and moon has been represented by Tarascans, as well as other Mexican peoples, as that of the male and female elements. Another noteworthy fact was that some old men referred to the Soldier Captain and his three assistants as 'Wakúxecha'. This was the only time during our stay in Ihuatzio that we heard the name of the dominant group in the ancient Tarascan state mentioned. The 'Soldados' indeed wear eagles embroidered in gold thread on the backs of their tunics. If it should be possible to associate the 'Soldados' not only with the Spaniards, but also with the ancient 'Wakúxecha' and their (sun) god Kurikaweri as opposed to the 'Moros', representing purépecha (or nahuatlaca?) with their (moon) goddess Xarátanga, we should be inclined to conclude that the 'Soldados' symbolise conquerors in general, the 'Moros' the subject groups. These symbolic representations are closely connected with the people's concept of the universe and of other religious and philosophical concepts existing within this Tarascan population group. More attention will be paid to these matters in the next chapter.

A survey of the entire cargo-hierarchy from Ureti up to Mesa de Campo has been given in the foregoing pages. The fulfilment of one of the major commissions, which, as has been said, take two years to complete, affords access to the higher executive offices. On December 12th the Mesa de Campo is 'pasado', and is consequently eligible for one of the chieftainships the next year. Before describing the traditional chieftainship in Ihuatzio we shall have to deal with the practical application of the cargo system.

Like young men in any other community a young man in Ihuatzio need not face the task of gaining a suitable position as an adult member of his community unaided, because there will always be blood relations and ceremonial relatives to stand by him. Their social status and economic resources determine the extent and efficacy of their support. This help and his own as well as his wife's ambition and diligence will affect the degree of his subsequent social success. The son of an Urétspeti, a wapánekwa-chief, is apt to be elected as an Uréti. It will also be easy for the son-in-law of an Urétspeti to be nominated in the latter's wapánekwa, especially if his wife is a member of one of the women's organisations. The Urétspeti, who is an important man, will generally have found his children important ceremonial relatives, and his sons usually marry daughters of other important families. Since the way in which a commissioner is able to perform his task depends considerably on the support given by his nearest relatives, the cargo system seems to be conducive to a strongly oligarchic form of government. However, the system is not as simple as it appears to be at first sight. There are factors which may prevent or hamper the inheritance of status, and impede the course of events as I have just described it. In the first place the social prestige resulting from the performance of a cargo depends on the cargo itself, but also to a great extent on the way in which it has been executed. Every commissioner ('carguero') is always compared with his predecessors and with commissioners equal or about equal in rank. When he falls short of the usual standards, it will be some time before he is called upon to undertake a new commission. Another uncertain factor for a commissioner is his own financial position as well as that of his relations and other supporters. A crop may fail, but it does not affect the demands made by the ritual of ceremonial feasts. Indeed, it appeared a few times after heavy hailstorms that the population showed an even greater desire to propitiate the gods by insisting on a strict performance of the ritual, and by bringing greater offerings. In periods of economic recession the Orénarikwecha[13] who have named the cargueros, and the commissioners themselves may be unable to estimate the actual amount they can afford to spend on their commissions, which may then prove to be too burdensome. This was the reason why between 1948 and 1956 the village found it most difficult to maintain the unrestricted application of the cargo system, when prolonged droughts, the after-effects of the eruption of the volcano Parícutin, and the rapidly increasing migration of labour to the United States seriously affected the economy of the village. In those days many cargueros found it impossible to fulfil their obligations, and some of them left the village to live elsewhere in order to escape the public disgrace caused by their failure. Others left the village as soon as they suspected that they would be charged with a cargo. Then some began to decline the offer of a commission. Others were able to perform their duties only by the sale of all their lands and sometimes even by raising a loan on their house and garden, so that at the end of the year they were financially ruined. It was then that resistance of a minority of the population against the cargo system first manifested itself. It is true that nearly all traces of opposition to the system have since disappeared, but this could only happen because the chiefs and principals were sensible enough to take the wind out of its sails by slightly mitigating the demands made on the cargueros. Most of our informants told us that demands were no longer excessive and the festivities less expensive than they used to be. However, the villagers were apt to present these matters to Crefal workers in a more or less misleading way; yet the large amount of data that we collected on this aspect from various sources induce us to assume that more money and labour used indeed to be spent on the feasts than today. Nevertheless the amounts of money that cargueros have to find are still astonishingly large.

An Ureti will find a few hundred pesos quite sufficient, but this sum is large enough for people whose weekly earnings hardly ever exceed 30 to 40 pesos. The Ayudantes and Tiputádox need a few thousand pesos for the year they are charged with the care of their 'saint'. Of course, the greatest demands are made on the Captains of St. Francis and their assistants. In each of the last few years they spent some 20.000 pesos (U.S. $ 1600,—) on the feast celebrated on October 4th and the following days, and an additional sum of about 10.000 pesos on ceremonial occasions during the rest of the year. When a man has passed all the stages of the cargo-hierarchy he will have paid, according to an estimate by one of the village chiefs, "no less than 40.000 pesos (U.S. $ 3200,—), and we may be sure that a smaller amount would not cover the cost. For the chiefs and principals are aware that strangers will usually consider these amounts spent on the feasts as waste of money; therefore they will generally try to represent the cost involved in the performance of the cargos as smaller than it actually is. The fireworks alone displayed by the Captains of St. Francis in 1963 cost more than 5.000 pesos.

So in some way or other a man who wants to attain the status of 'pasado' has to find at least 40.000 pesos, and it is easy to understand that in a village like Ihuatzio nobody will achieve this without the support of others. It might be imagined that fairly rich families can quite easily push one or more of their people through the hierarchy of commissions. Under certain conditions, for instance when there are not enough eligible men, a 'rich' father may be able

A wapánekwa cross.

The 'Soldiers' on October 4th, 1963.

to put forward his son, but when the father is only a rich man and has never borne a cargo himself, his ambitions are usually soon checked. Evidently the sons of 'pasados' are given preference over others, even if they themselves and their nearest relatives should be poorer people. It is a fact, however, that the new cargueros are preferably found among the richest families of 'pasados'. The principals seem to be intent upon keeping the economic differences between the people of high rank as small as possible, and try to prevent a man becoming a 'pasado' as well as a 'rich man'. Only people who are social failures can be allowed to be 'rich'. Therefore the norm, the official moral standard, is that a man should try to attain the status of a 'pasado'; he may be ambitious, though not openly, in the fulfilment of cargos, but he should refrain from desiring wealth either openly or in secret. Yet, most villagers cherish the more or less secret personal ideal of combining wealth with the status of 'pasado', an ideal, however, which it is very hard to reach with the system as it functions today. Nearly all cargueros are largely dependent on their relatives for the satisfactory execution of their task. This dependent position is another obstacle to the unconditional inheritance of status. A man who does not in every respect comply with the principal norms, or does not pay due respect to his elders, or is not humble and modest in his relations with other villagers, or has an untimely desire for influence and power; a man whose only fault is his lack of social adjustment, such a man will never receive ample support from his relatives for the execution of his commission. People who easily loose their self-control, who soon fly into a passion, or whose self-seeking ambitions are evident, people who act with great ostentation outside the relevant ceremonial field, or otherwise clearly deviate from the pattern of behaviour considered as normal by the inhabitants of Ihuatzio, will find it difficult to rise in the hierarchy of commissions, and will never attain the status of 'pasado'. The cargo system therefore contains a strong element of social control. It is such a strict form of control that outsiders are inclined to call it social compulsion. Young men in Ihuatzio often give the impression of living under great pressure preventing them from developing their individual personalities.

The Captains of St. Francis as well as those of the other gods have the money necessary for the great feasts organised by them collected by so-called colectores. Each of the Captains of St. Francis has three colectores. These receive contributions mainly from members of their own wapánekwecha, and from their Captain's godparents of baptism and confirmation. Now why are members of a wapánekwa willing to contribute to the social success of another member? Various motives exist for this tradition. They have a strong sense of unity, so that the prestige enjoyed by one of them is more or less shared by the whole group, especially by those members who are closely related to the commissioner. Sometimes support is given in the expectation of receiving assistance in return. For a person who contributes substantially to the success of a commissioner by enabling him to spend large sums of money, might perhaps at some future time receive support from a pasado, or later still from an Orénañikwa, or perhaps even so high a personage as an Urétspeti. He or his children may be in need of help, and every person in Ihuatzio can easily imagine situations in which support received from older chiefs or principals and 'pasados' is indispensable, for instance when new appointments have to be made. In some cases the support is not in the first place meant for the commissioner himself, but to help somebody who is directly dependent on him. In that case the commissioner will often be supported by his wife's relatives and by the godparents (compadres) of his children.

In conclusion the author would like to say that few men in Ihuatzio can avoid commissions or other communal duties. Nearly fifty posts have to be filled in the cargo-hierarchy every year. The Wandárich' and the Katáhpecha occupy some twenty positions outside the system, while the 'pasados' (Hurámutich', Orétspetich') and the Orénañikwecha hold some twenty-five more functions. So at any time of the year there are nearly a hundred men occupying a function in the village. As there are about 500 men over 15 years of age, nearly one fifth of the number is in office all the year round, of which about ten per cent. are in charge of a cargo.

7   *The Hurámutich', the rulers*

The actual rulers of the village are the older 'pasados'. They are mostly called Hurámuti (Ruler, Leader) for short, but on ceremonial occasions they are addressed with their official title: 'Acha Maruata Xanta Krusiecha ixu anápuecha', i.e.: 'August Lord of the Holy Crosses of the people who live here'. This title is reminiscent of the numerous crosses that used to indicate the minor shrines of the wapánekwecha. The Hurámutich' are officially referred to as the august rulers of these shrines, and consequently of the wapánekwecha themselves. They are placed above the wapánekwecha, and are therefore real village chiefs and leaders of the whole village community. But they are also members of their own wapánekwa, in which they are Orénaříkwecha. So every Hurámuti is also an Orénaříkwa, but the reverse is not true, not every Orénaříkwa is a Hurámuti, for an old member of a wapánekwa who has led a blameless life but is not quite 'pasado', will certainly be considered as an Orénaříkwa. In such cases he mainly derives his authority and prestige from his old age as well as from the great number of relatives who honour him as the oldest member of the family. But his authority and prestige are restricted to his own wapánekwa, while in matters concerning the whole village he will have no voting rights. As a rule such an Orénaříkwa will never become an Orétspeti, because normally this function is reserved for a Hurámuti. These two groups of functionaries are also referred to as 'Principales'. In the last few years there were in Ihuatzio nearly twenty Hurámutich' and about ten other Principales. There are twelve active functionaries, elected from the group of pasados. They form the executive council of the village, and consist of the nine Urétspecha or wapánekwa-chiefs, and three other functionaries. The latter exercise authority only in matters referring to the administration of the village as a whole. They are the Prioste, the Alkande and the Acha Representante. The Acha Hefe might perhaps be mentioned as the thirteenth member of the executive council and the fourth principal with authority only over the village as a whole, but he should not strictly be included, as his status differs from that of the other twelve chiefs.

As has been said, the Prioste is the head of the Urétich', Kenich' and Wakérox. Consequently he is also head of the ceremonial centre and he lives there as long as he is in office.[14] The Prioste and his subordinates hold office for one year, from December 12th until December 12th of the next year. According to most of our informants he is always a pasado. Other people, however, most of whom belonged to the Kapitan wapánekwa told us that he must be a former Tiputado who has taken a vow that he will shortly accept a major commission. According to the latter information he needs not have passed the whole cargohierarchy to hold this office. We were also told that former Capitanes de Guadalupe were preferred for this office, but it is regrettable that we could not confirm this. The Prioste's authority is an internal one; he never represents the village externally, at any rate not in matters concerning the administration of the village. He supervises the whole staff of the ceremonial centre, with the exception of the Roman Catholic priest, who is of course not his subordinate. It means that the Prioste can also be looked upon as the head of all the women's organisations, because as has been said in the preceding chapter, they are closely connected with the ceremonial centre. His extraordinary position as 'internal leader' made it very difficult for us, as strangers, to come into contact with him. We did not succeed in having an interview with him before the end of the second year of our research, when we obtained his co-operation in taking a census of the members of the wapánekwecha. The Prioste usually tries to avoid contact with strangers and outsiders, and in this he is supported or perhaps coerced by the villagers. We were therefore never able to form a clear idea of some interesting aspects of his position. The Acha Alkande appeared to be higher in rank than the Prioste and it was the Acha Alkande who had great influence over his appointment, but the question remained unanswered whether the Prioste was directly responsible to the other village chiefs or ranked equal with them on account of his headship of another hierarchy. The subordinates of the Prioste at any rate rank lower than those of the Acha Alkande; in this respect the position of the Prioste is between that of the Acha Alkande and that of the Acha Hefe. Yet, judging from the respect paid to the successive Priostes in the three years of our study, we may assume their position to be closer to that of the Acha Alkande than to that of the Acha Hefe.

Usually the internal authority of the Prioste is great, and he is highly respected by the population. This may be due to his direct connection with the world of the gods, because he lives within the enclosed court of the temple. One of the reasons why this office is much coveted by the more ambitious men in the village may be its short duration. One former Prioste considered his year of office as the 'fulfilment of his life', 'his finest year' and 'the year in which he was nearest to God'.

No doubt a Prioste or a former Prioste exercises considerable influence over the appointment of commissioners. Owing to his close contact, during the year of office, with the generation of Urétich' in service, his vote carries much weight when later on these young men become eligible for other functions. Financially the office is not attractive. It is true that the Prioste is assisted in the maintenance of his residence and his household within the ceremonial centre, where he and his family live. But with the inefficient help of wapáne-kwa-members the Prioste is sure to have his own house, garden and lands neglected during his year of office. This situation nearly always offsets the advantage of the help he receives. If the Prioste is not a strong personality, or if for other reasons he does not command enough authority, and Urétich', Kenich' and Wakérox are not too eager to help him he will have to find paid servants himself.

In contrast to the Prioste the Acha Alkande,[15] also called Juez (= Judge), has an officially recognised municipal office, he is a Justice of the Peace in addition to his traditional function. As a matter of fact, in Ihuatzio this public office only exists on paper, and is completely subordinate to the traditional function. This means that the Acha Alkande is the head of the whole organisation of religious ceremonies, one could also say: head of the organisation of the festivities. So the Acha Alkande is the head of the genuine commissioners: the seven Tiputádox, the two Capitanes de San Francisco and their helpers. His tenure of office lasts two years, and like all other functionaries he takes office on December 12th. Officially, that is from the municipality's point of view, this office as well as that of Jefe de Tenencia (Acha Hefe) is supposed to begin on January 1st. These appointments, which are made in the village, are officially looked upon as 'nominations', and are always officially confirmed, although the municipal authorities in Tzintzuntzan sometimes require certain conditions to be fulfilled.

All informants were agreed that the Acha Alkande must always be a pasado. As a rule he is a man between forty-five and sixty years of age. Like that of the Prioste, his authority is concerned with internal affairs. But, as has been said before, we could not ascertain his exact relationship to the Prioste. As in the case of the Prioste, it was quite some time before we got into touch with this chief. In the summer of 1962, however, this barrier was also partly removed and resulted in rather friendly relations with the then Acha Alkande, who was fifty-four years old. We were introduced to him by the Acha Representante (see later sections), with whom we were on good terms. Both men were members of the Tsʌtsʌ'ki wapánekwa. In that year we were allowed to attend some meetings in the village and could thus watch the Acha Alkande and observe the way in which he exercised his authority. The course adopted by this chief, as by most other village chiefs, is very interesting. At a meeting of villagers, convened at the request of the municipal authorities or Crefal, all the people present first listened attentively to the explanatory talks given by representatives of the municipal corporation or by Crefal experts. Then for a long time some of the less important villagers were requested to express their opinions; they were household heads, who were not too young, as a rule not ranking higher than a Helper. Women present on such occasions always sat close together at the south or west side of the hall, and never took part in the proceedings. Often some Orénaŕikwecha attended the meetings, but they too, never took part. After considerable discussion the Acha Hefe often tried to conclude the meeting by giving a very vague summing up of the arguments. For the chiefs and principals try at all costs to prevent decisions or promises being made at such meetings. Only when there is a risk of the principals losing control of the situation due to the fact that villagers who have no right to do so make practical proposals, does the Acha Alkande intervene. He says that the matter will receive careful consideration and that a decision will be made known on a certain day (usually three or four days later). When he has said this, none of the villagers will take the floor again, and the discussions are de facto at an end. But another meeting is called for the same or the next evening with none of the 'strangers' present. Then the real discussions take place, and may sometimes be rather heated. The lower functionaries and people who do not hold any office at all, if they have anything to do with the issue put up for discussion, are again the first to explain their points of view. After hearing their arguments the nine Urétspecha and the three other chiefs take a decision, which is then represented as a 'unanimous decision of all the household heads'. This fiction of unanimity in the taking of decisions is always strictly adhered to. The ultimate decision of the Hurámutich' is not subject to any change, and this being known to all parties, everybody will give his vote to the 'summing up of the arguments', made by the Alkande or the Acha Representante at the end of the meeting. This system prevents outsiders from learning and, perhaps taking advantage of, the differences of opinion between villagers. Furthermore contacts between outsiders and principals are purposely reduced to a minimum.

In the years immediately preceding our study, Crefal specialists relying on very inadequate data on Ihuatzio, had been under the impression that the village was lacking in a working system of traditional chieftainship, that the community was deprived of almost any form of leadership, and was in process of disintegration. So they tried to improve conditions by giving a member of the Kapitan wapánekwa, who presented himself as a liberal-minded man, special training in social management. When he had completed the course organised by Crefal, he endeavoured to obtain a leading part in the village community with the help of the Crefal centre. He gathered around him a number of people who were dissatisfied with the cargo system. As a Wandari and on the whole a good speaker he enjoyed a fair amount of success, so that he had a large number of followers, nearly one fifth of the household heads in the years from 1958 to 1960. His ambitious attempts at gaining power and influence outside the cargo hierarchy naturally brought him into conflict with the Hurámutich'. These principals quietly awaited a suitable opportunity to get rid of him. It came when in 1961 the Kapitan wanted to consolidate his position by having himself elected as Acha Alkande. At this moment the Hurámutich' intervened. At a large meeting the Acha Alkande then in office delivered a long speech making it clear to everyone present that the Kapitan's real object was to acquire a powerful position for himself at the cost of those who, as commissioners, had devoted all their resources to the benefit of the community, that he did not shrink from making use of the support of strangers to attain a position of authority, without having made any sacrifice for the community. The Acha Alkande then continued to invite the Kapitan to undertake the greatest commission, ironically promising him that in that case he would second his nomination in two years' time. In conclusion he loudly told the assembly that in Ihuatzio nobody would ever be able to become Alkande without first fulfilling a major commission. His statement was confirmed by all Hurámutich' with great emphasis. The Kapitan had overreached himself by going to the extreme of advocating his own election as Alkande, and was now defeated before the assembly. For his social and economic position did not permit him to accept one of the major commissions, a fact perfectly well known to the then Acha Alkande. Moreover it was and still is very unusual for a candidate for an executive office in the village to advocate his own election. Such an act is entirely incompatible with the traditional pattern of behaviour, according to which the most eligible candidates are supposed during the time preceding the election to be seen in public as little as possible, or even to keep in hiding. The activities of the Kapitan were much more appropriate to a political struggle for power, and seemed to have as their main object the acquisition of the office of Alkande with the influence attached to it. Consequently they had raised great suspicion among most of the villagers. The Kapitan was soon deserted by the majority of his followers and by the end of 1962 his position had become so difficult that he was forced to leave the village, and settled in Pátzcuaro in needy circumstances. This incident is a good illustration of the power of the traditional system and throws some light on the way in which the Hurámutich' exercise their power in accordance with the system.

The Acha Alkande is a very important member of the traditional executive, not least because he instals the commissioners ceremonially in their office and supervises and judges their achievements. His judgement greatly affects the prestige that a commissioner will enjoy and the timing of his nomination for another function.

The Acha Representante is the chief who ranks highest in the traditional hierarchy of functions. However, he combines the highest indigenous office with the least important public office. In this public office of 'Representante de la Comunidad Indígena' (Representative of the Indigenous Community) he is entrusted with the management of the ancient communal lands of the village, which lie on the southern slopes of Mount Tariatak'heri (see chapter III, p. 110, note 11). His official function is therefore limited to the rare questions that may arise in connection with these communal waste lands, consisting of poor pastures and almost exhausted woodland of very little commercial value. Yet, however small their value may be, to a relatively poor village like Ihuatzio they are of some importance.

Much more important than his public office is the Acha Representante's traditional office. He is sometimes referred to as Orétspetin hurámuti maruécheri (Ruler of the august Principals). He is chosen from the former Soldier Captains and is the supreme chief of the village, the leader who, if necessary, acts as the external representative of the village. The villagers look upon him not only as their representative before the local government, but also as the chief who regulates the relations of the community with the outside world and protects the village to the best of his abilities from its evil influences. He is, as one of our informants expressed it, "like a tree that shelters us". In times when the village is threatened by outside influences, he will also be able in various ways to exercise his authority over internal questions, because it is his duty to organise the opposition to the threat. In certain circumstances he may even resemble an ancient war-chief.

He holds office for seven years, after which he is eligible for re-election. Information given to us suggests that he is usually a man older, sometimes much older, than forty-five before he is elected, and he often remains in office for the rest of his life. The man who was Acha Representante at the time of our investigations, from December, 1960 till October, 1963 had been first elected in 1950 and was in the second half of his second term of office. He was in his early sixties, a man at first inconspicuous to strangers, but on further acquaintance appearing to have a great ascendancy over the other residents of Ihuatzio. On the whole he was a sensible and moderate man in his social contacts, although he could occasionally be too crafty. Before we started our research the Crefal experts had hardly ever met him. There was a special reason for this. Most of the Acha Representante's private land was located on the opposite lake shore, near Tzurumútaro, better known locally as La Playa. He worked his own fields and those of the nearby State boarding-school, called Melchor Ocampo. From Monday to Friday he usually stayed at La Playa, which is much nearer to the Crefal centre than Ihuatzio. Mostly he was at home in Ihuatzio only on Saturdays and Sundays. As the Crefal working-hours coincided with the time he spent at La Playa, and the experts of the centre had no business there, it was possible for the Crefal staff, who had been working in Ihuatzio for nine years (1951-1960), to have no contact with the Acha Representante. They had hardly noticed this village chief, while the Centre remained entirely ignorant of his great influence. This influence soon became apparent to us, when we were in a position to come into direct contact with the Acha Representante; on working days we went to see him at La Playa, on Saturdays or Sundays in Ihuatzio. But for a long time it was difficult for us to get on with him; he had little confidence in strangers in general and the Crefal staff in particular. It was only during the third year of our stay that our relations with him assumed a more friendly character. Then he invited us on several occasions to see him in his home in Ihuatzio.

It is not easy on the grounds of our own researches to describe the general aspects of the office of Acha Representante. The predecessor of the present chief died a long time ago, and most people in Ihuatzio have only vague memories of this 'Mr. Representative', not to mention the earlier ones. We have therefore a clear picture only of the present Acha Representante, who has his individual peculiarities, just as his predecessors had theirs. His long tenure of office will make it possible for him to put the stamp of his personality on his period of office, a thing more difficult for the Prioste and the Alkande to achieve since they are in office for a short time only.

The present Acha Representante told us that in his opinion his first period of seven years was characterised by land disputes with Tzintzuntzan, and by attempts to revive the wapánekwecha. He made it appear as if he was the man who persuaded the wapánekwecha to resume their traditional activities in the service of the community. Other informants, however, described him as a real innovator. According to them collective labour done by the wapánekwecha was introduced during his period of office. Formerly, so they said, the wapánekwecha were only concerned with the care of the Gwatapera and the ceremonial centre and public works had never been carried out by these groups. The present Acha Representante was the first to employ the wapánekwecha in the struggle against Tzintzuntzan. He called up the men, wapánekwa by wapánekwa, went into the mountains with them to replace the boundary-stones that had been destroyed by the Tzintzuntzeños. Then he ordered barricades to be placed on the mountain paths from Tzintzuntzan to Mount Tariatak'heri, and in some places he had trenches dug to obstruct the transportation of stolen cattle to Tzintzuntzan. In this way the wapánekwecha got used to collective labour, and later the chief arranged for public works to be executed, such as enclosing the cemetery, building a school, laying on water for the ceremonial centre and paving and improving the roads to Sanabria and Cucuchucho. The sometimes violent struggles with Tzintzuntzan brought him a lot of personal inconvenience. A few times he was taken prisoner and detained for some days in the primitive gaol of the municipal capital, with no one to look after him. But his perseverance combined with his 'martyrdom' won him considerable prestige. Now his prestige had always been great, because he had had an impressive career as a commissioner, and had never refused to place his private means in the service of the community. The large expenses involved could always be made good by the good crops from his lands year after year, and by the income derived from his work for the boarding-school. His success can probably be accounted for not only by his personal diligence, but also by the fact that he owned relatively very fertile lands by the side of the lake, which are to some extent independent of rainfall. Many villagers considered him, however, specially favoured by the gods. He continued to give financial contributions on behalf of the community, even when he had become 'pasado'. Even today he spends large sums of money, by Ihuatzio standards, on communal activities and works. To outsiders it is strange and at the same time impressive to notice the great deference shown to him by the villagers, while in appearance he does not differ from an ordinary Indian farmer. Equally impressive is the silence of the audience when he takes the floor at a meeting. He is always the last man to speak. Yet he is not a good speaker, certainly not in Spanish, which he speaks badly, but even in Tarascan he is not considered to be a great orator. To people who are used to the European cultural atmosphere the deference and ceremonial with which he is surrounded on many public occasions at first give the impression that he is a high-handed ruler, who imposes his will upon others wherever and whenever he likes. This is by no means the case. As an executive he is supervised by the old pasados, and as a rule he will consult them as well as the Alkande before taking a decision. Moreover he will never take a decision before acquainting himself of the opinions the villagers may have on the matter. The traditional procedure at meetings as described earlier whereby those lowest in rank are to speak first, enables the principals to learn the different opinions in the village until the moment a decision has to be made. It is interesting to observe the great tension with which the Hurámutich' watch the reactions of the public at an important meeting. They play an intricate game with their subordinates, aiming at the ideal-typical unanimous vote. This aim is then attained in a more or less fair way by making it crystal clear to minority groups that their standpoint has no chance of being adopted.

The whole complex of relationships among the principals themselves and between the principals as a whole and the rest of population is characterised by reciprocity rather than by responsibility. The Acha Representante enjoys respect and consideration as a reward for the great sacrifices made by him for the sake of the community and because he is nearer to the gods. Of course respect is also shown to him because everybody prefers to have him as a friend rather than as an enemy, for it is undeniable that he is an influential man. Even though he is a man of influence, he cannot act arbitrarily, for he is himself too dependent on his blood relations, his wapánekwa and his cere-monial relatives, who supported him in his progress towards his present status. As a matter of fact, the concept of chieftainship as a means to exercise power is entirely alien to the inhabitants of Ihuatzio. They still look upon their chiefs and the latter look upon themselves as commissioners, as 'shade-trees', as experienced men and favourites of the gods, who are therefore the most suitable persons to protect the community against the powers that threaten it from within and without. The main pre-occupation of the chiefs and principals is the maintenance of the existing social system. When they see that one of their institutions is declining, they may be prepared to reform it provided the result will be a strengthening of the institution as such; for the rest they prefer to leave things as they are. We may well assume that since the beginning of this century there have been considerable threats to the continu-ation of the traditional system, and that under the pressure of such forces the social order in Ihuatzio has frequently been compelled to adjust itself to the new conditions. This fact and what has been said in the foregoing sections explains why, judged by our standards, the chiefs and principals of Ihuatzio are grumpy old men, who cannot refrain from finding fault with modern conditions of life and always hold up the past as an example.

The chiefs as protectors of the people, do not in fact bear responsibility, as we understand the word. They may make mistakes, but as long as they themselves are the greatest victims no one will blame them. We once witnessed the Acha Representante taking an entirely mistaken decision. It happened at the end of the second year of our researches, and our relations with this chief had just improved considerably. He had made a suggestion to build a health centre in co-operation with members of the Crefal staff and government officials. So a meeting was held to decide where the centre was to be built, and how it was to be financed. There was a difference of opinion in the village especially over the site of the centre. A great many men, among whom was the Acha Representante, wanted the centre to be built on the site of the old Gwatapera. But none of the speakers of lower rank made this proposal, because they were afraid of the parish priest, who was very much against the plan. At the end of the meeting the Acha Representante personally launched the idea of rebuilding the Gwatapera, "because it stood on communal ground". Nobody objected when he included the decision in his 'summing up of the arguments'. So it seemed as if in our presence it had been decided to establish the health centre on the site of the old Gwatapera. At that moment, however, some Hurámutich' and Orénarikwecha appeared to be clearly upset, because they evidently disapproved of what was going on, although they did not express their objections. A few days later it was clear that the Acha Representante had completely underestimated the influence exercised in this question by the priest with the support of the women's organisations. At the second and final meeting, at which we were not present, the Acha Representante's proposal was reversed, because it would prevent the priest from extending the adjoining private school. The Acha Representante then offered a piece of land of his own, which offer counterbalanced his defeat. He was praised for his generous offer, although it was not accepted, because the site was too far away from the centre of the village. Then a member of Rivera, whose wife belonged to TsʌtsʌꞋki,[16] offered a site in the middle of the village and this was accepted.

I have called the Acha Representante an 'external leader', and the Alkande and the Prioste 'internal leaders'. These concepts must now be defined more precisely. The Acha Representante deals with the relations between the village and the outside world. In this capacity his activities may also be concerned with internal issues, but as a rule this is only the case when external influences may affect internal conditions, or when internal measures may have consequences for the contacts with the outside world. Examples of the former case are the projects executed with the aid of Crefal and the government. Examples of the second case are the construction and paving of roads, and the placing of barricades on the mountain paths.

The two other chiefs are in control of internal matters. Their duties are aimed at the correct functioning of the system of commissions.

The chieftainships of the Prioste, the Alkande and the Acha Representante involve obligations similar to those of the commissioners. They are also called upon, although to a lesser extent, to contribute from their own means to expenses made on behalf of the community. The Acha Representante regularly receives sick people and their relatives in his house at La Playa. On their way to and from the hospital at Pátzcuaro they sometimes stay with him for several days. He is always expected to contribute generously when there is a collection of money. Only Orénarikwecha, Urétspecha and old Hurámutich' in general may consider themselves released from such obligations. The opinion is that these old men have attained a status and a degree of leadership that should release them from all financial obligations.

8   *The Roman Catholic priest*

The Roman Catholic parish priest, whose living is Ihuatzio, and whose parish includes some neighbouring villages, is of Tarascan descent. The language spoken in the village is his mother tongue. He is in his forties and lives with his sister in the priest's residence in Ihuatzio. He is a domineering man, who has also given evidence of possessing a calculating character. It seems that he takes the interests of the Church and the preaching of the Christian faith very much to heart, but some private personal interests also occupy a great deal of his attention. His office as well as his personal qualities have repeatedly led to conflicts with the village principals. Most of their differences have been prevented from being widely known, but there have been occasional open conflicts.

The Roman Catholic priest considers himself to be the shepherd whose duty it is to save the villagers as 'God's stray sheep' from ruin. But the pre-Spanish god in the shape of a wolf looks down from the gallery of the church-tower, upon the village below, as if to scorn this idea from the start.

The people of Ihuatzio look upon the priest as their representative or rather defender before Tatá' Thios (God the Father), Naná Maria (Mother Mary) and other great gods, just as they consider their principals as their protectors in worldly matters. So long as the priest sticks to his task of being the intermediary between the people and their gods, all is well, and he is the dear Tatá Cura (Father Priest) of the village. The present priest, however, does not like to confine himself to these limits and thus often causes trouble. During the three years of our study and before that time he persisted in trying to play a leading role in the village and to interfere in many matters which have from time immemorial belonged to the exclusive domain of the traditional village chiefs. His activities in this respect and his partial success had, before we started our researches, caused the Crefal staff to believe that he was the most important so-called 'negative' leader in the village, i.e. the most influential man to oppose the development projects. This fact and his own ambitions are the reasons why I have felt obliged to describe his function here, for, properly speaking, he does not fit into the traditional hierarchy of functionaries.

The Roman Catholic priest is or pretends to be an avowed opponent of the traditional system. He ignores its manifestations as much as possible. He even persisted in telling us that there were no wapánekwecha any more. Outsiders are told that there are no traditional chiefs in the village and he pretends to be the only and generally recognised unofficial leader of the community. The Hurámutich' know this, but because, as has been said before, they want to avoid any direct contact with strangers, they do not object at all. When in 1958 Crefal started its project of chicken-farming the priest promised to cooperate on the condition that he would also receive a credit and technical assistance. Mexican law, however, prohibits the granting of credits to priests, so his condition could not be complied with. Crefal experts said that he was offered technical assistance, but the priest denies this. From that moment the priest has rather strongly opposed the activities of Crefal in his parish. However, he could not prevent eighteen household heads in Ihuatzio accepting the credits and assistance offered by Crefal, and starting chicken farms. To demonstrate his opposition to the Crefal Centre he had some of his faithful followers build a large chicken run in the front court next to the main entrance of the church. It was an ostentatious way of building a competitive 'demonstration chicken run' and a means to prove to the Crefal specialists that he could put his plans into effect without their help. A large number of villagers, and some Hurámutich' among them, resented his using part of the ceremonial centre for commercial purposes, and they let no opportunity pass to show their annoyance. But the priest derived income not only from his chicken farm, but also from the sale of medicines which he was able to obtain cheaply through friends he had in the capital. Several informants told us that his sister practised as a physician, making diagnoses and writing prescriptions, without any qualifications to do so. If this information is correct, it is quite clear why the priest so strongly opposed the establishment of a health centre and did everything in his power to prevent the reconstruction of the Gwatapera.

From the foregoing one might conclude that the position of the priest was strong and his influence extremely great. But he also suffered great setbacks. All his attempts to eliminate the traditional ceremonials, the indigenous rites and the cargo system were in vain, as was his refusal to admit the indigenous groups of dancers to the ceremonial centre. His sermons, which made it perfectly clear that he strongly objected to the traditional festivities and the display of fireworks and the drinking-bouts failed to have any effect. Great as his influence in certain matters may be, in other respects he is bound hand and foot. He is not in a position to risk a long conflict with the Hurámutich'. As soon as he leaves his residence he faces the Prioste and his assistants; in the last resort his domestic staff does not obey him, but the chiefs and principals and even the sacramental objects and shrines are guarded by the subordinates of the traditional chiefs of the village. Only by a policy of divide and rule does he sometimes succeed in making his strong personal influence felt and he has often proved himself to be a past master of this art.

9   *Female heads*

Owing to lack of data little can be said about the female heads. One thing, however, was evident, namely that the prominent members of the women's organisations, and the most important women in general, were usually the wives or daughters of the male principals.

Some influential women were exceptions to the rule in that they owed their status to their fame as xurihkas (traditional curers and midwives). It was these qualities that gave the sister of the priest some influence in the village, which she used to form a religious society of girls under her guidance. This society, the so-called Hijas de María (Daughters of Mary), occupied itself with all sorts of social activities, for instance the organisation of bazaars.

Notes to Chapter IV

[1]   cf. Gilberti, 1559, p. 149: vretietsperi = persona de mayor edad (aged person).
[2]   Manuscrito Medina (unpublished) Sambrasko Hiwatse Ereti; Oración del Wandari. cf. Medina, and Van Zantwijk, 1963.
[3]   A Tarascan corruption of the Spanish word Diputados.
[4]   In the singular: Keni = 'He who climbs trees'; cf. Gilberti, 1559, p. 97.
[5]   A Tarascan corruption of the Spanish word vaqueros.

[6] Anticipating on the conclusion to be made in the next chapter, I have here used the term Gods and not Saints. The term santos or saints is here clearly used in a sense different from that usually attached to it by Roman Catholics. Furthermore it will later on appear that the concept of saint as it exists in Ihuatzio does not differ in essence from polytheism.

[7] cf. Ley Orgánica Municipal del Estado de Michoacán no. 102, Cap. X, artículos 69-79.

[8] Idem, art. 69.

[9] Idem, art. 70.

[10] Idem, artículos 72 y 73.

[11] Idem, art. 75.

[12] They are sometimes called San Francisco Capitán, or in a corrupted form: Sambrasko Kapitán.

[13] Singular: Orénaïikwa, which is probably derived from ori, uri = first, point, nose; and arini = to tell something to somebody. The compound noun therefore also means 'ruler'.

[14] "Prioste iachaati maruaskusindi Thiosio tatá kaxirekwam ka ïyamendu ambé imangui Thiosio anápweka" (Medina manuscript): "The Prioste has the control of the magnificent place of God and the priest and of everything belonging to it".

[15] Composed of Acha, which is Tarascan for Gentleman, Nobleman, and Alkande or Arkande, which is a Spanish-Tarascan corruption of the Arabian word al-qadi (judge).

[16] He was the household head who should have belonged to TsᴀtsᴀʼkI, because he lived in the grounds of his father-in-law, who was a member of this wapánekwa. He probably made this offer to try to recover part of the prestige he had lost (see chapter III).

V *the people of Ihuatzio in their universe*

In 1952 Pedro Carrasco published a study of the Tarascan religion and its social and economic implications ('Tarascan Folk Religion'). The study led him to conclude that "unorganized (non-Church) religion is comparatively unimportant among the Tarascans. Most religion in the Tarascan culture has to be described in terms of the Church, a national (and international) institution with its own ideology, personnel, organisation and particular interests".[1]

He regards Tarascan religion today as an essentially Christian faith, with a few significant pagan frills, but he does not recognise an all-embracing pagan structure in modern Tarascan religious thought.

Carrasco's study is based on wider experience, gained from more than one village community, than our investigation; yet the data obtained in Ihuatzio, although incomplete, lead to some reasonable doubt as to the validity of his conclusion, as far as Ihuatzio is concerned.

People in Ihuatzio do not make an essential distinction between social and religious functions. In the preceding chapter it has been seen that most of the principals and other prominent people hold religious-ceremonial offices in addition to those which we consider as ordinary administrative ones. Like Redfield[2] we might define community life in Ihuatzio as 'sacral' and consequently attribute a fair degree of 'folk-nature' to it. As we do not fully subscribe to the philosophy of life on which Redfield's theory of the Folk-urban continuum is based, we shall repeat our above statement in other words. The system of religious-ceremonial acts still forms a fairly well integrated part of daily life in Ihuatzio. People associate with the gods in more or less the same way as they do with important and influential people from their social environment. There is no essential difference between the way in which they treat and greet a chief, a principal, a 'pasado', or any other important person, and the way they address their 'saints'; at most there may be a difference in the degree of greatness. The fact that the images of saints are kept in the houses of the commissioners in charge of them is in accordance with the fact that the 'saints' are incorporated in the life of the community. The 'saints' are part of people's lives, they are directly involved in the daily life of the community, although they are of an order different from that of the villagers themselves. The principle of reciprocity, which plays such an important part in the social life of the villagers, to a certain extent also determines their relationship with the 'saints', or one might also say the 'gods'. Offerings are brought to the gods in the expectation of a reward: adequate rainfall, recovery from illness, success in social relations, a good catch of fish, fair earnings from trade, etc. If the offerings and the devotion shown remain unrewarded, the gods concerned are sometimes abused; in some cases their images are beaten or dragged along through the dust. Often such gods are threatened with reprisals. It should be noted, however, that these Tarascans in Ihuatzio adopt such an attitude only when they are convinced that they, on their part, have fulfilled all the obligations due to the 'saints'. But often this is not so, in which case they try to avert the anger of the gods by bringing greater offerings and showing more faithful devotion.

1   *The ceremonies*

A clearer idea of the position of the gods in the day-to-day life of the community can be gained from a description of the most important ceremonies during the administrative year:

December 12th:

During the great feast of the Virgin of Guadalupe, the saint who, in Ihuatzio, ranks immediately after St. Francis, the necessary new officials and new commissioners are appointed. Once in every seven years a new Acha Representante is installed in office, or the old Acha Representante's mandate is renewed. In alternate years a new Alkande takes up his duties, and, like the Acha Representante, he is installed in office by the oldest Hurámuti.

Then the Alkande does the same to the Prioste and the nine Capitanes: the two Captains of St. Francis and the seven Tiputádox with their helpers. On this occasion all the eleven images of the gods are carried from the houses of the retiring commissioners to the front court of the church, and from there to the houses of the new commissioners. First the three small images of St. Francis, which are nevertheless called the 'biggest', are carried by the retiring Soldier-Captain and his helpers in procession to the house of his successor. If the man who has been named by the Alkande and the Hurámutich' as the new commissioner accepts his appointment, he will respectfully meet the procession and receive the images after speeches have been exchanged. By accepting the images into his house he confirms the acceptance of the commission. The images remain in his house during his year of office, except on ceremonial occasions, when they are placed in the church. If everything happens in accordance with the wishes of the chiefs and principals, the above ceremonial transfer is repeated eight times for the new Moorish Captain and the seven other Capitanes or Tiputádox to receive the images entrusted to their care for one year. The seven Tiputádox ought to receive their individual images in the order mentioned in the preceding chapter, but according to several informants these occasions give rise to "endless disputes on the right sequence". Such differences occasionally result in minor incidents, but as a rule they do not cause great difficulties. A much more serious situation arises when a commission is refused. It happened in the last year of our study that the man who had been named by the Alkande and the other chiefs and the principals as a candidate for the office of Soldier-Captain tried to avoid this commission. When the procession with the three small images arrived at his house near the village square, he did not come outside, nor was the door opened. In spite of the efforts made by the then Wandari[3] and the Alkande to persuade the man to accept, he did not admit the images into his house. Then they were left in the street in front of his house, where they remained for some days. Many villagers consider this dramatic accusation on the part of the gods whose images are left standing in the dust as the greatest disgrace that can be brought upon a family. The chiefs and principals leave the images standing outside not only by way of a sanction, but also in the hope that under the pressure of public opinion the unwilling candidate may change his mind. Similar incidents in previous years prove that they are sometimes successful; and in some cases a near relative of the candidate may take up the image(s), which is then also considered an acceptable solution. But in the above-mentioned case nothing of the kind happened. After some time the images were removed to the front court of the church "as a disgrace to the whole village". This meant that the chiefs kept the commission open for application by any sufficiently qualified candidate.

The main reason that the above candidate refused the cargo was his ardent wish to use his hard-earned savings of 20.000 pesos to buy a house in Pátzcuaro. After the incident his social position in the village soon deteriorated and forced him to try to realise his intention as soon as possible, so that he might be able to escape from such hostile surroundings. But before he could carry out his plans the god began his punishment (this was at any rate the interpretation placed on the following events by the villagers). Soon after he had refused the commission his wife and daughter suddenly became seriously ill. But the man was determined to buy a house in Pátzcuaro; so a few days later he went to Pátzcuaro for the purpose. He got on the bus in Ihuatzio, carrying the money on his body under his clothes. Again 'the anger of St. Francis' struck him, for when he arrived at Pátzcuaro all the money was gone and never found again. Some time later his daughter died, and then his daughter-in-law fell ill. Her condition soon grew worse, and her husband, the son of the man who had refused the cargo, at last succeeded in breaking his father's resistance. They agreed that the son should undertake the commission and that the father should bear the greater part of the cost. The son went to the front court of the church and took the three images to his house. The chiefs and principals accepted this solution because after all that had happened the father would not be able to hold the high office himself; and for once they allowed a man who had not yet completed the necessary number of minor commissions to skip one rung of the hierarchic ladder. Thus it happened that the year 1963 witnessed an extremely young man in the office of Soldier-Captain. Within three days after the acceptance of the commission the wife and the mother of the new commissioner recovered their health.

The above-mentioned refusal took place on December 12th, 1962. All the other images were duly transferred to the new commissioners. Several informants told us that between 1948 and 1956 there had been frequent refusals of commissions, most of the unwilling candidates secretly leaving the village. Some did so even before the images were offered to them; they had gathered sufficient information to know when the fatal offer could be expected.

On December 12th the Prioste and his assistants are also installed in their offices. So are his subordinates, the Urétich' or Urecha, the external chiefs of the wapánekwecha. The retiring Prioste and his wife vacate the Priostería, the official residence within the front court of the church, and the successor and his wife move in.

Meanwhile the feast of the Virgin of Guadalupe is celebrated with dances and ceremonial addresses in the house of the commissioner and afterwards in the church. There are also the inevitable fireworks.

December 16th:

The feast of the IrΛts'Λ takes place on December 16th. On this day a cere-monial procession goes about the village. The wapánekwa in service arranges the ceremonies. Its Ureti of the previous ceremonial year, in a special dress, plays the part of IrΛts'Λ (probably: 'the wrinkled man').[4] The IrΛts'Λ wears a leather mask with patches of hair made to resemble an old man with a beard. A grey wig completes the image of old age. Over his trousers he wears the leather 'chaparreras' (= pointed pieces of leather hanging down from the waist to protect his legs in front and at the back). Further he has shoes instead of huaraches (sandals). According to local tradition these garments give him the appearance of a hunter. In one hand he holds a bell, in the other a stick. All his movements are accompanied by the ringing of the bell, while the stick which he stamps on the ground "serves to indicate his great age". Usually this 'old man' is a young man in disguise. He plays an important part in the ceremonies of the day, which are divided into two parts. First there is a dance performed by the elderly women of the wapánekwa on duty. They are the wives of the elderly members of the wapánekwa. The wife of the Ureti, herself as a rule a young woman, directs this group of women. The IrΛts'Λ dances between the women, calling them 'Maríkwecha' ('girls'), which is another reminder of his old age. On this occasion the women wear festive dresses, consisting of wide, bright red woollen pleated skirts, embroidered blouses, decorated with multi-coloured designs on the shoulders and over it the large shawl crossed on the breast.

They wear two plaits with bright-coloured ribbons braided in. One of the shoulder-ornaments has a weaving-reed tied to it. They wear ear- and neck-ornaments and on their heads new sombreros. They are barefooted. The way they are dressed and decorated is in complete accord with the festive dress of marriageable girls. The dance-group starts from the residence of the new Ureti. Accompanied by a great many members of the wapánekwa and other villagers, the women go dancing through the village headed by the wife of the new Ureti. The IrΛts'Λ who accompanies them, makes a lot of noise, now and then chasing the bystanders apart or urging the 'girls' to hurry up. The explanation given for his performance was that he was chasing the coyote (prairie-wolf), the traditional village god (or perhaps the latter's 'fellow-being, i.e. his counterpart; see later sections), along the places where the wapánekwecha settled at the foundation of the present village.

During another part of the ceremonial the IrΛts'Λ is at the head of the pro-cession which consists of the Maríkwecha, the other members of the wapáne-kwa on duty, some musicians, and the on-lookers. This procession goes to the residence of the Prioste in the front court of the church. The women of the wapánekwa dance with the IrΛts'Λ to the music of Tarascan songs. In reward the Prioste gives them one or two bottles of strong liquor, which is consumed on the spot by the IrΛtsΛ, and the other male members of the wapánekwa and their ceremonial relatives and friends. The ceremony is repeated in the house of the priest and successively in the houses of the Acha Representante, the Acha Alkande, the Acha Hefe, the Captain of St. Francis and the seven Tipu-tádox or captains of the other saints. At first all is well and due respect is paid to the hosts, but when the procession is halfway through the village, many men of the wapánekwa on duty are drunk and the festival ends in disorder. On this day, however, the Acha Hefe and his assistants, the Katáhpecha, are very indulgent towards the members of the wapánekwa in duty. Only disorderly persons belonging to another wapánekwa run the risk of being arrested.

According to many informants every year it is the Rivérecha who take up their duties on December 12th. If this information is correct, the IrΛts'Λ can only be a member of this wapánekwa or of that of the Hwankrúsecha. Ac-cording to this system the festival of December 16th during the last two decades (1944-1963) must have been organised seven times by the former and thirteen times by the latter wapánekwa. In the years when December 12th is a Saturday, Sunday or Monday, December 16th will fall in the first period of service of the year. In other years the festival is in the second duty period and must consequently be organised by the second wapánekwa on duty.[5] Asked after the religious meaning of the festival of December 16th, some informants said that on that day they celebrated "the announcement of the coming of the Messiah". But the Roman Catholic church commemorates this fact on April 6th. A very old informant who belonged to Kapitan told us that December 16th used to mark the beginning of a series of nine daily ceremonies which were performed by the nine wapánekwecha on nine successive days before the crosses around the Gwatapera. After nine days it is Christmas, the fourteenth day of the religious-ceremonial calendar of Ihuatzio or the first day of the second period of thirteen days.[6] The numbers 9 and 13 are of special significance in the pre-Spanish forms of social organisation, as well as in the Mexican indigenous calendars.

December 25th:

Unlike December 16th, which is an entirely 'pagan' festival, the Christmas celebrations are clearly Christian in nature. High mass is celebrated and nearly everybody goes to church. In the afternoon and evening there are indeed performances of traditional dances, and on Christmas Eve the wapánekwa on duty provides the revellers with atole (a maize drink) and bread.

January 1st:

This day is celebrated as a thanksgiving day for the past year rather than as the first day of the New Year. Music, drinks and bread are again provided by the wapánekwa on duty. According to the pre-Spanish calendar January 1st is the first day of the second twenty-day period, for December 12th to December 31st inclusive constitute a period of twenty days. Some informants referred to the celebrations on January 1st as "the festival of the wapánekwecha". Evidently these groups then commemorate their own origin, or the origin of the entire composite organisation, but no further details could be obtained.

January 6th:

The festival of the 'Tres Reyes Magos' (Three Kings) is again the responsibility of the wapánekwa on duty. On this day some people give presents to children. According to the autochthonous calendar this is the last day of the second thirteen-day period.

The first movable feast (February): Virgen de la Soledad

This festival is organised by one of the seven Tiputádox, namely the 'Captain of the Virgin of Solitude'. In the morning this captain takes the image of the 'saint' from his house to the church. Ceremonial greetings take place in the front court and before the Priostería, the Wandárich' delivering the addresses. The chiefs and principals come there to pay homage to the image. Many villagers have already done this while the image was on its way to the church. Then the villagers come together in the ceremonial centre to attend the actual service.

In the afternoon the image is returned to the house of the commissioner in charge. He distributes bread and atole among the onlookers. As a rule traditional dances are performed, in front of the image inside the house and in the garden of the Tiputado. This feast is nine days before Shrove Tuesday.

The second movable feast: Madre Mayor

This feast falls in Lent and is also organised and directed by a Tiputado, the Capitan de la Madre Mayor. The ritual is the same as that of the feasts of the other saints.

At that time the Acha Representante and all the farmers go to the slopes of Mount Tariatak'heri to cut wood from the communal lands, and perform certain rituals. We were not allowed to attend this ceremony; nor could any further information be obtained about it. Some of the women who had remained behind in the village told us in 1963 that every year at about this time the men and the Acha Representante went into the hills "to pray for a timely start of the rainy season".

Palm Sunday is the beginning of the Semana Santa (Holy Week). Its celebrations are for the account of the whole village, that is to say for the account of the joint wapánekwecha. The women's organisations also make their contributions. They make embroidered articles and garments for the church and organise a bazaar. Fireworks and dances performed by members of the wapánekwecha form part of the celebration of Easter by the church.

The third movable feast, that of Nuestro Amo, is also held in the Semana Santa, and forms another part of a minor commission (Therúnchekwa sapichu). The image of Jesus Christ, which bears the name of 'Nuestro Amo' (Our Master),[7] is taken to the church by the commissioner in charge of it in a procession organised by him. In the church and in the house of the captain a ritual is performed similar to that of the other 'saints'.

The next movable feast, the Expiración, is another feast 'of the whole village', i.e. of all the wapánekwecha. This feast has only been celebrated since the Great Revolution (1910-1920). According to one of our informants the reason for having this feast was that "this saint delivered us from great distress, when we had prayed to him to help us and prevent the village from being destroyed by the federal troops in 1914". In 1962 the festival was held on April 24th and 25th. In a side street in the extreme west of the village a chapel had been set up made of tule mats two metres square. On the outside it was hung with pieces of pink and yellow silk and inside with white pieces of the same material. Inside hung pictures of Jesus Christ as the 'Santo de la Expiración' and of other 'saints', that of San Isidro Labrador being the most conspicuous. These pictures were surrounded by silvery and gilt cardboard stars with angels' heads. Under the picture of Christ a radioset blared light music for entertainment, broadcast by the Pátzcuaro Commercial Radio. In the afternoon rockets were fired and this went on throughout the evening.

At nightfall there was a procession to the little chapel. It consisted not only of people from Ihuatzio, but also of visitors from the Tarascan villages of Santa Fé and San Andrés Tziróndaro from the island of Jarácuaro. These visitors had brought decorated offerings, so-called coronitas (little crowns), and flowers, candles and incense or copal for the saint. The offerings were put before the little chapel. People sang and danced. There were 16 dancers from Jarácuaro, eight men and eight women, and three musicians, two playing violins, the third a guitar. These dancers and musicians from Jarácuaro, the island of the goddess Xarátanga, walked at the head of the procession – as they do every year –

when it was formed again to pass through the barrio of Ascensión on its way to the ceremonial centre. The offerings were taken up again and the procession set in motion. Two young men headed the procession, each wearing a mask representing the head of an ox. They danced, sang, and jumped about, as they led the way. They were followed by one of the village bands playing religious music interspersed with military tunes, and popular pasodobles. Then came the people from Jarácuaro, those from the other villages and from Ihuatzio. When they had reached the church the priest came outside to meet them in the front court. The women who carried the offerings knelt down, the priest pronounced the benediction and immediately retired into his residence. Meanwhile the church was filled with villagers, but a space in the centre was reserved for the participants in the procession. The latter now delivered their coronitas, flowers, candles and incense-burners, which were put before the altar. People sang, after which groups of dancers from Jarácuaro gave performances in the front court. The dancers wore bright clothes; men as well as women had wide silk skirts, the men wearing silk trousers under them. The two leaders of the dancers wore red cloaks, the dancers azure, pink or white ones. They all wore silvery or gilt crowns with little mirrors fixed on them.

The feast was continued the next day . By the side of the church, against the outer wall of the front court, stood booths where people sold drinks and snacks. The proceeds of the sale went to the church. This part was organised by the 'Hijas de María', an association of girls and young women under the direction of the sister of the priest.

In the evening a pastorela, a pastoral play, was performed by people from Santa Fé. After this many people indulged in strong liquor until they got drunk. Others sang Tarascan songs and performed traditional dances, while again the banging of rockets and squibs enhanced the joy of the revellers.

May 3rd:

In the neighbouring village of Cucuchucho the feast of Santa Cruz (Holy Cross) is celebrated on this day. Many people from Ihuatzio take part in it. According to some old informants there used to be ceremonies in Ihuatzio on that day before the wapánekwa crosses, and before the yákatas in the old ruined city, in which many Tarascans from other villages, also from Cucuchucho and from the islands, took part. This piece of information was endorsed by elderly informants on the islands. One of the chiefs on the island of Yunuén also told us that on this day his parents used to go to Ihuatzio to worship the sun, the moon and the stars. They used to go to the yákatas at night. In the autochthonous calendar this is the last day of the eleventh thirteen-day period, as well as the day on which the Pleiads disappear from the Mexican firmament.

June 13th:

The feast of St. Anthony, the fourth 'minor commission' of the year, is again the responsibility of a Tiputado, the Capitán de San Antonio.

June 16th:

On this day in 1963 the Warucha (fishermen) held their festival, which was mentioned in the third chapter. The most important fishermen of Sagrado Corazón had met a few days before and agreed to celebrate the festival of their 'destino' (occupational group) again after an interval of seven years. The fishermen from Ascensión joined them and together they hired one of the two village bands. The musicians and five dancers and the leaders of the fishermen walked at the head of the procession which, on the feastday itself, went along the streets of Ihuatzio, calling at the houses of all the village chiefs and Capitanes. The houses should have been visited in the order mentioned before, but as usual there was an argument about the order of precedence of the Tiputádox. We witnessed the ceremony in the house of the Captain of Guadalupe, who was visited immediately after the chiefs of the village. The house was in the barrio of Ascensión. Playing their instruments, the musicians turned from the street into the yard of the Captain of Guadalupe's house. The Captain had given orders for a long table and chairs to be put there, while the women of his family were busy preparing atole. The musicians greeted the host briefly and established themselves in the garden, while the five dancers entered the garden, dancing. One of them was dressed like a Tuřix,[8] or Katrín (townsman, mestizo) and resembled a hunter rather than a fisherman. He was referred to as 'Owner'. Another was called 'Helper'. Both men wore masks. If the mask worn by the 'Owner' unquestionably resembled a Katrín, that of the 'Helper' seemed to represent a Tarascan. Two other masked dancers were disguised as young women dressed in Tarascan pleated skirts and hats. The fifth was a young boy who performed his dance in a structure representing a fish and made of wood and paper. The other dancers pursued him with a long gill net, a cherémikwa, while the 'fish' escaped every time by diving beneath the net, until as a proper conclusion of the dance he got entangled in it. While these dances were being performed in the garden, the heads of the fishermen sat down at the table on the invitation of the Captain of Guadalupe. The Captain himself sat at the head of the table, with his Wandari on his left, and on his right the Wandari of the fishermen. Both 'priests' then made speeches in Tarascan. The 'priest' of the fishermen placed a Xikalpechtle (a lacquered bowl) filled with charales (small whitefish) before the Captain, who then muttered a Tarascan formula over it. Then the two 'priests' took up the bowl and, holding it at the level of their mouths, quickly pronounced a formula. We were unable to obtain the texts of these ceremonial speeches and formulas. The only thing our informants told us was that everything was said and done to ensure a good catch with the help of St. Mary of Guadalupe. While this ceremony took place, the women provided all the people present, fishermen, dancers, musicians, and onlookers with atole and bread. After these had been consumed the dancers entered the house of the Captain, and at the same moment a large quantity of copal was burned in front of the image of the Guadalupana. The dancers saluted the saint, and almost invisible in the smoke they again performed their dance in front of the image, which stood in the light of candles on the north side of the room, facing south. On the opposite side sat blood-relations and ceremonial relatives of the Captain. The women sat or squatted on the west side, the men on the east side. There was hardly any space left for the dancers to perform their movements. The dance lasted as long as the copal burnt. The four adult dancers knelt before the image and then left the room. They thanked and said goodbye to the Captain and his wife. The leaders of the fishermen and the musicians also took their leave, and the audience followed their example. Then the procession went to the next Tiputado to the accompaniment of music, and amidst the noise of squibs and jumping crackers.

July 29th:

Santa Marta's Day is the special festive day of the nine Urecha or Urétich', the external chiefs of the wapánekwecha. For that day every Ureti seeks from his blood relations or ceremonial relatives a Wandari ('priest', 'speaker'), who will speak on his behalf during the ceremony. With this Wandari and his nearest relations and co-parents the Ureti makes preparations to receive the Orénarikwecha and the other members of his wapánekwa. Under the direction of the Urétspeti, who is the internal chief of the wapánekwa, the Orénarikwecha, the Principals, honour the Ureti by paying him a visit. They are accompanied by the Wandari of the wapánekwa and are followed by other wapánekwa-members. When they are all assembled in and around the Ureti's house, his Wandari begins to speak. He rises, while all other people are seated, holding their hats in their hands.

"How are you, my co-parents? Our 'First Lord' (= the Ureti) and those who are the most prominent members of this wapánekwa considering that this is the day of activity on behalf of the virgin Santa Marta; and the Ureti, seeing that on this day of the year they have spoken to him saying that he shall be the man to keep watch at yonder altar of the virgin Santa Marta, and to bring it firewood, candles, incense or copal in a censer; and also those whose presence here today has been approved by God the Father (Tata Thiox) and who are his chosen people; be it said on their behalf that, assembled as members of the same wapánekwa, we shall all listen to the Holy Gospel, chanted by our venerable Priest at the hour of Holy Mass in the House of God, the church. Our Lord Ureti has invited you to his house that he may inform you of these matters. He does not offer you things of great value, only a token of his affection, in which God himself helped him (at this moment the Ureti's Wandari hands a bottle of tequila[9] to the Urétspeti), hoping that you will be kind enough to accept it". Then all say: "Thus it is, it is our wish, let it be so".

Then the Wandari of the wapánekwa rises to his feet to answer this speech, saying: "Yes it is as you have told us, co-parent; that is what should be done, when the day of the feast of our Lady Santa Marta has arrived, and thus it is possible for somebody to be elected as our Lord Ureti, who watches over yonder altar of our Mother all the year round, and who has today, with the consent of our Chief, assembled the whole wapánekwa and given it a purpose. This has been done and I have come on behalf of the Chief not to ask the least valuable nor the most valuable things, but if you are prepared to give us a small present, we shall be pleased to accept it. This is my answer, let it be so!" [10]

After the ceremonies in their houses the nine Urecha, led by the Ureti of the wapánekwa on duty, go to the altar of Santa Marta in the temple to take their offerings of candles and copal.

August 15th:

Virgen del Tránsito (Assumption of the Virgin Mary) is the fifth 'minor commission' of the year, and the celebrations are again the responsibility of a Tiputado, the Capitán de la Virgen del Tránsito. It is a fairly important feast. Unfortunately we were never able to be present, and the data collected are incomplete. According to the autochthonous calendar this is the last day of the nineteenth thirteen-day period.

September 10th:

San Nicolás de Tolentino is the sixth 'minor commission' of the year, its festivities being organised by the Tiputado concerned. As the festivities always took place during our absence in other parts of Mexico, further particulars on this festival are also lacking. In the autochthonous calendar this is the last day of the twenty-first thirteen-day period.

September 15th and 16th:

The celebration of National Independence Day in Mexico. Every year the teachers of the State school try to make this a general festive day in the village, but they have never been able to call forth any response outside their own classrooms. This was even more evident with regard to the celebration of the day of the national flag and other national festivals. Since 1962 the staffs of the development brigade have also made serious attempts in this respect, but so far they have been equally unsuccessful.

October 3rd, 4th, 5th and 6th:

The feast of St. Francis, the festival of the great commission. No other festival in Ihuatzio is comparable to that of the 'patron saint' of the village in size and significance. For four days it completely engrosses the attention of almost all villagers. The annual economic surplus of the community is largely spent on these days. The bands hired by the two Captains of St. Francis start their activities on October 3rd. In 1963 the Soldier-Captain had a local band, the Moorish Captain had one from the Tarascan Mountains. The next day, October 4th, is the feastday proper, when the most important ceremonial celebration takes place. In the morning of that day each band starts by giving a performance in the house of the Captain who hired it. Then the bands go round to all the village chiefs, after which each remains in the house of its Captain's Mesa de Campo. At a moment that has not previously been announced the Captains and their Helpers appear before the public which has assembled in the front court of the church to await the arrival of the Capitanes. The crowd is sharply divided into two sections, the men on the east side, the women on the west side. Only two or three little boys climbing a tree on the west side to have a better view relieve the picture. Suddenly between the poor houses and adobe huts the pomp and pageantry of traditional glory emerges before the silent crowd, which is waiting in eager suspense. The two Captains approach from opposite sides with the images in their charge, each attended by a large retinue of principals and other high dignitaries. The Soldier-Captain, his Alférez, his Sargento and his Mesa de Campo (who is the Moorish Captain of the preceding year), all are dressed in dark blue, gold-stitched uniforms in Napoleonic style and three-cornered hats to match; their tunics are adorned with golden eagles, the symbol of Tata Huriata, our Father the Sun. The Soldier-Captain carries a large sceptre topped by a moon.[11] The other three men carry the three small images, the Mesa de Campo carrying the so-called 'smallest'. Meanwhile the musicians blow their trumpets and beat their drums, the sound of their music and the bangs of the ceremonial fireworks making a deafening noise.

From the other side the Moorish Captain approaches. He and his men wear four- or five-tiered hats covered with some silky material and hung with flowers, mirrors and strings of pearls; a silver moon or a lyre crowns the hats.

Their lower jaws are hidden behind bright scarfs hanging down from their headgear. They wear tight sleeveless waistcoats over their white shirts, and trousers with fringed legs, protected by chaparreras richly mounted with silver figures, those of the Captain also having silver fishes as decoration. Their foot-wear consists of short boots with spurs. The Captain carries a sceptre with a silver moon, the symbol of Nana Kutsi, our Mother the Moon. The Alférez carries the largest image of St. Francis. They, too, approach amidst the sound of trumpets and drums and fireworks, altogether an imposing accompaniment to the procession. The Soldier-Captain and his men enter the front court of the church through the eastern gate, placing their images on the east side of the enclosed court. The Moorish Captain and his retinue enter the ceremonial centre by the other, the northern gate. The image they carry is placed on the west side of the court. The two groups of four men perform dances in front of their own images, then approach each other in a sham fight. This takes place before the main entrance of the church, before the Coyote-god and the reliefs of María of Guadalupe, of the Sun and the Moon on the church-front. Then the two groups take their images into the church, where they also take their offerings. When the ceremonies are over, each group returns to the house of its Captain.

Before the ceremonies each Captain has ordered a so-called 'Castle' to be built in the village square, just outside the front wall of the church court. This 'castle' is a tall wooden structure with fireworks. In 1963 the rainy season continued much longer than usual. It should have been over in September, but on the morning of October 4th dark clouds were hanging over the village, promising heavy showers soon after midday. At about noon both groups were ready to start a second performance of dances in the front court, but the 'Moors' showed little enthusiasm, expecting the rain to start at any moment. Their Captain was still in his own house, but his Alférez and the Mesa de Campo were waiting in the house of the Acha Representante. This Mesa de Campo, who had been Soldier-Captain in 1962, was a son of the Acha Representante. Their Captain being absent, the Alférez decided to go home for a while, much to the annoyance of the Acha Representante. Presently the Moorish Captain arrived on horseback. Then the Acha Representante invited us to come in, and personally treated us to atole and sweet bread. The band, which appeared to have been hired through his good offices, was there, too. The Moorish Captain being a ceremonial relative of his, and his own son being the Mesa de Campo, he was very interested in a perfect performance of the ceremonies by the 'Moors'. He was very nervous, because the Alférez's absence delayed the start of the dances. That year the office of Moorish Sargento had remained vacant, as there was no candidate. This fact already placed them at a disadvantage; furthermore tradition would have it that the Captain should have at least two assistant dancers before any dance could be performed. As has been said on p. 149, the Soldier-Captain of 1963 was a very controversial person, but he proved to have his men well under control, and soon his band announced another dance by the 'Soldados'. Surrounded by his three Helpers and with his father walking one step behind him, the Soldier-Captain crossed the village square. All at once the clouds broke and the sun shone on their brilliant uniforms. A murmur went through the crowd. The light thrown by the Tata Huriata (Our Lord the Sun) on his representatives in these circumstances was taken as a sign of His approval and a rehabilitation of the Captain and his family. Now it was assumed that the 'Soldados' would naturally carry the day. And when the public are of this opinion, they are sure to win, because it is their reactions on which the Alkande bases his judgment of the performances of the opponent groups. The sun shone as long as the dance of the 'Soldados' lasted, and when they had finished, the clouds closed again, or perhaps it would be better to say: the 'Soldados' danced as long as the sun shone. Meanwhile the Acha Representante had twice sent for the Moorish Alférez, but when at last the latter left his home, it began to rain and soon there was such a heavy shower that a performance in the open air was impossible. Almost soaking wet the Alférez entered the house of the Acha Representante and was at once reprimanded for being late. The village chief was very upset, especially because the precious 'castle', which had cost a lot of money to build, and on which the 'Moors' had set their hopes to excel the 'Soldiers', would probably fail to function in the heavy rain. The Moorish Captain was now compelled to perform his dance inside before a small audience. In the afternoon there was a bout of hard-drinking, the elderly men in general and all the principals in particular soon getting completely drunk. This indulgence in strong liquor continued for two more days. The 'Soldiers' also won the competition between the two musical bands.

In the autochthonous calendar the last day of this great festival is also the last day of the twenty-third period of thirteen days.

November 1st and 2nd:

All Souls, or 'Day of the Dead' (Día de los Muertos), as the Mexicans call it. It is another 'festival of the whole village', that is a festival not connected with the cargo system. It is an important festival in all Lake-Tarascan villages, especially for the fishermen. When the ducks, which come to Lake Pátzcuaro from the north, arrive in time, the fishermen from the lake villages gather in the night of 1st to 2nd November for a large drive. In the nineteen-forties about a thousand canoes took part in the annual drive, which is still held almost exclusively in the Bay of Erongarícuaro. In the nineteen-fifties the number of canoes was reduced to not much more than half that figure. The weapon used in this hunt is the ancient spearthrower, which dates from Toltec times. In Nahuatl it is called atlatl, the Tarascan name is tsʌpahki. With it long spears, each with a point consisting of three barbs, are thrown. In the early morning of November 2nd the ducks are cooked and laid on the graves of the dead together with bread, sempoalxochitl ('twenty flowers')[12] and candles. Unfortunately in 1961 and 1962 the ducks were late, so we were unable to witness a duckhunt.

On the first day the deceased children are commemorated. All the nearest relatives and co-parents go to the graves of the deceased children, bringing bread, sweets and flowers. The children who died in the past year receive the most. The second day is the great feastday. According to the Tarascans their ancestors return to the earth on that day to join the celebrations of their descendants and relatives. 'Arbolitos' (little trees) are brought to the cemetery on November 1st. These are not real trees, but decorated wooden structures hung with buns and other delicacies for the dead. They are put on the graves, and the relatives sit on the ground, burning candles, watching over the graves and waiting for the dead to come. Towards sunrise of November 2nd they have a festive meal, eating their own offerings, for after all "these have already been sucked by the dead".

According to the autochthonous calendar this festival falls on the last day of the twenty-fifth and the first day of the twenty-sixth periods of thirteen days.

On the latter day the Pleiads make their re-appearance in the Mexican sky.

The ceremonial year in Ihuatzio is concluded with the last cargo festival, that of María de Guadalupe, when the newly appointed functionaries take up their duties and a new year begins (December 12th).

There are many more ceremonial festivals in Ihuatzio unconnected with the calendar. It is the Wandárich' who are in the first place responsible for them. During the ceremonies connected with births, baptisms, entrance into the wapánekwa, marriage preparations, weddings and funerals these officials make speeches traditional in form and content.

As in most other indigenous Mexican communities, a proposal of marriage is made through the intermediary of a blood-relation or a ceremonial relative, and is accompanied by the customary presents of food (bread and fruit), expressing the reciprocal ties between the two families concerned. Bride-capture does occur in Ihuatzio, but is probably less frequent than in other Tarascan communities, for instance Cherán. As none of these ceremonies is much different from corresponding ones already described by researchers for neighbouring areas, it will be sufficient here to refer to the existing literature on the subject.[13]

2   *Occult conceptions*

The people of Ihuatzio appeared to be much more reticent on the subject of occult or 'magic' conceptions than the inhabitants of the nearby islands. On the islands unsolicited mention was made of witchcraft, one person accusing another member of the community of being an evil wizard; in Ihuatzio, however, people at first maintained emphatically that such things were unknown in their village; this was further evidence of their reluctance to confide in outsiders. Not only the social aspects of their day-to-day life, but also the religious aspects, which are so closely connected with them, were kept secret. However, the extensive occurrence of 'magic' conceptions in Indian communities all over Mexico and on the islands in the neighbourhood of Ihuatzio in particular, justified the supposition that they would also be found among the people of Ihuatzio. As a matter of fact the idea of reciprocity in their relations with the 'saints' may, from a European point of view, be considered as a 'magic' conception. The author would like to note, however, that like Van Baal[14] and others, he considers magic an expression of religious feeling and inseparably connected with religion. Like Van Baal, the author prefers not to restrict the concept of religion to acts and conceptions implying unconditional respectful obedience to a higher power, but likes to attach a wider meaning to it.[15] After some time the reluctance of our informants was partly overcome. One of the earliest indications of the existence of 'magic' conceptions was noticed when we tried to buy pre-Spanish objects. We knew that in the nineteen-forties an expedition sent by the official Mexican archaelogical institute to investigate the ancient ruined city had been forced to leave by the inhabitants[16]. As we were anxious to know the reason for their opposition, we told several of our informants that we would like to buy some pre-Spanish relics. Most of them said that "it was a long time since such objects had been found"; some said that "they were not for sale", others maintained that "'ídolos' could not be sold, as it would make the soil that had contained them infertile". The last piece of information was endorsed by the answers given by forty Ihuatzio farmers, whom we had approached on the subject. Most of them re-bury the ancient images of gods (Thares) and other pre-Spanish objects which are often found in their fields.

Other traditions in the village suggest the existence of magic conceptions. The two temples, that of Tata Huriata (Our Father or Lord The Sun) and Nana Kutsi (Our Mother or Lady The Moon) are said to be visited by an evil being about noon.[17] The creature is half bird and half mammal, and every one who sees it will die on the spot. Therefore no inhabitant will ever pass the temples in the middle of the day; moreover nobody will approach them bareheaded.[18]

There is a story about magic phenomena and actions which runs as follows:

"One day a young man and an old man went into the mountains of Cherán.[19] When they had walked a long time the young man became very thirsty. Presently he saw three girls carrying jars of water. The young man rushed towards them, leaving the old man behind. When he came to the well he asked one of the girls to give him her jar, which she did. The young man eagerly brought it to his lips and quenched his thirst, but when he wanted to return the jar to the girl he could not get it down again. He could not remove the spout from his lips. Meanwhile the old man had also reached the well, and because he was a magician and a curer, he at once understood that the young man had been bewitched by the girls. He made himself strong and succeeded in separating the jar from the young man's face. The old man and the young man spent the night in a neighbouring village. The young man laid himself down on a mat and soon fell asleep. The old man lay by his side, but did not sleep; he kept watch over his companion. Soon three owls came flying along; they were the 'fellow-beings'[20] of the three girls. The old man tried in vain to catch them. Then he changed himself into a mule, but in this disguise he was also unsuccessful. Then he changed himself into a dog and succeeded in frightening the owls. He asked them: "Why do you keep troubling this young man?" Their answer was: "Because we are in love with him". Then they fled".

This story is interesting for two reasons. First for the atmosphere of magic it calls forth and second for its social implications. According to elderly informants the story is told especially by fathers to their marriageable sons to prevent them from making marriage preparations on their own authority. The amorous adventures of Tarascan boys and girls are usually restricted to superficial contacts when the girls go out to fetch water, for this is about the only opportunity girls have of being out of doors on their own. The frequent bride-captures in the area, which nearly always take place with the prior consent of the girls, are usually arranged during such meetings. The elders of the village disapprove of the practice, because the tradition is for marriages to be arranged by the parents and co-parents, with the approval of the community, thus ensuring the greatest benefit for the boys and girls themselves. The above story obviously supports the 'official' norm. The young man is inexperienced and 'weak', and rushes recklessly to his own ruin as soon as he runs away from the 'strong' old man. The latter is the great rescuer and guardian. Although three girls are in love with him, the young man does not win any one of them in that way.

The magic concepts underlying the story are in full agreement with the more general autochthonic Mexican cultural pattern. Aztecs, too, and many other indigenous peoples, usually mention owls as evil 'incarnate spirits', doing a lot of harm.[21]

Older people are generally 'stronger' and better able to control their 'fellow-beings' than younger people. The old men who are 'pasado', i.e. who have fulfilled all commissions, are the strongest. They are expected never to abuse their strength and to use it only for the benefit of the community, in other words, to practise 'white magic' only. On the lake-islands some elderly men of authority were accused of having applied their magic power to achieve personal ends. We did not hear such complaints in Ihuatzio, which does not necessarily mean of course, that such accusations were not made. Therefore the question of whether black magic is ever practised must remain unanswered. But as we have already seen, there is no doubt that people believe that magic influences may be harmful. Some informants ascribed the misfortunes of the man who refused to accept a commission in 1963 to the magic intervention of the chiefs and principals of the village. Others, however, regarded the incidents as an act of direct retaliation on the part of the insulted 'saint'.

Another instance of intervention by a higher power is the following story from the time of the Great Revolution (1910-1920). It is often told in the village and is also found in the Medina manuscript or Sapichu Wandantskwa Hiwatse Eréteri (the poor style of the manuscript has been brought out in the translation):

"One of the old men told me that during the Revolution, when the units of the generals Inés Chávez, Francisco I Madero, called 'the belts' or 'the coloured people', who were the federal government's troops, came into this village of Ihuatzio to fetch the people for their struggle against the rebellious army leaders, some of those soldiers entered the house of one of the commissioners of St. Francis. And one of the Soldiers found in the niche the three 'Santitos'.[22] He took one of them, the 'middle-sized' one, puts it into his bag and continues to carry out the task he has been ordered to do. After some time they leave the village, taking the road to the cemetery. About three hundred yards past the cemetery the soldier who had stolen the image fell ill. He suffered from intense and unbearable colic pains. More dead than alive he asked his comrades to take him back to the village, that he might get something to alleviate his pains. So his comrades had to return, still ignorant, like himself, of the secret he was carrying about with him. Soon the soldier who had stolen the image strangely enough found himself in front of the commissioner's house without realising that he had taken the same way back. Then he remembers his shameful deed, takes the image out of his bag and puts it back where it belonged. It was easy to find the place because they found some salt on the spot where the image had stood. There was nobody in the village to ask for help, for all the people had fled. The sick man's companions used the salt to treat a hideous ulcer on the poor man's belly. This soothes his pains, and when he feels well enough to walk, they start again. By the time he passed the spot where he had first felt the pain, it had completely gone, and he escaped from death safe and sound. (It is said that afterwards this soldier had to desert his military unit). When he realised that a miracle had happened through him he regretted what he had done. In all battles and fights he always invoked the help of St. Francis, his favourite saint. A few years later, when he was no longer in the army, he returned to the village to thank the saint for the help rendered during his military career. Then he also told some people in the village what had happened to him. Therefore many men apply for this cargo of St. Francis. They want it, it is their desire to have it, and they fulfil it notwithstanding the cost it involves. For there are people who sacrifice what possessions they have for the fulfilment of this commission. Then they fall into poverty and never get on their feet again".

3   *The concept of the Universe*

Before attempting to describe the concept of divinity in the philosophy of the Tarascans of Ihuatzio, we shall try to give a brief idea of their conceptions of the universe, which is so closely connected with the former. As it was very difficult to get the people of Ihuatzio to talk about these matters, one of the methods of obtaining information that we resorted to was that of pictorial representation, a method which has often been applied by researchers. Remembering the great reluctance of adult villagers to discuss these ideas with outsiders, we first approached children. The co-operation of the schools was obtained, and some two hundred children from six to fourteen years old from Ihuatzio and the neighbouring villages were asked to make a drawing of the earth, heaven and the next world. This yielded 153 drawings made by the pupils of both the State and the Roman Catholic schools. Later we also received 27 drawings made by adult members of the community. The results were most surprising. With their primitive means of expression the children had depicted all the essential elements of the pagan conception of the universe, which had been so meticulously kept secret during verbal contacts. Not one tenth of the 153 drawings reveals anything reminiscent of a Christian con-

The Lord of the Underworld
(*9-year-old boy*)

ception of life in the next world. The great majority (139 drawings) represent the pre-Spanish conception of the underworld, with here and there an additional next world among the Sun and the Stars. Most of the drawings showed one or more snakes to indicate the abode of the dead. In ancient times the snake (akwitse) was the typical Tarascan symbol of death.[23] The akwitse was also the 'fellow-being' of Xarátanga, the Moon Goddess.[24] Some of the best drawings are reproduced here. A nine-year-old boy represents the God(dess) of the dead, the Ruler of the underworld seated on a monster, a five-headed snake, passing through a gate with a retinue of dead people. This masterly picture of the indigenous conception of the next world, drawn by a boy born

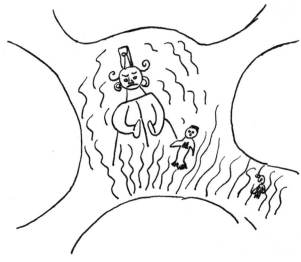

The Queen of the Realm of the
Dead (*14-year-old girl*)

Heaven
(*11-year-old girl*)

in 1954 expresses better than words can do the part which the ancient conception of the universe still plays in the minds of the villagers. The drawing
made by a 14-year-old girl clearly illustrates the realistic autochthonous
conception of the realm of the dead as a place of the decomposition of the
dead bodies (the Ximoayan of the Aztecs).[25] An 11-year-old boy shows both
heaven and hell, representing the dead who go to heaven by crosses accom-

The Heaven of the God

The Underworld (Hell)
(*11-year-old boy*)

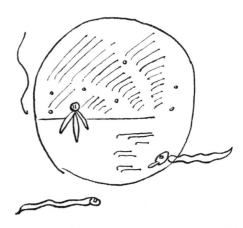

Glory
(*11-year-old girl*)

panying the celestial bodies. The idea that the dead can be admitted to the
retinue of a heavenly body existed even before the coming of the Spaniards.[26]
The same idea is expressed by an 11-year-old girl, whose drawing is also reproduced on this page. The way in which 'glory' (la gloria) has been depicted
by another child of eleven is particularly interesting in that she has drawn the
next world with in it the same strange snake with a bird's head which is also
found on pre-Spanish Tarascan pottery, the Tirípeme Kwarencha, the Tarascan
equivalent of Ketsalkoatl (Quetzalcoatl) as the envoy of the Sun and messenger of war (Pungarancha).[27]
The adults made slightly more differentiated drawings. These also contain
birds flying from the crosses in the cemetery up to the Sun. These birds were
explained by the people who had drawn them as the dead who pass into heaven.
A similar idea existed among the pre-Spanish Aztecs: the dead warriors either
returning to the earth as birds or accompanying the Sun. These representations already suggest a degree of identification of the chief god with the Sun.
This was confirmed by the unambiguous caption one of the children wrote to
his drawing of the sun, the moon and the stars: "in heaven is God, the Stars
and the Moon". Of course, it should be remembered that this entirely Indian
concept of the universe may have survived in this form only in the minds of
the children, while adults may have other ideas as well.
In the drawings made by adult villagers the earth and life in it were always

centred around the lake and the surrounding area with the vault of heaven rising directly from it. Their conception of the world does not extend far from their own familiar surroundings. They have only a vague idea of the size of the Mexican territory, not to mention that of foreign countries. A strong tendency is noticeable to represent their own familiar area as large, and remote areas as small. This was even done by the migrant workmen, who had seen parts of the United States.

4   *The Gods*

The chief deity in the pantheon of the inhabitants of Ihuatzio today is Awán-daeri ka echéreri Kweráhperi, the Creator of heaven and earth, the Tata Thiox, the Father God. The pre-Spanish creative deity was called Kwerawáhperi, and was represented as a woman. According to Corona Núñez the addition of -wa- means 'in the womb'; so the name meant 'creating in the womb', thus indicating the female nature of the deity.[28] In Ihuatzio today there is apparently some confusion over the sex of the creative deity. Most informants refer to Kweráhperi as a male god; others take the god to be female, ranking her with Mary, the mother of God. Like the Aztecs and the Toltecs, the ancient Tarascans probably conceived of the creator as Ometeotl, the Twofold God, who possessed male as well as female aspects.[29] A striking fact was that many villagers spoke freely of Kweráhperi, while they were as a rule reticent on other aspects of their religious thinking. They were generally convinced that their ideas about Kweráhperi were in perfect agreement with the Christian concept of Divinity. This probably accounts for their communicativeness in this respect.

Although the Kweráhperi is regarded as the supreme deity, he is not the most prominent god in the local ceremonies. Like the Aztecs of Motecuzoma and the pre-Spanish Tarascans, the inhabitants of Ihuatzio today are little inclined to apply to the Supreme God in prayer or worship. He is too remote from ordinary human life on earth. Many of the other gods are much nearer to them and more easily approached. This is true especially for the so-called 'saints'.

The term Tukupacha, which Gilberti's dictionary gives as the translation of the word God[30] is, as far as we could ascertain, unknown to the inhabitants of Ihuatzio today.

A number of cosmic deities of the ancient religion still occupy prominent places in the minds of the villagers, although naturally their worship has largely been superseded. Tata Huriata, Father Sun or Lord of the Sun, and Nana Kutsi, Mother Moon or Lady of the Moon, are well-known deities even today. The Moon Goddess is sometimes still referred to by the ancient name of Xarátanga. In these, as in some other cases, it is difficult to find out whether the use of a word is really based on tradition or results from the fact that some fairly well-read inhabitants have been able to lay hold of Tarascan history books. In many Indian communities in Mexico with a percentage of literate people higher than the national average. this fact often presents difficulties to socio-anthropological researchers. Several informants showed a tendency to identify Tata Huriata with Jesus Christ and Nana Kutsi with a kind of Virgin Mary. Some informants also considered the Tata Hóskok'eri, Father Great Star (Venus) to be a god. Some called the stars in general (the Hóskoecha) "our ancestors", which view agrees with some of the children's representations of heaven. The coyote, too, the Wolfgod, was considered by many as a deity. Some called him 'un Dios' (a God), others 'un Santo' (a saint). In the pre-Spanish religion the Wakux (eagle), the Hiwatse (wolf) and the Akwitse (serpent) symbolised the Sun or the Sky, the Earth and the Underworld respectively. As such they were also connected with the three capital towns of the Tarascan empire: Tzintzuntzan, Ihuatzio and Pátzcuaro.[31] The wolf symbolised Ihuatzio and perhaps also the aspect of the tribal god Kuríkaweri which was especially associated with this town. As we have seen, St. Francis is given prominence among the 'saints'. In Ihuatzio he has probably replaced Kurikaweri, whose main temple stood there and who was especially venerated by the inhabitants of ancient Ihuatzio. In this connection it is noteworthy that every person in Ihuatzio knows the name of the major pre-Spanish Tarascan tribal god, the god of the Wakúxecha, and never confuses him with Kweráhperi, as the mestizos frequently do. However, we did not notice any form of worship, or even any religious feelings, in connection with Kurikaweri. All informants described him as belonging to the past, as "the God of our ancestors". We do not mean to say, however, that there is no respect or even religious veneration towards Kurikaweri; the only certainty is that we did not notice any expression of it. It was evident, however, that our informants were more reluctant to speak about Kurikaweri than they were with regard to other gods; it is therefore quite possible that in this respect they were hiding something from us.

As was mentioned in the preceding chapter, Ihuatzio knows two – or perhaps four – saints of the name of St. Francis. The three images in the possession of the Soldier-Captain may be taken as a substitute for the ancient tribal god Kurikaweri, who was also associated with several forms of tripartition (see chapter II, p. 30). The St. Francis of the Moorish Captain, however, is considered by the villagers today as a different 'saint'. The ritual and the associations connected with this 'saint' suggest that, as is the case in San Francisco Péribán,[32] he has replaced the most important deity but one in pre-Spanish Ihuatzio, namely Xarátanga, the Moon Goddess. This explains why the St. Francis whose image is the biggest but who is nevertheless the 'smaller', that is the lesser god, is associated with the moon. It is possible that these two 'gods' were originally connected with two prominent wapánekwecha. The seven 'saints' in the charge of the seven Tiputádox may have replaced the other seven wapánekwa-gods. It is, to say the least of it, noteworthy that the number of 'saints' connected with the cargo system corresponds with the number of wapánekwecha. Unfortunately the nine gods worshipped in the nine pre-Spanish wapánekwa-sanctuaries are not mentioned in the available historical records, at any rate not in this connection. It is possible that María de Guadalupe owes her fairly prominent position to the corresponding position of Kwerawáhperi in the ancient Tarascan pantheon.

Many questions connected with this subject have remained unanswered, in the first place because the available ethno-historic data were inadequate, and in the second place because our imperfect knowledge of Tarascan prevented us from making a thorough investigation into the philosophical aspects of the religious system today. It is, however, beyond doubt that in Ihuatzio the 'saints' are worshipped as gods. To the people they represent powers which are, at least partly, beyond empirical observation. They are brought into relationship with social as well as cosmic concepts and are part of the universal order, which determines the Tarascan world view: the tripartition of the universe into heaven, earth and underworld. The nine 'saints' are heavenly gods, although they bear earthly implications and may in ancient times have belonged to the earth. The Christian church today probably only worships such heavenly gods. Santa Marta, the patron saint of the nine Urecha, may be an exception; she may originally have been an earth goddess. The gods of the underworld have in any case been removed from the ceremonial centre. They are only remembered in folk-lore and witchcraft. The gods of the earth, too, such as the Rain God, the Wind God, the God of the Lake are mere shadows of their former selves and have lost much of their glory. They are only remembered when serious events remind the people of their existence. The villagers sometimes try to protect the crop in the fields from damage by hailstorms by frightening (or propitiating) the Rain and Thunder Gods by letting off fireworks. The fishermen sometimes bring small offerings to the lake, when there is a heavy storm and the high waves are dangerous to the dugout canoes. The ancient pagan-sacral atmosphere has largely disappeared. This may be due partly to the progress of Christianity, but the independent road to Redfield's 'disenchantment', the decreased 'charm' of the close relationship between social life and an empirically indefinable reality, should not be left out of consideration in trying to explain that disappearance. Several modern ethnographic works dealing with indigenous Mexican population groups draw the conclusion that their religion is characterised by 'syncretism'.[33] If all original elements are considered to be autochthonous and the concepts and ceremonies, or parts of them introduced since the Spanish conquest are looked upon as instances of 'modernisation', it is of course, easy to describe the religion today as a mixture of autochthonous and Christian elements. Moreover an attempt can be made to determine the respective degrees of autochthonous and Christian influences. But this would not lead us any further. Any religion will show some degree of syncretism. Even if it should be possible to know that say 40 per cent of a religion consisted of Christian elements, this knowledge would hardly increase our insight into that religion. Syncretism resembles acculturation, transculturation or a blending of cultures, in that it is a term used to indicate a very intricate complex of social processes and phenomena. Of greater essential significance is the question of whether a religion such as that of the inhabitants of Ihuatzio has retained the essential elements of the autochthonous religious system, or whether its original religious foundations have been replaced by fundamentally Christian or other elements. The same question could be put in this way: 'Have the newly introduced Christian and other elements become integral parts of, or been adapted to the ancient indigenous religious structure, or is the religion an essentially Christian structure with autochthonic elements as additional appendages? As has been said before, our study of this matter was not thorough enough to justify a satisfactory answer to the question. It is possible, however, to give a partial answer, which may be useful for a more accurate definition of the problems for future investigations. The results of our study justify the conclusion that the following inherent foundations of the Tarascan indigenous religion still form essential elements of the religious life of the inhabitants of Ihuatzio today:

1   the concept of the tripartite universe (heaven, earth, underworld);
2   polytheism;
3   magic control;
4   a cosmic relationship of earthly phenomena (the opposition of Sun and Moon, which is reflected in the relations between the Soldier- and Moorish Captains);
5   the worship of the dead;
6   the concept of 'fellow-beings'.

One fundamental aspect of the pre-Spanish Tarascan State religion has completely, or at any rate largely, disappeared: the worship of the tribal god Kurikaweri, with its offerings of firewood and human sacrifices, and the Gwatapera, the women's quarters dedicated to him. This part of the indigenous religion was abolished by the Spanish conquerors, and the God, who had raised the Tarascan people to the status of a God-chosen nation with a special position in the world, disappeared. In this respect the Christian conquerors were successful. But no victory is complete and final when the power of the enemy is only partly destroyed. And a partial victory is only consolidated if the victor succeeds in replacing what has been destroyed by a permanent element of his own. We must, therefore, examine the position of Roman Catholic Christianity in Ihuatzio today.

1   The Christian concept of Divinity exists in so far as it is in agreement with the indigenous concept of the Creator. The only effect of Christian influence in this respect has perhaps been the change of Kwerawáhperi into Kweráhperi. As the idea of trinity was not unfamiliar to the ancient Tarascan religion, its existence today in certain forms should not be attributed merely to Christian influences. The concept of the Holy Ghost is, indeed, alien to the villagers. Their ideas on the subject are those they have about

Kweráhperi. To the Tarascans of Ihuatzio God is not associated with Love; this idea is strange to them. As a matter of fact, the question may be asked if the God of the Christians has ever been preached to them as a God of Love.

2 The concepts of sin in general, of original sin, and Divine grace are hardly understood in the Christian acceptation of the words. To them a man has sinned if he has made a stupid mistake, and his 'expiation' consists in accepting and taking the consequences of the mistake, while his 'purification' is nothing more than the lesson he has learned from the mistakes he has made.

3 The term 'soul', called mintsita in Tarascan, is not understood in the Christian sense either. The word mintsita is also used for the 'heart'; it refers to the source of life in man; and not only in man, animals also have a mintsita.

Many Christian rituals and ceremonies are applied in their outward forms, and have no doubt replaced many autochthonous rituals and pre-Conquest ceremonies. Just as churches have replaced the ancient temples, so the fire-burners on the altars of Kurikaweri have been replaced by candles; but the Wolf God, who looks up to the ancient town on the mountain slope from the gallery of the church-tower is more significant than the heathen cocks perched on church-steeples in Europe. Indigenous religious ideas are still very much alive, they fill the hearts of these Tarascans, leaving little room for Christianity. But in order to survive the old religion had to appear in largely Christian garments. This has been done as far as possible, but it was most difficult to achieve with regard to the worship of Kurikaweri, made even more difficult because the Spanish heresy-hunters considered it as the greatest evil. This picture is based on the data we collected. A more detailed picture of the characteristic qualities of the religion of the inhabitants of Ihuatzio will only be obtained after a thorough study of the religious expressions in the Tarascan language. Yet an outline of the religious life of this Tarascan population group can be gained from the data collected in Ihuatzio. In some respects it differs considerably from that given by Carrasco. In Ihuatzio the Roman Catholic church as an institution has been incorporated in a rather firmly closed Indian organisation with a predominantly traditional character (see the following chapters). But Christian conceptions have been able to penetrate only to a limited extent. It is true that the polytheistic religion of the Tarascans has undergone drastic changes in Ihuatzio, too; it has lost several of its original elements and gained new ones, but up to now it has retained its specific Indian character. This is the main reason why we do not consider it as a fundamentally Christian religion.

Carrasco gives interesting examples of stories about souls guarding treasures,[34] about the people's attitude towards money[35] and the appearance of the Devil in various guises.[36] According to him these are especially Christian elements. Very similar stories and other data were also told us by Ihuatzio informants. The relationship between the Devil on the one hand and God (or the Gods) on the other, however, is also very suggestive of the indigenous principle of a dualistic organisation (cf. pp. 219 and 235), particularly since the agraristas are associated with the former and the traditionalists with the latter.[37]

Notes to chapter V

[1]   Carrasco, 1952, p. 23.
[2]   Redfield, 1941, pp. 352-355 (7th ed., 1959).
[3]   See chapter IV, p. 116 and appendix 2.
[4]   cf. Gilberti 1559, p. 64: irárukwa = wrinkle.
[5]   More information on this matter is contained in chapter III. It should be noted that in 1948, '49, '53, '54, '55, '59 and '60 December 16th fell in the first duty period.
[6]   The religious-ceremonial calendar of the indigenous peoples of Mexico and Central America comprises units of 260 days consisting of 20 periods of 13 days, and also of 13 periods of 20 days. In ancient times festivals often took place on or just before the last day of such periods (cf. Sahagún, 1955; Anderson and Dibble, 1952). It may be interesting to note that, as the following survey shows, at least seven fixed festivals in Ihuatzio today follow this rule:

12-XII : first day of the year (María de Guadalupe).
16-XII : 5th day of the first thirteen-day period (IrΛts'Λ).
24-XII : last day of the first thirteen-day period (start of Christmas festival).
  1-I : first day of the 2nd twenty-day period (New Year).
  6-I : last day of the 2nd thirteen-day period (Twelfth Night).
  3-V : last day of the 11th thirteen-day period (Santa Cruz).
13-VI : second day of the 15th thirteen-day period (San Antonio).
16-VI : fifth day of the 15th thirteen-day period (Festival of the fishermen).
29-VII : ninth day of the 18th thirteen-day period (Santa Marta).
15-VIII: last day of the 19th thirteen-day period (Assumption of the Virgin Mary).

10-IX : last day of the 21st thirteen-day period (San Nicolás).

4-6-x : last day of the 23rd thirteen-day period (San Francisco).

1-2-XI: last day of the 25th thirteen-day period and the first day of the 26th (All Souls).

Among the days following the above-mentioned rule are Roman Catholic feastdays generally recognised as important and some less important ones. These data alone are not sufficient to justify any valuable conclusion; yet they may be interesting in connection with the question of why December 12th, of all dates, has been chosen as the commencing day of the ceremonial and administrative year.

[7] In the sense of 'boss', 'owner'.

[8] Turix = originally 'the black one', 'negro', but in Ihuatzio today it is a nickname for whites and mestizos. (cf. Gilberti, 1559, p. 128).

[9] Tequila, a strong native liquor, resembling gin.

[10] For the Tarascan texts see Medina and Van Zantwijk, 1963.

[11] One would have expected a sun, in accordance with the other symbols of the sun.

[12] Sempoalxochitl is a large kind of French marigold; in Mexico the traditional funeral flower; Caryophyllus mexicanus (Hern.) or Tithonia tubaeformis (Cass.). cf. Simeón, 1963, p. 71 and Schultze-Jena, 1957, p. 334.

[13] Beals, 1946, p. 177 ff.; Foster, 1948; Rendon, 1950.

[14] Van Baal, 1960, p. 9.

[15] Idem, pp. 4, 5. For instance his definition: "Religion is the structure of conceptions associated with an empirically undefinable reality, and all acts which imply the existence of such conceptions . . .". See also Van Baal, 1947, p. 19.

[16] Personal information by Dr. E. Noguera in 1957.

[17] Originally the Mexican indigenous peoples reckoned a day to last from noon till noon the next day.

[18] The Aztecs of Milpa Alta today also believe that the 'sombrero' protects a man against evil magical influence. cf. Van Zantwijk, 1963 c. pp. 26, 27.

[19] The Lake Tarascans consider the Mountain Tarascan village of Cherán as an important centre of witchcraft. cf. Beals, 1946, p. 156 ff.

[20] = Kwincha, Tsikwámecha, comparable with the Na'nawaltin of the Aztecs. See Van Zantwijk, 1960, pp. 57-60.

[21] cf. The Tlakatekolotin (Human Owls) of the Aztecs.

[22] Santitos, literally 'little saints'. Owing to Indian, especially Aztec, influences the Mexican diminutive has a meaning which differs from the meaning attached to it in Western Europe. In Nahuatl the diminutive may also express politeness, or create a friendly atmosphere dependent on the situation in which the term is used.

[23] See Corona Núñez, 1957, pp. 99, 100.

[24] Idem, p. 74.

[25] See León Portilla, 1956, 1959.

[26] Aztec warriors who were killed on the battlefield and Aztec women who had died in childbirth went to heaven as attendants of the sun; they did not go to the underworld (miktlan).

[27] See Corona Núñez, 1957, pp. 32, 33.

[28] Idem, p. 71.

[29] See León Portilla, 1956, 1959.
[30] Gilberti, 1559, p. 298.
[31] cf. Corona Núñez, 1957, p. 86.
[32] Aguirre Beltrán, 1952, p. 78.
[33] See e.g. Aguirre Beltrán, 1957, p. 134; Plancarte, 1954, p. 70, picture-page: "Un sincretismo entre ideas y creencias cristianas forma la religión del tarahumara"; Rojas González, Berragán Aviles and De la Cerda Silva, 1957.
[34] Carrasco, 1952, p. 45.
[35] Idem, p. 47.
[36] Idem, pp. 49-50.
[37] Idem.

VI   *social external contacts*

1 *Contacts with other Tarascan groups*

Ihuatzio today maintains various traditional contacts with several other
Tarascan or originally Tarascan villages, for instance Jarácuaro, Cuanajo,
Pareo, Pacandan, Tzintzuntzan, Erongarícuaro, etc. Some of these social
relations may extend back to pre-Spanish times and have originated from the
regional patterns of organisation of those days. We have seen that Ihuatzio
was one of the three administrative centres of the Tarascan empire, and consequently occupied an important position. The contacts of Ihuatzio fishermen
with the inhabitants of Erongarícuaro and the Mountain Tarascans who visit
the market there are no doubt of ancient origin. The people of Ihuatzio have
always maintained relations with the inhabitants of the islands of Pacandan,
Yunuén and Janitzio: the islanders used to hold religious services before the
yácatas in the ancient ruined town, and today they come to Ihuatzio to buy
fishing-nets. Probably these contacts also date back to pre-Conquest days, as do
the relations which the weavers of tule sleeping-mats and makers of other
products of tule handicraft maintain with the inhabitants of Tzintzuntzan and
Pátzcuaro. Another custom which may be of historic origin is the following.
On certain occasions the people of Santa Fé, San Andrés Tziróndaro and
Jarácuaro come to Ihuatzio to bring religious offerings. The author's attempts
to find out whether this tradition had started in colonial times, or even before
the Conquest, were unsuccessful. Tarascans from Cuanajo and Pareo also
sometimes bring religious offerings in Ihuatzio. An interesting fact in this
connection is that Jarácuaro, Pareo, Santa Fé, Pacandan and Tziróndaro were
places of special religious-ceremonial significance before the arrival of the
Spanish conquerors.[1]

Mountain Tarascans occasionally come down to the villages in the Lake Pátzcuaro basin. The curers from Cherán are the most frequent visitors.

Many residents of Ihuatzio have contacts with other Tarascans both in and outside their own village. They meet regularly in the markets at Pátzcuaro and Tzintzuntzan. As has been said before Ihuatzio fishermen meet Mountain Tarascans on market days in Erongarícuaro, and have their traditional duck hunts on November 1st together with Lake Tarascans from the islands and elsewhere. Every year in February a great many people from Ihuatzio participate in the great festival of Rescate held in Tzintzuntzan, where they meet many Tarascans from La Vuelta.[2] Ihuatzio is famous among Tarascans for its musicians and singers. Therefore the village bands are often invited by other Tarascan communities to take part in and lend a more festive air to celebrations. Many of these musicians have been to all parts of the Tarascan area.

Many Lake Tarascans, the inhabitants of Ihuatzio among them, like to visit Cherán, which is the largest pure Tarascan village and the main centre of witchcraft. The village enjoys some prestige and is sometimes held up as an example of a village with a typically indigenous character. This atmosphere is enhanced by manifestations of indigenous material culture.

Relations between Ihuatzio and the village of San Pedro Cucuchucho, 3 kilometres to the west, are of a special nature. They are traditionally antagonistic and resemble those between the two barrios of Sagrado Corazón and Ascensión. Just as informants from Sagrado Corazón told us that "until a few years ago those people of Ascensión could not pass through our barrio", so we were told that in former days the people of Cucuchucho were barred from the whole area of Ihuatzio. Several elderly informants said that residents of Cucuchucho were 'bad people'. This antagonism between the two villages arises partly from a conflict over the boundaries of their communal lands. This quarrel, however, cannot be the principal cause of their differences, for it was mentioned only incidentally. At least the greater part and probably the whole of San Pedro Cucuchucho had its origins in San Pedro Ihuatzio, which village occurs in a sixteenth century document.[3] The present village is situated almost as far from the ruins of the pre-Spanish town on the mountain-slope as modern Ihuatzio itself. There are two small yácatas quite close to the present village of San Pedro Cucuchucho. People from this village told us that until about forty years ago the social organisation of their village was absolutely the same as that of Ihuatzio. It was the Roman Catholic priests who broke down the wapánekwa system. The wooden crosses, which used to play an important role in Ihuatzio, had a similar function in Cucuchucho, which still has eleven such crosses, six within the enclosed front court of the church and five by the roadside.

The inhabitants of Cucuchucho also consider the ancient ruined town as the ceremonial centre of their ancestors.

Cucuchucho has a little over 600 inhabitants, who are very poor; seventy per cent. of the occupational population are tule weavers, twenty per cent. farmers, and ten per cent. fishermen. Its community life resembles that of Ihuatzio, but disintegration of the traditional system has made more progress. It has retained a cargo-hierarchy, which is, however, no longer connected with the barrios and wapánekwecha. The majority of the household heads are followers of Sinarquismo,[4] and the extreme Right-wing priest of Ihuatzio has a considerable influence in this village of his parish, more than in Ihuatzio. The people of Cucuchucho seem to be more interested in local political problems. Some years ago a Tarascan from this place, who could neither read no write, was made mayor (presidente municipal) of Tzintzuntzan, albeit through a strange political manoeuvre. Just as in Ihuatzio, many men from Cucuchucho left the village a few years ago to migrate to the United States as 'braceros' (migrant workers); yet the village is on the whole averse to contacts with outsiders. Although sharp dissensions exist between members of the community, largely based on personal rivalries between the leaders of the village, no interference from outsiders is tolerated, and the inhabitants show great solidarity in their attitude towards the outside world. Some years ago the news got abroad that a man who had stolen a cow had been executed in the village. Tarascan traditional law had prevailed over Mexican codified law. The government authorities made investigations; at first some village chiefs and principals were imprisoned, but eventually they were released after the intervention of Crefal. Some time afterwards, however, the village chiefs were more cautious in dealing with some one who had stolen money. Instead of executing him in the centre of the village, a duck hunt was organised on the lake and the man was killed 'by accident'.

Some people in Ihuatzio accused the inhabitants of Cucuchucho of being 'matones' (i.e. killers, murderers). Boundary disputes between the two villages are said to have claimed victims on more than one occasion. Even as late as 1962 we heard of such a case.

It is a striking fact, however, that many people from Ihuatzio came to Cucuchucho to attend the great festivals on May 3rd and June 29th, but that Ihuatzio remained closed to the people of Cucuchucho. The present relations between these villages may be remnants of their institutionalised relations in the days when they both belonged to one greater pre-Spanish organisation, in which Ihuatzio played the more important part. (As has been said before, San Pedro Cucuchucho used to be called San Pedro Ihuatzio).

It has been said that the rivalry between Ascensión and Sagrado Corazón does not exclude a certain degree of solidarity between the inhabitants of the two barrios in external matters. Likewise the inhabitants of Ihuatzio and Cucuchucho feel that they belong to a larger Tarascan community, in spite of the contrasts between their villages. Towards non-Tarascan outsiders they feel that they are above all Purépecha. This is clearly illustrated in the following song, which is very popular in both villages and is often sung on festive occasions:

Tirínguintsatsahki

Será muy xierto, mare,
ke somos naturalitas;
noskhe huchá k'heri Puré'pecha,
noskhe huchá, mare!

No mengwatatantsʌ
tirínguintsʌtsʌhki
yekárantania.

Tsipen, tsipen mare!
hurá andápara kwéntani
hánikwa sapichun erontania.

Noskhe huchá k'heri Puré'pecha,
noskhe huchá, mare!
No mengwatatantsʌ
tirínguintsʌtsʌhki
yekárantania.

Flower of death

It may be true, my dear,
That we are mere natives;
But we are (also) the great Purépecha,
That is what we are, my girl!

We never tire
Of sowing
The Flower of Death.

Rejoice, rejoice, my girl!
It grows and rises
When the rainy season is approaching.

We are the great Purépecha
That is what we are, my girl!
We never tire
Of sowing
The Flower of Death.

The contrast between the first two lines, which are sung in Spanish, and the next Tarascan ones strongly emphasises the ethnic difference: to the people whose tongue is Spanish we are 'mere natives', but in reality we are the 'k'heri Purépecha'. We are never tired of honouring our dead; do not be sad, for we shall remain the great Purépecha.

2 Contacts with other indigenous population groups

Several inhabitants of Ihuatzio have been in touch with members of other Indian, non-Tarascan peoples, and most adults in Ihuatzio have their opinions about neighbouring indigenous population groups. They have the most emphatic opinion about the Aztecs:

"Aztecs are bad people; they used to come to Tzintzuntzan and Ihuatzio and other places in Michoacán, and they ate the people";

"Aztecs are proud and domineering people";

"Aztecs always try to dominate other people, they are not to be trusted".[5]

Such statements were numerous, and, indeed, most inhabitants did not like the Aztecs. The stereotype of the man-eating, domineering and arrogant Aztec is, presumably, largely based on tradition and a sense of the past. The Tarascan ancestors of the people of Ihuatzio, however, had little to learn from their Aztec contemporaries: they even surpassed them in cannibalistic practices. Yet, even today part of the Tarascan opinion is confirmed by the Aztecs themselves. In nearly all Aztec villages in Central Mexico which we visited people appeared very much to look down upon the Tarascans. One informant from Milpa Alta D. F., on hearing of the author's appointment to a lectureship at Pátzcuaro, remarked: "I am glad you are going there; they are a poor lot and badly in need of someone to put things in order". This Aztec was by no means richer than the average Ihuatzio householder.

In spite of their above-mentioned views on Aztecs, the Tarascans often feel some admiration for their former arch-enemies. Some called them "the real Mexicans, the kings of the country"; "the best soldiers in Mexico"; "handsome people", etc. Today contacts between members of the two population groups are rare and incidental. Many Tarascan travelling merchants have been to Aztec villages in Guerrero, to the Nahuatl-speaking villages on the Michoacán coast, those in the east of this state, and those in the states of México and Jalisco. Some people from Ihuatzio have also visited the Aztec-speaking parts of Puebla, Morelos, Hidalgo and other states. These contacts were most frequent during the war activities between 1910 and 1930. In those days many Aztec soldiers invaded Michoacán.

The Otomis and Mazahuas enjoyed scant regard, though they were not looked upon as "bad people". Some inhabitants of Ihuatzio who have probably read some litterature on the history of their country claim to cherish friendly feelings toward the Pirindas or Matlatzincas, once the allies of the Tarascan princes. The Yaquis are considered to be bloodthirsty people, an opinion arising from the way their army behaved during the Great Revolution.

On the whole Tarascans have a vague sense of solidarity with regard to the other, non-Aztec, Indian groups. There was, however, only a small minority who included the Aztecs. Some people still identify the Aztecs with the present federal government, "the authority from Mexico".

3 'Catrines' or 'Turíxecha'

The Tarascans of Ihuatzio refer to the non-Indian Mexicans, the mestizos (people of mixed descent) as 'Catrines' or 'Turíxecha', but these are not synonyms. The term 'catrín' in Mexico refers to a pretentious inhabitant of a town, who obviously lacks sympathy for peasant life: it also means a 'dandy', a man dressed in a conspicuous way and pretending to be a refined gentleman. The performers of certain traditional Tarascan dances who represent mestizos and ridicule them are also called 'catrines'.

People in Ihuatzio use the word to refer to the urbanised mestizos of Pátzcuaro, Morelia and other towns, and generally to refer to people, including Tarascans, dressed like 'western' townspeople. Strictly speaking, the word is not an equivalent of the term 'mestizo', since the latter refers to racial distinctions. Yet all informants at first maintained that the words were synonymous. This is not surprising, because these and other words dating from colonial times originally referred to racial distinctions, but have gradually acquired meanings largely based on cultural differences. When Mexicans today use the terms 'indio', 'mestizo', 'tarasco', etc. they want to stress the differences of culture between the population groups rather than their racial differences. So in

Ihuatzio the word 'catrines' only applies to Mexicans from urban areas, who do not speak an Indian language; it never refers to pure Indian or mestizo peasants, even if they have been assimilated to the cultural pattern of the mestizos. The word has a decidedly unfavourable connotation, since implications are attached to it which are the reverse of some of the standards and values so highly appreciated by these Tarascans, such as acceptance of commissions on behalf of the community, piety, faithful adherence to the principle of reciprocity, honesty in trade, conjugal faithfulness and reverence for the aged.

In speaking Tarascan, the inhabitants of Ihuatzio call the mestizos 'Tuříxecha' (singular: Tuřix). This nickname is rather strange. The literal meaning of the word Tuříxecha is 'the Blacks'.[6] One would expect the name to refer to negroes, and this may have been so in the past. The word 'catrines' was given as the Spanish equivalent of Tuříxecha, which was not quite correct, because Tuříxecha has a wider meaning; it can be used to refer to all non-Tarascan strangers, such as whites, mestizos and others. It is unknown how the word Tuříxecha came to be used as a nickname for mestizos. Is it possible that the name which first referred to the numerous negroes who had also been imported by the Spaniards into Michoacán, came to be used for strangers in general? This is indeed possible. But it should be borne in mind that black was the colour of Kurikaweri. The servants of the 'black god', the priests of Kurikaweri and some high State dignitaries before 1522 were dressed in black. It is therefore possible that in pre-Spanish times the name was used to refer to authorities and after the Conquest came to be used for colonial rulers and their descendants. The dark clothes worn by the sixteenth-century Spaniards may have prompted or fostered the use of this nickname.

The people of Ihuatzio have been and still are being taught to distrust the Tuříxecha. Every Tuřix represents a danger, a threat to the indigenous, Tarascan identity of the people, to the social order in Ihuatzio. Most Tuříxecha are enemies of the gods of Ihuatzio, they worship other gods or, worse still, they are atheists, unbelievers, enemies of every religion, they are troublemakers, cruel and warlike people, who prefer to use force instead of peaceful negotiation to attain their ends. It is best to avoid all contact with them but, if this should not be possible, to keep it to a minimum.

'Bracerismo', that is labour-migration and the resultant contacts with North

Americans, however, has helped to develop a somewhat more varied picture of the stranger, especially among the younger people. Many of them distinguish between Spaniards, mestizos, 'gringos' (the common Mexican name for their neighbours in the north), Europeans and 'latinos' (Latin Americans), and have formed stereotyped ideas of them. It is noteworthy that these more or less xenophobe Tarascans have on the whole a more favourable opinion of North Americans than of the Mexican mestizos, in spite of the often unpleasant experiences of migrant Tarascan workers in the United States. Probably this is brought about by their poor relationship with the mestizos. Their defensive attitude to the increasing influence of the catrines explain their efforts to seek support from others. Tarascan workers migrating to the north often experience more opposition from their Spanish-speaking compatriots than from the North Americans. The Tarascans of the Ihuatzio area often tell foreigners that Tarascan is not a difficult language at all and that it is very much like English. This statement has no linguistic basis whatever, but it illustrates the relationships described above. It may reveal an attempt on the part of the Tarascans of Ihuatzio to identify themselves with other people who are also different from the catrines. Informants who had lived in the United States for some time as braceros often proved to have been very selective in their observations. One of them, describing Chicago, only mentioned the great lake, the ocean of fresh water, the fish caught in the lake, the boats that he saw there, the parks and trees in them, especially fruit trees and flowers. He did not mention the sky-scrapers, the busy traffic, the big department stores, or other typically urban aspects of the city. This report and other accounts given by 'braceros' clearly show that they had only incidental contacts with the North Americans.

The picture which the inhabitants of Ihuatzio have formed of the mestizos is, of course, largely based on their experiences with population groups in the neighbourhood of their village. Most inhabitants of the centre of Pátzcuaro treat them in a patronising way. They address the Tarascans familiarly, whether they know them personally or not, a thing they will never do when talking to other mestizos. The situation here differs from that in some other Indian areas in Mexico with a centre of mestizos; the Tarascans of Ihuatzio also speak in a familiar way to the mestizos. If the mestizos more or less look down upon Tarascans, the Tarascans of this district do not feel themselves inferior to the mestizos at all. On the contrary, they are convinced that they are leading more virtuous and on the whole better lives than the mestizos. Therefore they regard the mestizos, who are mostly much wealthier people, as clever thieves, who have gained their riches in a way unacceptable to them. Unlike many other Indian groups in Mexico, these Tarascans are not ashamed of using their own language. On market days in Pátzcuaro Tarascan is heard everywhere in the centre of the town. On such market days, when they have the most intimate and most varied contacts, we can see most clearly how far apart the two worlds of these ethnically different groups are. There is hardly any sign of interest in or sympathy for each other's problems, ideals or ideas. Their short commercial encounters are the only contacts between on the one hand the shopkeepers and intermediary traders of Pátzcuaro, who are mestizos or people of almost pure Spanish descent, and on the other hand the Indian farmers, fishermen and artisans. Their relations are strictly confined to bargaining over prices.

The Tarascans of Ihuatzio and the mestizos and assimilated Indians of Tzintzuntzan have a wider basis for mutual understanding, because their ways of life and ideas have very much in common, in spite of the fact that the traditional social system in Tzintzuntzan is in an advanced stage of disintegration. Yet the two groups are much more sharply opposed owing to their greatly conflicting interests. The disputes over the boundaries on the slopes of Mount Tariatak'heri, which have been mentioned earlier, and the reluctance of the inhabitants of Ihuatzio to be subordinate to the municipal authorities of Tzintzuntzan give rise to frequent incidents, which often end in minor and sometimes in serious acts of violence.

4 *The church*

As the inhabitants of Ihuatzio are nominally Roman Catholic and the priest lives in their village, this community as a parish forms part of the greater ecclesiastical organisation, at least nominally. But from what has been said in preceding chapters it is clear that in practice this does not amount to much. The priest regularly receives instructions from his superiors, for instance from the Bishop of Morelia, and passes on to his parishioners all the information intended for all the 'faithful members of the church'. So far the ecclesiastical organisation works perfectly. But in Ihuatzio it fails to pass the last link between the ecclesiastical authorities and the 'faithful', for here the church as a local institution is part of the whole body of traditional forms of organisation. To the villagers the church building is the most important part of their ceremonial centre, which, however, comprises more than the church alone. It also contains the official residence of the Prioste, that of the priest, the front court, and until a short time ago, the Gwatapera. The templo, or Thioseo ('place of God') is their chief place of worship and thus plays an important part in many activities of the community. Its connections with the community are established through institutions: the Priostería, the Capitanías (the 'genuine' commissions) and the wapánekwa services. In such circumstances the Roman Catholic church as an international institution can exercise but little influence in the village. The church in the wider sense of the word has only one direct subordinate: the priest, and he has no authority over the organised groups within the community, since these obey the traditional chiefs and the Hurámutich'. The villagers consider the church as well as the other parts of the ceremonial centre as communal property. Everything inside the church building is also village property. So are los imágenes (the images of the saints).

In Ihuatzio the Roman Catholic Church is faced with the people's suspicion of every foreign element in the village. It is therefore important that the village priest is himself a Tarascan. The villagers look upon him as one of their external leaders. To them he is first of all their representative before the ecclesiastical authorities, and their representative before the Tata Thiox rather than the representative of those ecclesiastical authorities and that god in their village. And even in the latter capacity his internal authority is limited; only the chiefs and principals can decide in what respects the community shall accept or reject the authority of the priest.

5   *The municipality, the state and the republic*

The people of Ihuatzio consider the politico-administrative units to which the village officially belongs as mostly troublesome aspects of the hostile outside world. During the time of our study in Ihuatzio we noticed very little interest on the part of the people in the political controversies and problems in their municipality, the state and the federal republic. At the municipal elections of 1962 only 37 of a total number of 900 voters polled. It is true that the U.N.S. (Sinarquistas) had issued an instruction to its members to abstain from voting, but even if all the members and fellow-travellers of the party in the village had cast their votes, the poll would have been less than 35 per cent. of the people qualified to vote. The majority of the people have no interest in any of the political parties.

On the whole the people feel that the municipal institutions have been imposed upon them and do not work in the interest of the village. The Mexican system of government involves almost inevitable imperfections in the lowest administrative units. Officially the administrative system is strongly decentralised, and normally the Municipio libre can only be governed by its own citizens. This means that a remote rural municipality with a large proportion of illiterate inhabitants can offer only few candidates for administrative offices. Sometimes there are none at all. Moreover the Presidente Municipal ('Mayor') is not immediately eligible for re-election. Until 1963 a new mayor had been elected annually, then the period of office was extended to three years. Although nominally municipalities enjoy a high degree of self-government, rural councils have very limited financial resources at their disposal, and this restricts their activities.

Municipalities with both Indian and mestizo communities as a rule have councils consisting mainly of mestizos. Usually this is a direct consequence of the better relations between mestizos and the national and regional party-organisations; sometimes it may be due to better knowledge of Spanish and a better education. Tzintzuntzan is no exception to this rule, although the situation here differs from the general pattern in that mestizos and Tarascans have similar levels of general education. Another unusual feature is that although this village is the municipal capital, it can hardly be called the centre of the municipal district. The main business centres are Pátzcuaro and Quiroga. As has been said in the general introduction to this study, the municipality of Tzintzuntzan is an artificial product created with sentimental motives.[7] Soon after the creation of this municipality in the nineteen-thirties, Ihuatzio began to get into difficulties. Until that time the village had been located in the northern extremity of the municipality of Pátzcuaro, so that it was easy for the village chiefs to keep aloof from the local authorities in Pátzcuaro, who on their part showed little interest in Ihuatzio. Tzintzuntzan was then part of the municipality of Quiroga, and the boundary between the two municipalities also separated the communal lands of Tzintzuntzan from those of Ihuatzio, the two ancient Tarascan capitals. With the formation of the new municipal district of Tzintzuntzan the above mentioned municipal boundary disappeared. This gave rise to the disputes over the boundaries of the communal grounds, which have not been settled to this day.

The mestizos in Tzintzuntzan regard the Tarascans of Ihuatzio as stubborn and difficult people, not open to reason and constantly causing trouble. All our non-Tarascan informants in Tzintzuntzan believed that only fear could induce the inhabitants of Ihuatzio to be co-operative, and that it was useless to consult with them. The inhabitants of Ihuatzio openly called the mestizos of Tzintzuntzan thieves, accusing them of stealing cattle, secretly removing boundary-posts, illegally collecting taxes and tempering with emigration papers and labour permits of braceros. However serious these differences may be, neither party on the whole likes to push matters to extremes. The authorities in Tzintzuntzan showed a fair amount of understanding of the traditional system of administration in Ihuatzio and always agreed to the nominations submitted by the principals for the offices of Juez and Jefe de Tenencia and their deputies. The inhabitants of Ihuatzio on their part, though reluctantly, paid some small local taxes.

Since General Lázaro Cárdenas came into office, first as Governor of Michoacán, then from 1934 till 1940 as President of Mexico the Lake Tarascans have been more aware of the existence of their own state and the federal republic. During both periods of office Cárdenas preferred to live at his estate 'Eréndira' in Lower Pátzcuaro, showing great interest in the indigenous population of the district. This brought about the first direct contact between this population and the Governor and future President. Cárdenas is still extremely popular among the Lake Tarascans. Many of them fail to see any inconsistency in combining their membership of the extreme-right-wing U.N.S. with a great liking for the left-wing General Cárdenas, which is another significant illustration of the fact that they are scarcely politically-minded.

The understanding that the people of Ihuatzio have of the state and federal institutions has hardly increased. To them authority at these two levels is embodied in the persons of the Governor and the President, and, if they know about the existence of institutions like the Houses of Representatives, their ideas about them are very vague indeed.

6 *C.R.E.F.A.L. and the problems attached to development projects*

When in 1951 the Regional Centre of Fundamental Education for Latin America (c.r.e.f.a.l.) was established at Pátzcuaro and commenced its activities from the 'Eréndira' estate, which General Cárdenas had kindly put at their disposal, many people in the whole district had great expectations of its success, although some of them were indeed a little critical. The moral support given by 'Tata Cárdenas' was in general a good introduction for the Crefal staff and their students and facilitated their first contacts with the inhabitants of nearby villages. Some Right-wing groups in Michoacán, however, were hostile, and their connections with men in the Roman ecclesiastical hierarchy enabled them to begin an agitation against the Centre. In some villages the priests told their parishioners that Crefal was a centre of communist and anti-clerical activities. Here and there people co-operating with Crefal were threatened with religious sanctions, even with ex-communication. Because of this opposition Crefal was confronted with great problems in the first few years of its existence, but after some time the agitation subsided, thanks partly to the fact that the Centre had dismissed the staff-members who had extreme Left-wing sympathies.

Ihuatzio and Cucuchucho have from the first been among the most difficult villages for Crefal. In the first few years most of the Crefal activities were carried out in Ihuatzio. The director of the Crefal team in those days was a man who was in favour of direct material action as far as the practical side of the development projects was concerned. With the help of some villagers who sympathised with Crefal (they were the people mentioned before who refused to accept commissions) the team worked hard to install electric cables and telephone ducts, to dig wells and build latrines. In general they followed the same method which was applied by General Cárdenas when in the nineteen thirties he tried to develop the district: the Crefal team decided what were the most urgent needs of the community and arranged for the works to be carried out. This policy has the advantage that visible results are usually attained within a fairly short time. But in most cases it involves great risks. Without considerable financial resources and a large staff this method can only be applied incidentally, that is in a few localities only. Furthermore the organisation carrying out a development project in this way has itself to see to the means to continue it, as usually the villagers are not prepared to undertake the maintenance of new works, which have been more or less thrust upon them. This aspect was neglected in the nineteen-thirties; consequently the district abounds in disused water conducts and mills, and broken road surfaces, not to mention the monumental, but entirely decayed community-halls and schools built in many villages. Before 1960 Crefal, too, was quite unable to guarantee adequate continuity; but then, such a task would not be in accord with the original plan and the nature of the Centre, because even then its activities were mainly directed towards the training of Latin American staffs for development projects instead of the actual execution of works in areas allocated by the Mexican government. Furthermore the difficulties met in Ihuatzio were enhanced by the fact that Crefal had omitted to make thorough investigations into the intricate social and religious organisation of the village community and was therefore unfamiliar with it. The Hurámutich' and Orénaříkwecha watched the activities of Crefal with increasing suspicion. Owing to the historically-determined situation in Ihuatzio this suspicion had existed from the very beginning, but when the teams set to work, ignoring the chiefs and principals and showing no interest in matters to which the villagers attached the greatest importance, the feelings of distrust naturally increased. Things went from bad to worse when Crefal experts and students began to support the opposition to the cargo system, which, as we have already seen, was leading to excesses. If at first the attitude of the principals towards Crefal had more or less been one of indifference, it gradually changed into complete disapproval. The Crefal team became more and more an exclusive refuge of 'dissident' persons in the village, those opposed to the traditional system.

After some years the Centre started a chicken-farming project in several villages. Controlled loans were granted by one of the Mexican banks to the new regional co-operative association of chicken-farmers. Each member built a model henhouse under the direction of Crefal and started business with 200 chickens. The Centre provided information and instructions and gave further aid. This project was directed by the agrarian specialists of Crefal and became a great success in several villages, but not in Ihuatzio. Here only 18 people joined the project, chiefly young men, followers of the ambitious member of the Kapitan wapánekwa, who was afterwards to be defeated when he tried to become Alkande.[8] Moreover the chicken project started a quarrel between Crefal specialists and the village priest.[9] Altogether the situation became so difficult for Crefal that no students were sent to Ihuatzio in 1959 and 1960. In Cucuchucho students' activities had been terminated some time earlier.

When in the second half of 1962, after our researches had been going on for more than eighteen months, we succeeded in establishing fairly intensive contacts with some of the most important chiefs and principals, the latter unreservedly expressed their opinion about Crefal. Their grievances against the Centre were:

1 that it had accomplished nothing of essential value in the village;
2 that members of Crefal staffs and students had in the past made many promises which had never been fulfilled;
3 that some specialists and students of the Centre had tried to prevent the people from executing their duties towards the community;
4 that the students had been doing the same things for ten years without ever completing anything;
5 that Crefal was causing discord in the village;
6 that the co-operative society's earnings from the chicken project were greater than those of the individual members.

With four of these points the author was in full agreement;[10] the first and the last are open to question. The fifth grievance betrays some anxiety about the infringement of social control, which the chiefs and principals consider to be embodied in their own authority. Such situations indeed involve a risk of social disintegration. This problem will be dealt with again in the last chapter.

Thanks to my students' devotion to their work and the entirely different policy in dealing with the problems, which we had been able to apply at the beginning of the new programme of the Centre in 1961, some improvement was brought about in the relations between Crefal and the village. From that time the emphasis was shifted from the execution of works under the direction of specialists and students to the social study of the village and so-called 'technical assistance'. With regard to this very limited assistance we always took care to consult the village chiefs: by doing so some of their objections could be removed. Nevertheless the lack of continuity and the almost entire absence of funds allowed only very little scope for really effective activities. These could be extended, it is true, when at our instigation the 15th Indigenous Development Brigade was stationed in Ihuatzio. But this also created a new problem, because the introduction of the federal government's social and cultural policy, which aims at national integration, might in the long run constitute a threat to the authority of the traditional chiefs.

Personally the author agrees with the majority of the inhabitants of Ihuatzio that the activities of Crefal in the village had by no means been a complete success. This also applies to the three years during which the author was charged with the direction of the Centre's activities in Ihuatzio. In that period the Centre was sometimes a nuisance rather than a convenience to the people of the village. This was especially true for the year 1961, when the students were exclusively engaged on making investigations. There was some improvement afterwards, but our work did not mean a great deal to the villagers. Of course, they had no idea of the value of our study, while the practical results of our activities were small, as they were bound to be, considering the circumstances and the lack of funds.

To the people of Ihuatzio 'los del Crefal' or 'los crefaleanos' are a kind of Turíxecha, who after all the years of contact are no longer considered dangerous, although it is still necessary to keep an eye on them and be on your guard. One of the most persistent suspicions against 'those of Crefal' is that they are supposed to pass on all kinds of information to the government. The customs and ideas of Crefal specialists and students which often differ greatly from those of the people of Ihuatzio are another constant source of distrust. The villagers are well aware that many of the social, cultural and religious customs which they value highly and many of their norms clash with those of 'los del Crefal'. They know quite well that the people of the Centre generally disapprove of the great displays of fireworks, the use of liquor, and other aspects of their religious festivals. Therefore they feel that the presence of the students and lecturers in the village is a hindrance to their social life. The women are as a rule even more suspicious than the men, for which they have good reason. They know that women among the catrines have a lower social status than they themselves enjoy in their own community. Any change towards the norms prevailing among mestizos is a threat to their own position. Therefore the women are conservative and usually less open to the cultural influences of the national majority, in spite of the fact that it is they who have more contacts with the catrines through their regular visits to the markets and their trade in tortillas.

Notes to chapter *VI*

1 Jarácuaro (Xarákwaro) was the centre of the Xarátanga cult (Corona y Núñez, 1957, p. 74) and of the worship of five other Deities (see: Relación de Michoacán 1541, p. 118); Pareo was the religious centre of the Tirípeme Kaheri, the God of the south (Corona y Núñez, 1957, p. 29); Santa Fé or Wayámeo, the first centre of the worship of Kurikaweri in the lake district, place where the original tribe was divided (Relación de Mich., 1541, p. 24; Corona y Núñez, 1957, pp. 25-30); Pacandan was the home of the cult of Chupi-Tirípeme, the God of the Centre (Corona y Núñez, 1957, pp. 27, 28); Tziróndaro was the place where the 'holy' road to Tzacapu began, along which the Kasonsí had to walk during a certain annual ceremony (Corona y Núñez, 1957, p. 24).

2 This is the common name to indicate the villagers and hamlets between Tzintzuntzan and Cucuchucho, for instance Ichupio, Tarerio, Ucasanástacua, etc.

3 Doc. 1593 Mex. Just 94 Archivo General de Indias, Sevilla.

4 cf. chapter II, pp. 47, 48.

5 "Son mero malos, pues antes vinieron por acá a Tzintzuntzan y comieron a la gente. Son orgullosos, tratan de dominar, tiranizan a la gente pues. No son de confianza".

6 Gilberti, 1559, p. 128.

7 See: chapter I, p. 12.

8 See: chapter IV, pp. 93, 94.

9 Idem, p. 99.

10 This is not meant as disapproval of the activities of the author's predecessors. It is impossible afterwards to judge whether in the given circumstances they could have done any better.

VII   *the Tarascan identity*

The results of this study of the social system of the inhabitants of Ihuatzio have
implications in two entirely different fields. They call for a more thorough
consideration of the ethnological and historical background of the Tarascans,
and for some remarks on the complex of problems connected with community
development in these and similar circumstances. These two aspects of the
study may seem to be almost unrelated at first sight, but they have proved to
have common ground in the social and cultural identity of the community
studied and of that of the larger Tarascan population group to which it belongs.
An analysis of this Indian identity will be the starting-point for a more detailed
description of the two above-mentioned aspects.

The word 'identity' is here used in a relative, not an absolute sense. The
Tarascan identity is critically compared with that of the mestizos, as the identity
of an ethnic minority compared with that of the national majority. It refers to
the whole complex of elements or aspects of social and cultural life which
differentiates Tarascan society from that of the mestizos. So the concept of
identity, as it will be applied here, is not confined to the specific characteristics
of the group, to aspects and qualities only found within that particular group
or community. Nor is it used in the restricted sense of a complex of original
cultural and social aspects of the group which are the outcome of the au-
tochtonous character of a society. Four centuries of autonomic developments
in a variety of fields have contributed to form the identity of the present-day
Tarascan society.

The main aspects of the identity of the Tarascan community of Ihuatzio have
been described in the four preceding chapters. They can be summarised as
follows:

1 Leadership (traditional chieftainship) is entrusted to the most devoted and successful servants of the community (the commissioners), to men who, aided by blood-relations and ceremonial relatives, have made great sacrifices on behalf of the community. Their spirit of sacrifice is judged from the work, goods and funds they spend on behalf of the community as officials within the religious and ceremonial system. In this respect a festival in Ihuatzio resembles a potlatch. Prestige depends in the first place on the fulfilment of 'cargos'. Riches do not lead to a high position in the social scale, unless they are spent on behalf of the community.

2 Prestige, in addition to being associated with the completion of commissions, is also connected with old age. The latter connection is found among many peoples, but is almost entirely lacking among mestizos. A group of influential old men, like the Orénaŕikwecha in every wapánekwa in Ihuatzio, is a phenomenon unknown in mestizo villages and towns.

3 Another feature of the identity of Ihuatzio is the existence of dual forms of organisation within the village community. Dual organisations may be antagonistic or complementary. The two barrios and the two Capitanías of San Francisco are examples of the former; the system of chieftainship, consisting of internal and external leaders, contains instances of the latter. The principle of duality is also found in the strong tendency to barrio-endogamy.

4 The village community is divided into 9 wapánekwecha with predominantly religious and ceremonial functions, although they may also be called upon to carry out public works. These groups, which are based on relationship as well as on territorial grounds, form the foundation of the social organisation and are one of the most important aspects of the individuality of the village.

5 The village community is a fairly closed entity in which the elements introduced from outside have not been able to destroy the traditional social system. Most of the originally foreign elements have been encapsulated; their influence is limited and they have been made subservient as far as possible to the interests of the community. Thus the Roman Catholic church has been made part of the ceremonial centre, thereby becoming subjected to the inherent traditional system of the village. The same thing has happened to the municipal administration. The Wandárich' and the

village chiefs perform functions which in mestizo communities are performed by the priest and the municipal council.

6   The Tarascans of Ihuatzio have views on the universe and a number of religious concepts different from those of mestizos.

7   The identity of the villagers is largely derived from their adherence to the Tarascan language and, although to a much smaller extent, from their particular Spanish dialect, which differs in some respects from that of the mestizo villages in the surrounding area.

8   Ceremonial relationship (compadrazgo), which is an important feature also in mestizo communities, has a character of its own in Ihuatzio. On the whole there is a greater variety of motives for establishing ceremonial relationships. Usually these are more meaningful than they are in a mestizo community.

The above survey of the main aspects of the identity of Ihuatzio leads to the question of how they fit into the general pattern of Tarascan identity, or whether Ihuatzio is an exception among Tarascan villages. To answer this question a comparison has to be made between several Tarascan communities with regard to the above eight points. Many people living in areas around Lake Pátzcuaro were convinced that Ihuatzio possessed an indigenous character quite peculiar to the village. A close examination of the data on some other Tarascan villages may show how far this popular view is correct (cf. appendix 1).

San Jeronimo Purenchécuaro, a village of about 1500 inhabitants, is one of the largest Tarascan villages on the northern shore of Lake Pátzcuaro, and strongly resembles Ihuatzio. One of the author's team, Miss N. B. González, collected the following data about the village. Like Ihuatzio Purenchécuaro is divided into two territorial barrios and into nine 'ceremonial wards'. The territorial wards have no names of their own, as they have in Ihuatzio, but are referred to as 'secciones' or 'sectores'. Each sector is subdivided into two 'cuarteles', so that the village is also divided into four quarters. Each of the nine ceremonial wards bears the name of a saint: San Jerónimo, Santa Isabel, San Pedro, San Salvador, Santa Guadalupe, (Santa) Concepción, Santa Magdalena, San Juan and San Miguel. So there are five male and four female saints. The first saint is also the patron saint of the village. San Jerónimo and San Pedro are the largest ceremonial wards and rank highest. The greatest festival in the village, that of San Jerónimo, is jointly organised by these two ceremonial wards. In this village the nine ceremonial wards are closed territorial units, five in one and four in the other village sector. The former sector is ranked higher than the latter. The Acha Hefe is a man from the former, his deputy a man from the latter sector. People still remembered that "in former days there used to be a tendency towards sector endogamy", but they doubted if it had ever been strictly applied. According to these informants no such binding regulations existed today. (It should be borne in mind, however, that people in Ihuatzio at first said the same thing with regard to their village). Besides sectors, quarters and nine ceremonial wards Purenchécuaro is also divided into eight 'manzanas' (localities), two in each quarter. It appears that this division has largely replaced the traditional division into nine ceremonial wards, because today the hierarchies of principals, chiefs and commissioners are largely dependent on this division into eight parts. There are eight manzana-heads with the traditional title of Teruhtsikuri.[1] They bear some resemblance to the Orétspetich' in Ihuatzio. There are also eight Semaneros, who are referred to, as in Ihuatzio, by the Tarascan word Oreti or Ureti. The village has two Priostes, one for each sector. Each is assisted by four Urétich' or Urecha, two for each quarter. Their duties and offices agree with those of their colleagues in Ihuatzio. The offices of Juez and Representante de la Comunidad Indígena in Purenchécuaro are less traditional in nature. The ceremonial year starts on August 24th. Then the so-called 'Colectores' are appointed, and these in their turn name the cargueros. Nominally the Colectores are elected by the general assembly of villagers, but in reality here, too, it is the chiefs and principals who elect them. The most important cargo is that of San Jerónimo; the commissioners organise the greatest festival, that of September 30th. The Captains of San Jerónimo are always men from the ceremonial wards of San Jerónimo and San Pedro. They have three aides, one from each of the three other quarters. These helpers bear the title of Anátakuri.[2] Then there are the captains of the other saints with their helpers. At the bottom of the hierarchic scale are the Caporales, who perform so-called 'penal cargos'. These are cargos which involve expenses without bringing any prestige as a reward. The Prioste and the Acha Hefe impose them on men who have refused a cargo, in order to give them an opportunity for partial rehabilitation. Christmas Day is also a major feast in the village; it is organised by eighteen cargueros: 4 Capitanes with 3 helpers each, and two Caporales. Moreover each Caporal is assisted by 6 vaqueros, so that no less than thirty men are charged with the organisation and the performance of the festivities. Informants estimated the total cost of the festival of San Jerónimo at Mex. $ 13000.—, and that of December 25th at a little over half the amount.

A more thorough comparative study of Ihuatzio and Purenchécuaro may yield further results. On the whole the inhabitants of Purenchécuaro are much more assimilated to the culture of the mestizos than are those of Ihuatzio. But this does not exclude the possibility that some elements of their culture may be more autochthonous. The differences in status between the ceremonial wards and the differentiation of their functions appear to be greater and more pronounced.

In 1961 and 1962 short comparative studies were made of two islands in Lake Pátzcuaro. The small community of the island of Yunuén (175 inhabitants), which is situated 8 km northwest of Ihuatzio has a very simple form of cargo system. Every year four commissioners are elected to organise the religious festivals and manage the local chapel. Then there are 4 to 6 Rezadores del Rosario (sayers of the Rosary), who conduct the divine services in the chapel. The commissioners are elected by the assembly of household heads. One of the four commissioners is elected as leader over the other three. The expenses to be borne by the cargueros are about 5 pesos per month for the maintenance and decoration of the chapel; 400 to 500 pesos for the festival of Guadalupe, which is held here on January 12th (!); the same amount for the Candlemas festival (Candelaria) on February 2nd; and about 60 pesos for Christmas. The group of old Principales has lost much of its influence. Leadership today is based on personal qualities and merit. No official distinction is made between internal and external leadership. In this little island, which was not populated (or repopulated) until 60 or 70 years ago, we witnessed in 1961 and 1962 its division into two parts by the thirty-odd household heads. It was also decided that if in any one year the Jefe de Tenencia came from one part, his Suplente was to come from the other 'barrio' and vice-versa the next year. Soon a difference in status and some rivalry arose between the two parts. The islanders evidently thought that the independence of their own community would not be complete without the formation of two 'barrios', for such was the situation in the island of Janitzio, where most of the Yunuén families had come from. (In former days Yunuén was sometimes considered as a 'barrio' of Pacándani).

The nearby island of Pacandan(i) or La Pacanda has a more extensive cargo system and even a modest organisation of occupational groups. The great festival in Pacándani is that of Corpus Christi in July or early in August, when Tarascans from a wide area come to the island. Then each occupational group has its own ceremonial performance. The population of the island is divided into three 'destinos' ('destinies'):[3] laboristas (farmers), chinchoreros (seine fishers) and chirímecueros (trawl-net fishers). Each occupational group supplies one carguero and a band. This island is also divided into two territorial barrios. Each barrio has a chief and a Colector, who collects the money for certain festivals. In Pacándani the performance of cargos leads to much higher prestige than in Yunuén. Relations between the two islands resemble those between Ihuatzio and Cucuchucho, but the island populations are not as sharply divided.

Beals's study of Cherán contains a considerable amount of information on the traditional religious and social organisation of that village.[4] The following is a brief summary of the most important features. The traditional administrative hierarchy is headed by a number of elderly Principales or Aches (classical Tarascan: Acha-echa), who have held the offices of Prioste and Colector. These principals form an administrative body, called the Cabildo. From its own members the Cabildo elects a chief of all the principals. He is the traditional supreme chief of the village community. There are three executive chiefs of lower rank: the above-mentioned Colector and his subordinates, the Prioste and the Keng(u)i. The Colector and the Prioste are appointed by the Cabildo; the Colector in his turn appoints the Keng(u)i. They hold office for one year, from December 8th till December 8th of the next year. After completing his year in office, the Colector becomes a member of the Cabildo, and the Prioste takes his place as Colector. The Keng(u)i, as long as he is in office, lives in a community-hall within the ceremonial centre. These three chiefs manage the religious centre of the village and supervise the work done there. The Prioste appoints the Wananches, girls in the service of the religious centre whose task it is to perform certain traditional dances. They are required to have previously participated in the 'dance of the viejitos' (old men) before they can be chosen as Wananches. One of them leads the group and bears the title of Xunganda. (In former days in Ihuatzio there also used to be a group of girls called Wanánchatiecha; they were in charge of part of the worship of Guadalupe). The 'saints' of Cherán and the cargos connected with them can be divided into two groups:

I The 'Saints', who are owned by the Cabildo. They are the following six (given in the order in which Beals mentions them)
1 Santo Niño (Holy Child), December 25th;
2 La Virgen de las Nieves (the Snow Virgin), August 5th;
3 La Virgen de Guadalupe, December 12th;
4 San Isidro (the patron saint of the ploughing farmers), May 15th;
5 San José (St. Joseph, the patron saint of the woodworkers), March 19th;
6 Santa Inés (the patron saint of the stockfarmers), April 21st.
The six commissioners having charge of them are appointed by the Cabildo. The carguero of Santo Niño has the most important commission and is highest in rank after the Cabildo. Usually the image, which like those of the five other Santos is regarded as the property of the Cabildo, is kept in the maize storehouse of the carguero. The latter has to give presents to the Turi'a (Negrito) dancers and to the Wananches; further his expenses will amount to about Mex. $ 1600.—. As a rule he is supported by his brothers. The other cargueros have lower expenses. In Cherán the commissioners take up their duties on the feastday of their saint or the day after. The cargos of the Cabildo are usually undertaken for the prestige attached to them. The commissioners of the patron saints of the occupational groups are usually drawn from these groups, but not always. Beals mentions as an example that the commissioner of San Isidro need not be a farmer.

II The worship of at least six of the saints in Cherán is not directly dependent on the Cabildo. Their cargueros, who often accept the charges to redeem a vow, are appointed by the Aches of the respective occupational groups or by Principales especially charged with these appointments. These commissions and the commissioners in charge of them are:

7 San Rafael (patron saint of the traders), October 24th. As a rule this carguero is a trader, but in 1940 he was a maker of fireworks from Pichátaro (!).

8 San Antonio (patron saint of the mule drivers), June 13th. One commissioner.

9 San Anselmo (patron saint of the panaleros or honey-gatherers).
This saint has two Mayordomías or cargos. One of the cargueros is always a man from one of the two upper barrios, the other from one of the lower barrios, upper and lower referring to the difference in altitude. Only gatherers of honey can perform these cargos. There are two images of San Anselmo, one for each commissioner. In 1940 the honey-gatherers of the lower barrios chose four Principales to nominate the candidates for the cargo. The upper barrios chose only one Principal or Acha for that purpose. The Priest chose the cargueros from the list of candidates. In 1940 the nominal carguero from the lower barrios was a boy of four who was retarded in growth, which fact induced his father to take a vow. In such cases the father or another man enjoys the honour and the prestige attached to the actual performance of the duties. A boy who has been a nominal 'carguero' can never claim having performed the commission. The four Aches or Principales of the lower barrios have to fulfil some financial obligations.

10 Tres Reyes (Twelfth Night), January 6th.
In 1940 the carguero was a man who had fulfilled the commission of Santo Niño the year before. In each case the acceptance of the cargo was due to a vow he had taken. The cost involved is nearly Mex. $ 700,—. This mayordomía or cargo is apparently 'owned' by three Principals. The cargo dates from 1938, when these three Principales "were inspired by God to organise a feast", and one of them undertook the commission. The carguero of 1940 was the third, and his successors for the next two years had already been appointed.

11 Santa Cecilia (patron saint of the musicians).
One carguero chosen from the musicians of the village.

12 El Milagroso Santo Niño (The miraculous Holy Child).
This cargo 'belongs' to a certain family, the carguero being a member of the family.

Cherán and Ihuatzio have the same patron saint, St. Francis, but in Cherán this saint is not connected with the cargo- or mayordomía-system. His feast is financed by the four territorial barrios. At the end of August the Presidente Municipal (the 'Mayor') appoints four Chief Comisionados, one from each barrio. Each of them chooses from 5 to 15 assistants from the men of his own barrio. The cost is divided between the barrios. In 1940 the two low-lying southern barrios had to provide one band each, the north-western barrio provided the 'castle' (fireworks) and the northeastern gave the wax for the candles. Furthermore the inhabitants had to pay contributions in money to the Comisionados. People who refused to pay ran the risk of imprisonment. When the total contributions are insufficient to cover the cost of the festivities, the Comisionados have to supply the deficiency from their own private means. The Comisionado of each barrio has to appoint and equip one Moro dancer. Further each barrio has a young comisionado who is responsible for the barrio's contribution to the building of a bull ring.

The barrio-organisation also plays a part in some other festivals. On the first Saturday after Easter the village celebrates the fiesta de la Octava. For this festival each barrio appoints five to eight comisionados, who collect money to hire bands. Official and unofficial cockfights are part of the festivities.

Before Palm Sunday the Colector takes a boy from each barrio; they have to cut green palm-leaves from the tropical lowlands. Each boy takes a girl, usually his girl friend, to help him prepare a special festive dish. Each boy has to make a wooden cross about five feet high. These crosses are hung with specially decorated eatables, little bags and little maize-cake cloths and thus decked are carried by the boys on the day of the festival. The girls carry sticks hung with tropical fruit, brought by the boys. Sometimes the girls also carry a water-melon or a honeycomb on their backs. On this occasion the barrios show a strong competitive spirit. The girls are judged as to which carries the heaviest burden and which of them has made the largest maize-balls. Some communal services on behalf of the community are also organised according to the barrio-division. The maintenance of the waterworks and the cleaning of the cemetery are the traditional tasks of the barrios.[5]

The feast of Corpus Christi (fiesta de Corpus) is organised by the occupational groups. The most important occupational groups, those of the arrieros (mule drivers), the travelling merchants, the shopkeepers, farmers, cabinet-makers and makers of wooden planks each appoint eight Comisionados in each of the four barrios. Each group of 32 Comisionados collects money from the members of the occupational groups to hire a band. This money is readily given. The bakers, weavers, butchers, shopkeepers [6] and honey-gatherers are not obliged to supply a band, though they sometimes do so. The honey-gatherers have special obligations. A fortnight before the festival they carry the two images of their patron saint, San Anselmo, to the hamlet of Cosumo. They camp out in the forests, making merry at night and collecting bees' nests in the daytime. A short time before the feast these are brought back to Cherán. Two wooden structures are built, called kata'rakwa. The two largest honeycombs are put on top of the structures, and the others are put in a net, which is hung around them. During the festival they are carried about the village, and then sold. On this day there is a fancy market where members of occupational groups sell traditional merchandise and are 'paid' with pieces of bread, chewing-gum, etc. Some youths collect the 'market tax', also consisting of pieces of bread, pieces of wood, and such things; another group of young men attacks them with wooden pistols and rifles, and robs them of part of the 'tax' collected.

Some traditional forms of rivalry and ceremonial fights have become institutionalised and are displayed as part of some of the festivals. During the pre-Lent Carnival period girls sell painted eggs which they have filled with confetti: young men buy them and break them on the girls heads. Then boys and girls throw confetti at each other. During the transfer of the office of Kieng(u)i both the old and the new officials are represented by an old man. Both old men are accompanied by a woman disguised as an old woman. The old man who represents the new Kieng(u)i criticizes the achievements of the retiring Kieng(u)i, while the latter's representative defends his past year of office. A noteworthy point of resemblance with Ihuatzio is the fact that differences exist between the Cabildo and the village Roman Catholic priest. At the time of Beals's study of Cherán they led to a sharp open conflict.

Beals's study also contains data concerning the village of Angahuan collected by Silva Rendón.[7] Angahuan has a hierarchy of offices with the following ranks: Alcalde, Regidor, Kámbiti, Petahpe or Biskal, Mayores, Kieng(u)i and Anyítakwa. Furthermore there is a body of elderly principals comparable with the Cabildo in Cherán and the Hurámutich' in Ihuatzio. Its members bear the title of Tarénpenya or Principal. The management of the ceremonial centre is entrusted for one year to the Alcalde of Angahuan. During his year of office the Alcalde has to organise six festivals, among which is that of Santiago, the patron saint of the village. The last festival is held on the day when the Tarénpenyas elect a new Alcalde. The Alcalde is assisted in the fulfilment of his duties by the Regidor and by his own relations.

The Kámbiti finances the celebrations during the Holy Week (Semana Santa) and has to decorate the main altar with fruit from the tropical lowlands (the ceremony of the Wirímutakwa). On Easter Eve an important ceremony takes place under his direction. The boys and girls of the village form two separate groups going about the village, the girls carrying the image of María Magdalena, the boys that of San José (St. Joseph). The groups meet at certain points of the village and run races, carrying the images. The Kámbiti is the head of a club of girls, who are called Tsʌtsʌ'ki hatsirati. During his year of office they supply the flowers for the altars and during the Holy Week they serve a refreshing drink, called charape by the Tarascans, to the congregation.

In February the Petahpe invites the young men of the village to his home and serves a maize dish, called iskitl in Aztec and kanita takunhi in Tarascan. On this occasion he calls upon the young men to clean the village well. On the day of their communal labour he treats the young workers to rice and pork and provides them with music.

To become a Mayor a man has to give a feast in honour of Santiago, and to give a performance as a Moro-dancer. The Mayores have to supply the village chiefs with fire-wood; then their wives have to grind maize and fetch water for the festivities organised by the Alcalde, Kámbiti and Petahpe.

The Kieng(u)i is the immediate subordinate of the Alcalde, his task being the cleaning of the ceremonial centre and the decoration of the church. He is head of the Anyítakwas or Semaneros. These are charged with the care of a community hall, called Yurixo ('Place of Blood', or 'Place of the Virgin'). They are divided into groups according to blocks of houses, each group being on duty for one week. Every week a group of seven or eight families goes to a building next to the church. One of them prepares the meals for the others and for the sick people of the village.

The Anyítakwas of the first two weeks in December have to find and pay for

The Soldier Captain in 1963.

'Soldiers' dancing in front of the parish church (October 4th, 1963).

a group of Pastorela dancers; those of the second fortnight in December supply a rival group of dancers.

The villages so far mentioned are divided into two or four territorial barrios. But there are also villages with three barrios, for instance Patamban, Zicuicho and Pamatácuaro. Pamatácuaro has three territorial barrios, San Juan, San Diego and Espíritu Santo, where the ceremonial centre is situated. At one time Zicuicho and Atapan were dependent on Pamatácuaro. The executive village-chief bears the title of Alkandi and ranks highest in the cargo-hierarchy. He has three Consejeros (Counsellors), one for each barrio. The village has a group of young girls in the service of the Virgin Mary; they, like the girls of Cherán, are called Wananches. Cargos are undertaken after marriage. In the first year of their marriage young men have to invite the Alkandi and his Consejeros for a meal. Furthermore they have ritual obligations on Palm Sunday. The cargos of San Juan and San Diego are annual ones. After these a man can accept the cargo of Corpus Christi (also annual), after which he is eligible for the office of Alkandi. Above the Alkandi is a body of old Principales.[8]

The village of Pitchátaro has the following offices: at village-level there are the Colector and Prioste, whose duties are similar to those in Cherán, a Kweni as the carguero of the Holy Virgin, a Haindé, a Fiskal, and a Petahpe. As in Ihuatzio, several commissioners are called Therúnchitiecha. Wanánchatiecha, the maids of the Virgin Mary, are also found here. The village used to be divided into barrios or wapátsikwecha, each under the direction of an old Principal, called Ehpu. Every wapátsikwa had, like the wapánekwecha in Ihuatzio, an Ureti or Semanero.[9]

Finally the above-mentioned aspects will be considered as far as it is possible, for three mestizo villages in the Tarascan area which used to be pure Indian communities, but where the Tarascan language and some other indigenous cultural characteristics have been reduced to minority positions. A clear and correct survey of the remnants of the traditional system of Chilchota (or Chilchotla) has been given by Pedro Carrasco.[10] Probably this village was originally inhabited by Nahuatl-speaking people.[11] Its ceremonial organisation is closely connected with the two oldest and largest territorial barrios: San Juan and San Pedro. There are two more barrios: Urén and Chapala, but these are later additions, and are evidently unconnected with the traditional organisation. The lowest rank in the cargo-hierarchy is that of Mayordomo del Hospital, the commissioner being charged with the care of a community hall which can be compared with the former Gwatapera in Ihuatzio. The tenure of office is one year and the office is barrio-linked; one year the commissioner comes from San Juan, the next from San Pedro. The following rank is that of Mayordomo de Santiago, the keeper of the patron saint of the village. This commissioner is also alternately supplied by San Juan and San Pedro. Men who have completed both Mayordomías or cargos are, with the old Principales, admitted into the Cabildo. The next office in the cargo-hierarchy for the men of San Juan is that of Karachakape, Carguero de San Roque and for the men of San Pedro that of Carguero de San Nicolás. After completing these cargos the commissioners can hold the office of Vaquero. Each Vaquero is required to have two female relatives serving as Wánanchatis or Roseras. Of these four Wánanchatis one bears the title of Pendompari and another that of Capitamoro. These two are always from different barrios, the offices changing annually between San Juan and San Pedro.

The highest office in the cargo system here is that of Regidor; there are two, one from each barrio. After the completion of this cargo the commissioner is a Tarépiti or Principal. In addition to the real commissioners there are, as in Ihuatzio, some lower functionaries, of whom the most important is the Chichiwa (probably an Aztec title), who plays a part in the worship of the Santo Niño before and at Christmas. The Fiscal manages the livestock of the Virgen del Hospital and is also a sacristan. The Topil (an Aztec title) rings the church-bells and assits the Mayordomo del Hospital. Each Regidor has two messengers: the Petahpe or Mayor, and the Katapi. The latter also has to drive away dogs during festivities, in which office he is called Wichariri. A man aspiring to a ceremonial office can apply to either Regidor, adding to his request a gift consisting of bread, chocolate and an alcoholic drink. The Regidor consults the Cabildo about the application, but he cannot accept the presents before the applicant has actually been appointed. The Regidores also have some judicial functions with regard to the Tarascan population of La Cañada, the area around Chilchotla.

On December 12th the new commissioners are installed in their offices at a ceremony in the Hospital when the wife of the Mayordomo of the building places crowns on their heads. The meeting of the Cabildo at Candlemas (Candelaria), February 2nd, is the most important fixed meeting of the year. Then the Principales and all the ex-Mayordomos of Santiago assemble in the morning in the enclosed chapel court of the Hospital. There they find the two Regidores, seated at either end of a long table covered with tule mats. On arriving, members of the Cabildo kiss a roofed cross before the chapel, then they cross themselves before the Regidores and kiss their staffs. The men sit down on either side of the table. Their wives are gathered as a separate group arranged in the same order of precedence, but they squat on tule mats around a row of similar mats; they do not sit on chairs like the men. The Wánanchatis give everyone present two pieces of sugarcane, and a bottle of strong liquor to each Regidor. Then the Regidores deliver ceremonial speeches, called wandakwa (so on this occasion they act as Wandárich'). Then the people eat and drink, while the Regidores receive blessed wax. They continue drinking until about 5 p.m., after which they go to the home of the new Mayordomo de Santiago, where the drinking goes on for some hours more.

On February 4th the Wánanchatis summon the boys and girls of the village to gather firewood for the Hospital. The boys and girls go into the mountains under their direction and collect enough wood to supply the needs of the Hospital for a whole year.

On the day before Shrove Tuesday the image of San Nicolás is transferred from the house of the old to that of the new Carguero. The new commissioner assembles the young men on the Cerro Viejo (Old Mountain) to gather flowers of the Kanínxikwa-plant. He treats the boys to maize cakes with beans and pork. They also get some strong liquor for the journey. When they come back to the village music is played and fireworks are let off in their honour. The flowers are woven into three triumphal arches; one is set before the entrance to the house of the new commissioner, one before the door of the room where the image stands, and one in front of the image itself.

On Shrove Tuesday the Vaqueritas ('cowgirls') are relieved. They are virgins who are supervised by the Vaqueros; there are two from each barrio. On that day red vanes are put on the rooftops of the old and new Vaqueros. Every boy who can get one down receives a bottle of brandy. The boys carry bulls made of tule mates, and hold 'bullfights' in the streets. Each barrio has two 'bulls' and a band to accompany them. The boys give the girls sugarcanes and the girls give them chapatas (a tamal made of Wawtli, or amaranth) in return. As in Cherán, boys and girls have sham fights with eggshells filled with confetti. These fights used to be wilder than they are today.

On Ash Wednesday the commissioners used to gather in the houses of the Vaquero and the Karachakape, in whose gardens lay heaps of oranges, lemons, ashes and earth. The men and women rolled the fruit about in the ashes and earth and then threw them at each other. When the skirmishes became too heated, one of the women beat a stick on a wooden board, calling 'peace': then the fight ended.

Here, too, the Wánanchatis or Roseras are the maids of the Holy Virgin and the keepers of Her image. They supply the chair and the flowers for the image when it is carried in procession. The Pendompari carries the standard of the Virgin, and the Capitamoro carries a wooden structure richly decorated with flowers. They walk in front of the image. Before them, at the head of the procession, goes the Fiscal accompanied by a thurifer.

On Palm Sunday there is a procession to the wells with an image of Jesus Christ sitting on a donkey which bears the name of San Ramos. The young men who a fortnight before went out to cut palm leaves also go to the wells.

In April the young men are summoned by the Regidor to clean the well. The boys make music and girls bring them food.

After their return from the Ascension Day festivities in Huáncito the honey-gatherers announce the approach of Corpus Christi with music and a traditional cry (the pitákuri). Two days before the feast bread is baked in all households. On the eve of Corpus Christi each barrio hires a band. In the morning of the feast the girls bathe in the well; in the afternoon girls and boys come together and exchange fruit and knick-knacks. The next day members of several occupational groups throw all kinds of things at the onlookers. The butchers kill a goat and throw blood at the people. One of the butchers, disguised as a coyote, steals a piece of meat, and the others chase him across the village square. The honey-gatherers give away honeycombs or sell them, led by their head, the Kuríndure.

On the feastday of the patron saint of the village, Santiago, the Moros and Soldados perform dances. The Moros always come from the barrio of the Mayordomo (or commissioner) of Santiago, the Soldados from the other. On the previous night they give a performance in the house of the Regidor. In the evening of the feastday the Wánanchatis serve a meal (the tsíndakwa ceremony).

During the festival of Guadalupe (December 12th) there is a reconciliation ceremony between boys and girls, after which they call each other brother and sister in pairs.

The traditional celebrations of Christmas Day and Twelfth Night are particularly the responsibility of the Chichiwa. On Christmas Day he is assisted by the Wánanchatis.

Tzintzuntzan, the most important historic capital among the three Tarascan administrative centres, is today a village smaller than Ihuatzio. Culturally about 85 per cent. of the population are mestizos, 15 per cent. Tarascans. Foster published a detailed and as clear a survey as possible of the traditional social and religious ceremonial organisation of the village.[12]

Its cargo-system used to be well developed and was of great social significance, but during the past twenty-five years it has gradually lost some of its characteristics and functions. Tzintzuntzan has or had eleven major cargos with a great many commissioners:

I   The Cargueros of La Soledad (Commissioners of (the Virgin of) Solitude). It was the most important cargo until 1942, when the priest reduced its importance. Before 1942 there were four commissioners:
1   the Mayordomo de la Soledad,
2   the Diputado (Deputy),
3   the Escribano ('Scribe'),
4   the Fiscal.

II The Cargueros of La Judea. This became the most important commission since that of La Soledad lost its former significance in 1942. It has five commissioners:
1   the Cinturión,
2   the Mayordomo,
3   the Capitán (Captain),
4   the Alférez (Ensign) and
5   the Sargento (Second in Command).

They are sometimes popularly referred to as 'Cargueros de Habas' (Broad bean commissioners).

III   The Cargueros of San Francisco.
In spite of the fact that, as in Ihuatzio, St. Francis is the patron saint of the village, this cargo does not rank highest in the hierarchy. It is borne by eight commissioners. The chief commissioner is called Mayordomo; the others have no special title.

IV   The Cargueros of San Isidro.
There are six commissioners, the chief commissioner having the title of Mayordomo. The others are referred to as Acompañantes (Escorts). All six must be Tarascans from the neighbouring village of Ichupio.

V   The Cargueros of the chapel of Guadalupe.
This chapel is in Ojo de Agua, a village bordering on Tzintzuntzan.
Originally there were three commissioners:
1   the Carguero of San Bartolo,
2   the Carguero of La Magdalena and
3   the Carguero of San Pablo.
San Bartolo, La Magdalena and San Pablo were three barrios of Tzintzuntzan which apparently had a special status (see a later section). In the nineteen-forties this arrangement was abolished and replaced by one of twelve commissioners, three from Ojo de Agua, the others from Tzintzuntzan. These twelve cargueros have smaller financial obligations than their three predecessors.

VI   The Cargueros of San Miguel.
They used to come from the barrio of that name. Today the commissioners are boys between 10 and 15 years old, who have limited obligations.

VII   The Cargueros of the Kenguería.[13]
These commissioners disappeared at the time of the Great Revolution (1910-1920).

The Kenguería had the following functionaries:
1 the Mayordomo of the Kenguería,
2 the Prioste,
3 the Escribano.

Foster's informants did not quite remember whether it was the Mayordomo or the Prioste who had to reside in the community hall. These commissioners were appointed by other commissioners, the Mandones (see a later section), on San Andrés's Day (November 30th). Some female functionaries were also appointed on that day. The Cargadoras, whose duty it was to carry the image, were married women; the Sahumador(a) (female thurifer) and the Campanita (female bell ringer) were young girls. The great festival of the commissioners of the Kenguería took place on December 8th, the day of La Purísima Concepción de María Santísima (The Immaculate Conception of the Most Holy Mary), the patron saint of America in colonial times, and up to this century the favourite saint of Spanish settlers and rulers, but since superseded by the Indian María de Guadalupe. Large quantities of food and drink were consumed in the Kenguería during the festivities, while as many as five bands gave rival performances. At Candlemas (February 2nd) the wife of the Prioste painted the faces and fingernails of drunken officials a bright red. When the victims noticed what had happened they fled home shamefaced.

VIII   The Barrio Captains (Capitanes de los barrios).
According to a document preserved in the Archivo de las Indias in Sevilla Tzintzuntzan had in 1593 fifteen barrios, which were then already centred in and around the present location of the village, although the pre-Spanish barrios may have been more widely dispersed.[14] The decrease in the population also reduced the number of barrios. Until about 1915 seven barrios still played a part in the religious ceremonial system. They were: San Bartolo, San Pablo, La Magdalena, San Pedro, San Juan, Santa Ana and San Miguel, of which the first three occupied special social positions. The administrative head of a barrio was the Cabeza (Chief), who was appointed for life and was often succeeded by one of his sons. In his house he kept an image of Jesus Christ and that of the barrio saint. Next to the barrio-chief there was a Capitán (Captain), who served for one year and was considered to be a commissioner. All the Captains of the village as well as the commissioners of the Kenguería

met at 3 a.m. every Saturday to say a prayer which was called the Kénikwa. The Prioste summoned them for this prayer and they all went to the Kenguería with a wooden box full of flowers. After this service, at sunrise, they carried the images of San Francisco, San Nicolás, La Virgen del Rosario and La Virgen de la Purísima around the temple court.

IX   The Cargueros Mandones (the Ruling Commissioners).
There were six of them. Two came from each of the three barrios: San Bartolo, San Pablo and La Magdalena. Two of them distributed pozole[15] on the Saturday before Carnival, two others on Easter Eve, and the other two on the day of the Invention of the Cross (May 3rd). On Shrove Tuesday they hung five or six dozen chickens on the beams in their houses and led a procession which started in San Bartolo and passed through all the barrios. They paid for all the food, drinks and fireworks of the Festival of St. Francis.

X   The Cargueros of Nuestra Señora del Rosario (Our Lady of the Rosary).
The three commissioners were:
1   the Mayordomo of Our Lady of the Rosary,
2   the Capitán (Captain) and
3   the Fiscal.
They joined the Kénikwa on Saturday mornings and played a part in the festival of Corpus Christi.

XI   The Commissioners of the Cross (Cargueros de la Cruz).
There were also three of them:
1   the Capitán de la Cruz (Captain of the Cross),
2   the Alférez (Ensign),
3   the Sargento (Second in Command).
They helped the commissioners of Our Lady of the Rosary with the festival of Corpus Christi. The Captain provided pozole on the first day, the Ensign on the second and the Sargento on the third day of the festival. They also provided a band; and made fun of the people, pulling off hats and shawls and teasing women. These commissioners were appointed on December 12th.

A particular development of circumstances in the village has made the feast of Nuestro Señor del Rescate the most important social religious manifestation in Tzintzuntzan. It is of regional importance, many people from neighbouring villages and even from Pátzcuaro participating in it.[16]
Until the Great Revolution (1910-1920) Tzintzuntzan had also had an influential group of old Principales, but they lost their influence in the turbulent years after 1914. Some occupational groups still play their part in the festival of Corpus Christi, but on the whole their participation has already acquired an unofficial and incidental character.

The village of Quiroga or San Diego Cocupao has largely lost its indigenous Indian character and has retained only a few remnants of its former traditional system. Some important aspects of the traditional organisation are still noticeable during some religious festivities and ceremonies in the month of May. During the first three days of the month the new Cargueros of the patron Saint, San Diego, are appointed. There are two groups of three commissioners, one from Upper Quiroga (El Calvario), the other from the lower part of the village. Each group consists of a Capitán, an Alférez and a Sargento. They organise the festival of San Diego, which is held on November 13th and during which Moros and Christianos perform dances.
Certain occupational groups are involved in the festivities held in the second half of May.
On September 29th the feast of San Miguel is still celebrated mainly by the inhabitants of the former barrio of that name, which has long disappeared as a social unit.[17]

Readers who have lost their bearings because of the abundance of titles and offices, especially because the same titles often refer to different offices in the villages compared, are referred to the chart given in appendix 1.
The comparison between the Tarascan villages of which data have been given on the preceding pages reveals a number of corresponding social and cultural aspects, which are partly responsible for the specific identity of these communities within the larger, national Mexican environment. The picture which is thus obtained of the more general Tarascan identity may be incomplete, yet it shows a fairly clear and varied outline of the situation.

The Tarascan communities described above, including Ihuatzio, show in a majority of cases ten important points of similarity:

1 In most villages there is, and in all of them there used to be, a connection between old age and social prestige. This is brought out most clearly in the position of the Principales, the old men of distinction, greatly respected in nearly all villages, men who can as a rule exercise a decisive influence on the course of affairs. Nearly all of them have been commissioners, so that it is often difficult to distinguish their old age as a separate factor determining their high social status. But in the villages described above the connection is quite obvious. In Ihuatzio: the Orénaïikwecha; in Cherán: the Aches; in Angahuan: the Tarénpenyas; in Chilchotla: the Tarépitich; in Purenchécuaro: the Principales, just as they formerly existed in Tzintzuntzan and Yunuén, and today, though less strongly, in La Pacanda.

2 In all these villages there is a connection between social status and the fulfilment of commissions. Villages differ as to size, social significance and the structure of the cargo-system, but they all reveal this connection. In most indigenous villages like Ihuatzio and Cherán a man must have completed a number of commissions before he is considered to have reached a social position which will qualify him for executive traditional functions. Usually the traditional offices are themselves counted as commissions. Chieftainship is a commission just as the direction and organisation of the worship of a 'saint'. The fulfilment of an administrative function is equivalent to the fulfilment of a task for the benefit of the community. The village chief, the official whose position is often far above that of his subjects, who is treated with great respect by the ordinary man or woman, nevertheless remains himself a servant of the community and has to obey the highest administrative body in the community, the council of old Principales, called the Cabildo in some villages.

3 Nearly all the villages had some forms of dual organisation, which may be antagonistic or complementary. Dual forms consisting of competitive units were found in:

Ihuatzio: the two territorial barrios;
the Moros against the Soldados;
the four 'central' against the five 'outlying' wapánekwecha;
the seven original as against the two 'alien' wapánekwecha;
the relations between Ihuatzio and Cucuchucho.

Purenchécuaro: the two Sectores;
the ceremonial barrios of San Jerónimo and San Pedro;
the barrios of San Jerónimo and San Pedro as against the seven others.

Yunuén: the two barrios;
the relations between this island and La Pacanda.

Pacándani: the two barrios.

Cherán: the Upper barrios as against the Lower barrios during the festival of San Anselmo;
the 'tax-collectors' against the 'robbers' during the same festival;
boys against girls during Carnival;
the old Kengui with his helpers against the new one and his helpers during the transfer of the office.

Angahuan: the running-match between boys and girls carrying the images of San José and María Magdalena;
the Anyítakwas of the first and second halves of December.

Chilchotla: the barrios of San Juan and San Pedro;
the sham fights between boys and girls on Shrove Tuesday;
ritual fights between men and women on Ash Wednesday;
the Moros as against the Soldados.

Tzintzuntzan: until about fifty years ago: three ceremonial barrios as against four others with a lower status.

Quiroga: the Upper village as against the Lower village;
Moros as against Cristianos.

Complementary forms of dual organisation were observed in:

Ihuatzio: the administrative system or the organisation of chieftainship, with its internal and external aspects (e.g. the distinctive Urétspeti – Ureti relations within the wapánekwecha); the continuation of the territorial bipartition of the village within the occupational groups;

the distinctive man-woman relations noticeable in several social and ceremonial fields.

Purenchécuaro: dual chiefship within the eight village wards (the distinctive Teruhtsikuri-Oreti relations); Priostes, Colectores, Caporales and Vaqueros distinguished according to Sectores.

Cherán: the Upper and the Lower village;

bipartition in the group of honey-gatherers; commissioners of the Cabildo and other commissioners; boys and girls separately charged with the preparations for Palm Sunday.

Chilchotla: the two original barrios (dual in some respects);

Vaqueros and Wánanchatis;

the two Regidores;

men and women (on several occasions);

boys and girls in the service of the Hospital;

boys and girls during Carnival;

boys and girls during communal labour in April;

boys and girls during the festival of Guadalupe.

Tzintzuntzan: the barrio-administration (Cabeza and Capitán);

the commissioners of Guadalupe, distributed over Tzintzuntzan and Ojo de Agua;

the male commissioners of the Kenguería and the female commissioners of the Holy Virgin.

4   A noteworthy resemblance between Ihuatzio and some other villages is the periodical exchange of an office or function between two or more parts of the village. In Ihuatzio this is done for the Soldier-Captain and the Moorish Captain with regard to the two territorial barrios, and for the Semaneros with regard to the wapánekwecha.

In Purenchécuaro the only unambiguous example is that of the Orecha in connection with the eight village manzanas. There may be more instances in the village, however.

In Yunuén the two barrios in turn supply the Jefe and his Deputy.

In Angahuan blocks of seven or eight households in turn supply the Anyíta-kwas for the Yurixo. Semaneros, who are here connected with the ceremonial wards, which in this village are called by the old Tarascan name of wapátsikwa, were also found in Pichátaro.

In Chilchotla the Mayordomo del Hospital comes from the barrio of San Juan in one year, and from San Pedro the next year. This is also the case with the commissioner of the patron saint Santiago, and the female functionaries: the Pendompari and the Capitamoro. The Moros and Soldados follow the same custom, since their functions are connected with that of the Mayordomo of Santiago.

In Tzintzuntzan the barrio-linked Cargueros Mandones served by turns on the three special Saturdays. The Capitán de la Cruz, his Alférez and his Sargento took turns during the three days' festival of Corpus Christi.

5   From the Relación de Michoacán it appears that the principle of tripartition played an important part in contemporary Tarascan society. It appears to be occasionally applied even today. In Ihuatzio the nine wapánekwecha are divided into 3 groups (4 + 3 + 2). Probably the wapánekwecha of Tsʌtsʌ'ki, Úskuti and Sánduri were formerly occupational groups; so it is possible that there used to be a tripartite occupational organisation, as exists in La Pacanda today. There are three traditional village chiefs: the Acha Representante, the Alkande and the Prioste. Then there are the three different images of San Francisco of the Soldier-Captain.

Cherán also has three traditional village chiefs: the Colector, the Prioste and the Keng(u)i. Three Principales 'own' the cargo of Twelfth Night (Three Kings), although this tripartition is probably based on the three saints, not, or not directly, on a traditional form of organisation.

As already mentioned, there are some villages with three territorial barrios.

Finally Tzintzuntzan had tripartite divisions connected with three ceremonial barrios with special functions. Furthermore it has tripartite divisions within some of the Mayordomías (Guadalupe, Kenguería, Nuestra Señora del Rosario and La Cruz). The concept of a tripartite universe was noted in Yunuén, La Pacanda, Purenchécuaro and Tzintzuntzan as well as in Ihuatzio. As in pre-Spanish times it consisted of:

a   Awándaro, the sphere of the cosmic Gods;

b   Echerendo, the worldly sphere or human sphere;
c   Chumiechúkwaro, the underworld, the sphere of the dead.

6   Several forms of multi-partition may be interesting for more accurate and thorough comparisons for which more exact data are indispensable. In this connection only a few examples can be given here.

Forms of organisation with fourfold divisions are not important (any longer?) in Ihuatzio. Mention can only be made of the four so-called 'central' wapánekwecha. In Purenchécuaro and Cherán, however, the territorial division into four parts is very important.

It is noteworthy that the ninefold division found in the wapánekwa organisation of Ihuatzio has its equivalent only in Purenchécuaro. Forms of organisation based on multi-partition and the differences between them in different villages can usually be interpreted only as remnants of pre-Spanish or colonial regional or national organisations. This offers a considerable field of investigation to ethno-historians, for no research of any importance has ever been carried out with regard to the structures of these wider organisations in the ancient Tarascan empire.

7   In several villages the territorial principle appeared to be a major factor in many social organisations. In Ihuatzio, Purenchécuaro, Yunuén, La Pacanda, Cherán, Chilchotla, Pamatácuaro, Pichátaro, Tzintzuntzan and Quiroga some forms of organisation are or were based on territorial ties. The internal influence of this principle was particularly strong in Chilchotla, while it remained an important factor in Ihuatzio, Purenchécuaro and Cherán.

This clear relationship between population groups or institutions on the one hand and parts of the territory belonging to the community on the other is unknown to the national mestizo society. Examples of this relationship are found in most barrios, the wapánekwecha and several Capitanías, such as those of San Francisco in Ihuatzio, of San Jerónimo in Purenchécuaro and of the Karachakape and San Nicolás in Chilchotla.

8   A community hall with a staff of commissioners of various ranks plays an important part in the social life of most of the larger villages. An excellent example is found in Ihuatzio, which has a Priostería with the Prioste and his

wife as permanent residents and the Urecha, Kenich' and Wakérox as temporary assistants. The former Gwatapera was a similar institution, where the Urecha, and their wives used to work. Cherán and Chilchotla still have so-called 'Hospitales', which were founded in many villages in the sixteenth century, first in Santa Fé, as hispanicised continuations of the old Gwataperas. In Cherán the Hospital is the permanent residence of the Keng(u)i, in Chilchotla that of the Mayordomo. In Angahuan people call their community hall Yurixo. The short description of it in Beals's study suggests that its tenant keeper is the Kieng(u)i, just as his equivalent in Cherán. At one time Tzintzuntzan had a Kenguería with a large staff. Comparable officials in several villages are, in addition to their ceremonial duties, charged with the care of one or more kinds of communal labour. It is noteworthy that informants in Purenchécuaro maintained that they did not remember any community hall with its own commissioner ever having existed in their village.

9   Another fairly general similarity has just been mentioned: collective labour on behalf of the community. In the description of Ihuatzio given before the collective execution of public works by the wapánekwecha and the communal services of the Urecha and their relatives have already been mentioned.

Yunuén and La Pacanda have an extensive system of communal services, carried out very intensively today due to fairly recent developments in the village which have received strong encouragement from Crefal.

In Purenchécuaro the barrios have compulsory services and a system of Semaneros equivalent to that of Ihuatzio. In Cherán people are obliged to contribute financially to the festival of San Francisco; further there are compulsory services of boys and girls for Palm Sunday; the maintenance of the waterworks, and keeping the cemetery clean and tidy.

In Angahuan there is the collective cleaning of the well under the direction of the Petahpe, and the regular services of the Anyítakwas.

In Chilchotla we also noted the collective duty of cleaning the well under the direction of a Regidor.

10   The final point of agreement between the villages is a very important one: the latent danger of a serious conflict between the traditional chiefs and principals and the Roman Catholic priests. It is true that only in Ihuatzio and

Cherán were overt sharp differences between principals and priests noted, but it is evident that they also occurred in Tzintzuntzan,[18] and in all places where a Roman Catholic priest is found in a traditional Indian community a conflict may reasonably be expected. The priest represents, or should at any rate represent, an organisation and a creed with aims and norms in many ways considerably different from those of the traditional Tarascan communities. The traditions tend to restrict the official powers of the priest and to supervise his activities, and not all priests are prepared to acquiesce. Several priests, however, appear to attach enough importance to good human relations and are prepared to delay the conscientious application of the social and cultural implications of their faith. Such priests will as a rule be able to avoid serious conflicts in their parishes.

It is now possible to return to the question of Ihuatzio's exceptional position in the area of Tarascan culture. The widespread popular opinion held by the mestizos of Pátzcuaro and Tzintzuntzan that Ihuatzio has an extremely con-servative population and that it is the most purely indigenous village in the whole region, is only partly confirmed by our investigations and comparative studies. The collected data reveal only two or three important respects in which community life in Ihuatzio is distinguished from the general traditional Tarascan pattern.

1   The extraordinarily great emphasis laid on the acquisition of prestige through the acceptance of commissions. In Cherán and other villages com-missions are usually accepted in consequence of vows taken; there are often sufficient candidates for commissions and Beals's study does not suggest that they are urged by motives of social success. In Ihuatzio vows play a minor part in the acceptance of commissions. Seldom if ever is it the main motive.

2   The semi-territorial principle of the wapánekwecha is a phenomenon peculiar to Ihuatzio today. Several informants ascribed this to fairly recent developments; according to them the wapánekwecha used to be closed territorial units.
If this view is correct, the former situation must have closely resembled that of the nine ceremonial barrios of Purenchécuaro. It is quite possible, however,

The Moorish Captain in 1963.

The 'Moors' of 1958 (from a photograph in the possession of Crefal).

that our informants based their interpretation of the situation in Ihuatzio today on their knowledge of conditions in Purenchécuaro and other villages.

3   Noteworthy in Ihuatzio is the almost universal occurrence of a clear distinction between internal and external chieftainships. This functional division is an ancient indigenous form of organisation in the Mexican cultural area. In spite of the absence in the studies of most other villages of unambiguous indications of the existence of a dual organisation of chieftainship in the Tarascan area, the question of whether it is peculiar to Ihuatzio remains unanswered. (Foster's data on Tzintzuntzan (see pp. 213-217) may perhaps be taken as an indication of the existence until recently of a dual barrio-chiefship). Other studies of Tarascan communities have on the whole shown little interest in ethno-historical matters and have consequently paid little attention to this aspect.

There are a few other less important, yet noteworthy conditions peculiar to Ihuatzio. Nowhere else do the officials who are here called 'Representative of the Indigenous Community' and 'Prioste' hold such high positions as in this village. Most of the villages compared in this study have a Representante de la Comunidad Indígena, but in none of them, apart from Ihuatzio, does he play a very important part in the traditional system. This development in Ihuatzio may be due to the people's extraordinary interest in matters concerning their communal lands, which also caused their original supreme external village chief to accept this office of Representative of the Indigenous Community when it was introduced in the nineteenth century.

In other Tarascan villages the Prioste is an official of secondary or lesser importance, but in Ihuatzio today he is held in high respect. Before the decline of the Gwatapera he may have had a less prominent position. After the decline of the Gwatapera the Urecha were removed to the Priostería, which may have enhanced the influence of the Prioste.

The investigations conducted in Ihuatzio, and the comparative studies, have shown that the distinctive aspects of the Tarascan identity are such important factors in the social and cultural life of several Tarascan communities that they have preserved a great deal of that identity.[19] Many Tarascans are inclined to base on it their claim to a distinctive position within the national Mexican society. Therefore these Tarascans will always resist any policy which in their opinion aims at eliminating their identity.

Notes to Chapter VII

[1] Gilberti, 1559, p. 115; teruhtsikuri = "perlado o superior de casa" (prelate or master of the house).

[2] cf. Gilberti, 1559, p. 13: anátakwareni = "tener obra, ser oficial" (to be in charge of some work, to be an official).

[3] cf. Ihuatzio; chapter III.

[4] Beals, 1946; pp. 131-156.

[5] Idem, pp. 108, 109.

[6] Beals also mentions shopkeepers among the main occupational groups with greater commitments; so evidently there is some confusion here. See Beals, 1946, p. 126.

[7] Beals, 1946, pp. 143, 144.

[8] The data on Pamatácuaro were supplied by Mr. Onofre Álvarez, a teacher of Tarascan descent from Atapan, Los Reyes, Mich.

[9] León, 1904.

[10] See Carrasco's contribution in Beals, 1946, Appendix 2, pp. 215-219.

[11] Aguirre Beltrán, 1952; p. 51.

[12] Foster, 1948; pp. 188-224.

[13] The word Kenguería suggests the existence of a Kengui, since the word means 'Building or place of the Kengui'.

[14] See the document: Mex. Just. 94, 1593 hoja 2: "La Ciudad de Cintzuntzan está repartida en 15 barrios. Pónense los nombres, por si fueren necessario nombrarlos en la Provisión. Todos tienen capillas de sus vacaciones y están dentro de la traza y sitio de la ciudad (the town of Tzintzuntzan is divided into 15 wards. Their names are given here, in case it should be necessary to mention them in the 'Provision'. All have chapels under their own control, and they all are found within the boundaries of the town proper.):

1 La Sanctíssima Trinidad,	9 Sanct Matheo,
2 La Sancta María Magdalena,	10 Sanct Lorenzo,
3 Sanct Miguel,	11 La Sanctíssima Trinidad Hatacurin,
4 Sancta Anna,	12 Los Reyes,
5 Sanct Antonio,	13 Sanct Pedro,
6 Sanct Joan Baptista,	14 Sanct Sebastián,
7 Sanct Pablo,	15 Sanct Bartholomé Yahuaro".
8 Sanctiago,	

[15] A corruption of Aztec posolli, a maize dish.

[16] A description of the way in which this festival is organised is contained in Foster, 1948, pp. 204-208.

[17] Brand, 1951; pp. 204-206.

[18] See Foster, 1948; p. 193.

[19] The picture of the Tarascan identity which is given in this chapter and which is based on our study of Ihuatzio and comparable data on other communities of Purépecha is noticeably different from Beals's conclusions drawn from his study of Cherán. In the conclusive chapter (only three and a half pages) of his study, bearing the title "Conclusions and further problems", Beals makes the following statement:

"Perhaps the most striking fact about Cherán is the essentially European origin of most of the culture and the relatively small number of traits of native provenience". (1946, p. 210). There are various reasons for the author to challenge this statement. The first objection concerns the formulation of the statement, since it seems to be based on the opinion, fairly often held by researchers into acculturation processes, that a culture is composed of autochthonous and additional alien elements. In the author's opinion the Tarascan culture and for that matter any culture should not be seen simply as the sum of elements of various origins. Such an approach may easily neglect the independent development and the creation of new elements, which make as many valuable contributions to the cultural identity as do the indigenous ones. Beals himself also refers to the existence of independent developments a few paragraphs further on in his conclusive chapter. The author's objection concerns by no means the whole of Beals's study, but only the formulation of the above quotation, and the contents of his conclusion. Beals holds that much of the Tarascan culture today is European in origin, and considers the European traits to constitute a more important part of the culture than the indigenous. This appears form the following statement added to the above-quoted one:

"Most of the material culture of Cherán is probably European. . . . . The economic specialization and trade patterns may be based upon aboriginal conditions, yet they are known to have been formalized by Europeans. Political and ceremonial organization are also European, although in part their origins represent Bishop Vasco de Quiroga's interpretation of Thomas More's 'Utopia'. The extensive compadre system is but an enlargement upon European ideas . . . Concepts of the supernatural, both in formal religion and in witchcraft, are certainly almost wholly European". (1946, pp. 210, 211).

Quite apart from the question of whether the objectives which Beals had in view and on which the above quotations are founded, serve a useful purpose, his conclusions should be judged for their validity; most of his statements are difficult to reconcile with the results of the author's own study. The material culture does not yield many points for discussion. Social and ceremonial organisation as well as religion, however, give ample occasion for comment. In this chapter the writer has given a fairly detailed account of his opinion that these aspects of the Tarascan culture are strongly indigenous. The question may be asked if Ihuatzio is very different from Cherán in these respects. This is not likely. Beals himself considers the Lake Tarascans to be more acculturated than the inhabitants of Cherán (1946, p. 210). His conclusions not only conflict with the data obtained in Ihuatzio, but also in the author's opinion with his own data on Cherán. The great importance of the barrio in Cherán as a matrix for the organisation of collective labour, the ceremonies and some activities of the occupational groups reveals significant indigenous influence. The whole complex of elements and ideas commonly referred to as witchcraft also contains so many indigenous traits that Beals's remark about them is hardly relevant. It is by no means the writer's intention to discuss the question of whether this or that village reveals a few more Tarascan and fewer European influences, or vice versa. As a matter of fact this is not very important. The essential problem is concerned with the extent and strength of the cultural identity. Beals's above-quoted conclusions seem to leave little room for the Tarascan cultural identity, yet no sooner has he made his conclusions than he recognises the existence of this identity, which he attributes to an "extensive reworking of its European materials" due to the "patterning influence of native ideas" (1946, p. 211). In this connection he refers to the strength of this identity, which according to him is due to the general and fierce attachment to traditions or customs (costumbres). Here Beals is in close agreement with the results of the present study. His conclusion, however, was made afterwards in the light of phenomena which he could not or not fully account for at the time he wrote his study. His lack of knowledge of or his lack of interest in the historic background will no doubt be partly responsible for it. Furthermore he himself remarks that he had collected insufficient data on the role of Tarascan women in community life, and that his study was one of the "masculine culture of Cherán" (1946, p. 212).

Thus rather much of the "patterning influence of native ideas" may have escaped his attention. The same thing happened to the author during his study of Ihuatzio, and further investigations of this aspect would be desirable. The compadre system in Ihuatzio, for instance, also seemed to follow old principles of patterning. (There appeared to be a tendency to seek ceremonial relatives within the wapánekwecha of the nearest female relatives (mother, wife).

It is interesting to note that Beals, after ascertaining the predominance of European elements or traits in Tarascan culture, calls this "the most striking fact about Cherán", which proves that he considers his own conclusion a surprising one.

After considering the results of the research in Ihuatzio and comparing them with data on other Tarascan villages, the author has reached a conclusion which is almost the opposite of Beals's:

The most striking fact about community life in Ihuatzio today is the persistence of fundamentally indigenous forms of organisation and planning, and a world view which is strongly determined by indigenous ideas and concepts. These forms and concepts are elements of a strong cultural identity, which is the outcome of its largely independent course of development, in spite of the fact that this Tarascan community has been obliged to accomplish great adjustments (or, if a technical phrase is preferred, in spite of its high degree of acculturation).

VIII   *autochthonous elements*
in the modern Tarascan identity

The ethno-historic part of this study has two aspects. On the one hand the historic approach was used in the second chapter in order to gain a better insight into the present social structure and organisation, and on the other hand a better interpretation of the old chronicles has become possible through data obtained in the field and by means of comparative studies.

As has already been said, the only major source of Tarascan history, the Relación de Michoacán, is far from complete. The document contains much information on the general aspects of the pre-Spanish Tarascan state and society, but the old functionaries from Tzintzuntzan supplied little more than a formalistic abstraction of their system of government. The Relación contains hardly any information on the lower level of villages and village wards. The fact that no direct connection can be clearly seen between on the one hand the state and society as described in the Relación and on the other the village-community of modern Ihuatzio does not establish that no such connection exists between the modern village-community and its pre-Spanish past.

A comparison between Ihuatzio today and a Nahuatlacan community, such as San Bernardino Contla in Tlascala, will reveal some differences but also some striking resemblances.[1] The calpultin (singular: calpulli) of Contla resemble the wapánekwecha of Ihuatzio. Even their numbers are the same. The numbers of lineages in the semi-territorial calpultin, however, are smaller. A note-worthy resemblance is the fact that in neither community are persons with the same family-name but belonging to different social units considered to be blood-relations. Contla appeared also to show a strong tendency towards local endogamy. The calpultin of Contla differ from the wapánekwecha of Ihuatzio in two respects: they have a marriage-regulating function (they are exogamous), and they have different positions in the organisation of festivals.[2] It is well worth noting that as a rule the Aztec calpultin today have no marriage-regulating function and, except in a few cases, never had it in the past.[3]

This study is not intended to make a comparison of traditionalist Tarascan, Aztec and other Indian village-communities. Such a comparison might indeed reveal a number of resemblances in social organisation and culture, and might lead to the definition of a general Mexican Indian identity. Without going to such lengths, we might, however, compare some data obtained in Ihuatzio with data from Aztec sources on the pre-Spanish communities of the central highlands. After all they are two peoples with close historic connections. Some Aztec historic sources contain much more information than the Relación de Michoacán with regard to pre-Spanish population groups and institutions comparable with the groupings and organisations in present-day Ihuatzio. These sources reveal interesting points of resemblance with Ihuatzio. Some quotations from the Códice Ramírez are given as examples: "As we have seen, there were in the front court of this great temple (of Witsilopochtli) youths of 18 to 20 years old, who were called votaries of God. . . . . . . These young men, who served in the temple of Witsilopochtli, lived frugal and pure lives and served as acolytes, handing thuribles, firewood and garments to the priests and high functionaries of the temple; they swept the holy places, fetched firewood, that the fireplace of the God might always be burning in front of the altar of the image of the God. Besides these young men there were boys who were pupils of the monastery and as such rendered compulsory services, such as decorating the temples and framing them with garlands of flowers and green twigs, handing washing-water to the priests, keeping the sacrificial knives and accompanying the almsmen, whom they helped to carry the sacrifices. All these boys had tasks, which they were in charge of (tenían cargo de ellos) . . . . . . Their service and the conscientious execution of self-affliction lasted a full twelve months. . . . . The second house of retreat stood opposite the first and was a house of chosen 'sisters', girls of 12 or 13 years old, who were called the girls of self-affliction; there were as many girls as young men (fifty) . . . . their tasks only consisted in saying prayers, sweeping the temple and every morning preparing the food for the image of the God and his priests, which food was collected by the boys (in the town). . . . . The girls served and exercised self-affliction for one year, just as the boys . . . . These boys and girls came from six wards specially appointed for the purpose; they could not come from other wards".[4]

The informants of Fray Bernardino de Sahagún told about the boys in the telpochkalli (The Young Men's home): ". . . . they went in closed groups to the place of their work to make clay tiles or build walls, to work the fields, or dig canals; they did this work together, or were divided into smaller groups. And they went into the woods to gather torches and take them to the Kwika-kalli (the 'State theatre').[5]

When the parents handed over their sons to the priests of the Kalmekak (literally: 'in the outbuildings', the schools with stricter education, located in the neighbourhood of the temples and directed by the priests) they said: ". . . . that this son of ours may have the task of sweeping and cleaning the house of our God".[6]

These young Aztec commissioners of pre-Spanish times show a surprising resemblance to the Urétich' or Urecha in Ihuatzio today. Their tasks and the duration of the cargos are the same. There are also differences. According to the above-quoted texts the Aztec boys and girls were always unmarried when they fulfilled their first cargo, whereas the Urétich' in Ihuatzio today are preferably newly-married young men. What was the situation among the historic Tarascans? It is a well-known fact that daughters of aristocratic Tarascan families served in a Gwatapera for some time. The Spaniards at first tried to abolish these institutions; later Don Vasco de Quiroga reformed them into his so-called 'hospitales'. The Gwatapera as a girls' home ceased to exist and with this the traditional ties between young girls and the temple disappeared. May this have been the reason for the first cargo to be shifted from the single girls to the newly-married couples, in order to retain the services of the young women for the church? If this was indeed the case, the resemblance between the original Aztec and Tarascan first 'commissions' must have been almost complete. Another important difference between the situation described in the above-mentioned Aztec source and the present situation in Ihuatzio is the degree in which the young people are connected with the temple. The Aztec boys as well as the girls lived together near the temple during the whole year. The Urétich' today work by turns, serving for only one week (as so-called semaneros), and they live outside the ceremonial centre. In this respect the Tarascan novices today differ not only from the Aztecs, but from their own historic predecessors, who lived in the Gwatapera. The Aztecs, however, also knew the system of working by turns. The Códice Ramírez, in mentioning the temple of Teskatlepoka, says among other things: ". . . . . . this temple, like the other, also had rooms for the priests to retire, for the boys and girls and the pupils . . . to live in. These halls were supervised by one priest only, who never left it and served as a semanero. If any temple should as a rule have three or four priests or other functionaries, each of them would serve there for one week without leaving it".[7]

This document mentions other resemblances with Ihuatzio today. When a ceremony was held as part of the worship of Witsilopochtli the old men, the priest and his acolytes and all other dignitaries left the temple in the order of their ranks and seniority, for there was a strict application of the rules of precedence, in connection with their names and titles".[8]

The sacred maize dough of Witsilopochtli was then eaten according to the same order of precedence. This passage reminds us of the importance attached by the people of Ihuatzio to precedence during some of their ceremonies. However, this resemblance may have a purely functional basis and may not be taken as proof of a common historic background.

The writings of Fray Diego Durán, which describe community-life in Te-nochtitlan, Tlaltelolco and Tezcoco, also mention conditions very similar to those in Ihuatzio today. Durán gives a more detailed description of communal services in the ceremonial centre of Tenochtitlan than the Códice Ramírez. He mentions a 'monastery' (communal home) for young men of 18 to 20 years old, doing all kinds of work in and around the temple of Witsilopochtli.[9] Furthermore he describes another group of temple officials, the 'Elokwa-tekomane', evidently the same men as those mentioned in the Códice Ramírez, for there were fifty of them at most, from six barrios, and serving for one year.[10]

Pomar gives a similar picture of the first cargos in Tezcoco.[11] This is what he says about the Telpochkalli: "Most of the sons of the common people were educated in other homes in the town, which they called Telpochkalli, which means 'boys' home", where they were taught the same norms and creed as the boys in the homes of the priests of the temple (the Kalmekak), except for matters of ceremony. Most of these boys as well as their fathers were employed in farming, which, after the use of arms, was their main interest. Some of these boys grew up to be valuable members of the community, called upon to undertake administrative and other offices and duties (cargos)".[12]

The main features of the cargo-hierarchy in Ihuatzio, and the norm of modesty applied to the higher authorities and cargueros, were also found among the Aztec priests. Sahagún's informants said:

"(for their appointment and promotion) descent is irrelevant, the main qualifications being good conduct. The main qualifications for a candidate, which are strictly adhered to, are that he is of good conduct, acceptable to the community, that he has a fine nature, that he is kind and humble, a man who inspires peace and happiness, who is resolute, who is never in a hurry and always acts after serious consideration, who has a strong and steadfast character, who always gives of his best, who is good company, the comfort and stay of those who are in sorrow, a charitable man, who feels sympathy for his fellow-men and shares their grief, a god-fearing man, devoted to his Gods and respecting them, a man who weeps, and grieves and sighs.

And if such a man is at the beginning of his career, he is called 'little sacrificial priest', afterwards he becomes a 'sacrificial priest', then a 'burner of fire' and as such he is already a venerable man, From such men are chosen those who are called 'Feathered Serpent' " (the High Priest).[13]

The Códice Ramírez describes a ceremony which was part of the worship of Teskatlepoka, in which the girls of the temple go about the village in a procession accompanied by an old man.[14] This ceremony resembles that of December 16th in Ihuatzio, when the Irʌtsʌ goes about the village with the girls of the wapánekwa.

The Aztecs had several forms of organisation, consisting of competitive elements (often dual), and resembling such organisations in the Tarascan area today.[15] The division of chiefship into specialised internal and external responsibilities also existed in Aztec society.[16]

The Relación de Michoacán contains sufficient data to give us an idea of the general historic background of the Tarascans. It mentions some principles of hierarchic order and organisation which are also recognisable in modern Ihuatzio, but gives only incidental information on the lower administrative offices and commissions, which alone does not provide sufficient indication of the existence of any pre-Spanish predecessors of the groupings and institutions found in Ihuatzio today. The striking parallels found in the much more detailed Aztec sources, however, justify the conclusion that some important groupings and institutions in present-day Ihuatzio have their predecessors even before 1522. The question now is whether the Aztec and Tarascan societies in general showed such great resemblances, or whether Ihuatzio, as one of the Tarascan administrative centres, had especially undergone many Central Mexican influences. A more accurate and much more detailed comparison between Ihuatzio and Chilchotla might throw more light on the specific consequences of Nahuatlacan influences in the Tarascan area. In the preceding chapter a limited comparison had been made between these two villages on the one hand and other Tarascan communities on the other; no striking differences have been found which could be explained on the grounds of the presence or absence of strong Nahuatlacan influences. It would be possible in theory to assume that important Aztec influences in the Tarascan area only occurred after the Spanish Conquest, but since sources from colonial times do not contain any such suggestion, the assumption must be rejected.

From the data considered above the tentative conclusion may be made that some Michoacán historiographers and ethno-historians, like Ruiz, have strongly exaggerated the specifically Tarascan aspects of their indigenous culture, which must be due to regional chauvinism. It is evident that Central Mexican influences in the whole Tarascan area were considerable, and that there were but few great differences between the Aztec and Tarascan social systems.

A comparison of the existing patterns of organisation in the Tarascan area with the pre-Spanish data contained in the Relación de Michoacán gives rise to the following remarks:

The vague and incomplete description in the Relación of the office of Okámbecha seems to suggest that the office most resembles the modern office of Urétich' or Urecha, the supervisors of the communal duties of the wapánekwecha and similar groups, among whom are the Anyítakwecha of Angahuan. The pre-Spanish Okámbecha may have been comparable officials serving in sections of territorial barrios resembling the present-day wapánekwecha, just like the Aztec Sentekpanpixke' in the divisions of the calpultin. The question of what was the connection between territorial groupings and kinship groups, which could not be solved with the scarce and vague data found in the Relación, has remained difficult to answer even now. People in Ihuatzio consider the wapánekwecha above all as kinship groups, while to the researcher the principle of territoriality often appeared in practice to be more important than blood-relationship. The two principles of kinship and territoriality are closely connected in the minds of modern Tarascans, even in their world view, and it is reasonable to assume that this was also the case in historic times. Ties which are fundamentally based on common local residence may thus be looked upon as kinship relations and be treated as such. It is possible, however, that real blood-relationship accounted for the inter-territorial ties between the Wakúxecha, who lived scattered all over the empire.

We saw in the preceding chapter that the present Tarascan identity consists of a mixture of autochthonous and more recent elements resulting from autonomous developments. The chief autochthonous elements in modern Ihuatzio are:

1 the wapánekwecha and the institutions connected with them, such as that of collective labour;
2 the commissions;
3 chieftainship as a commission and differentiated according to its internal and external functions;
4 the high social status of old people;
5 the division of the population into two competitive territorial groups;
6 remnants of 'magic' social control;
7 marriage-regulation by the parents of young people of marriageable age, sometimes preceded by bride-capture;
8 remnants of the pre-Spanish conception of the universe and the religious system based on it (tripartition of the universe; dualism; male and female deities; Wandárich').

Some other aspects of the identity of modern Ihuatzio are dependent either less directly, or hardly at all, on autochthonous developments:

1 the social position of women, which is much higher than that of mestizo women in their society. This situation extends back to pre-Spanish times, although some important changes have taken place since (the disappearance of the Gwatapera; the abolition of polygyny; the weakening of the economic position of this once dominant people compelled their women to make much greater efforts of labour);
2 the language;

Tarascan is still largely an autochthonous language, but has been influenced by Spanish and major independent linguistic changes;

3   the occupational groups;

during colonial times they adopted new forms and contents; what has remained of them today has colonial rather than ancient Tarascan characteristics;

4   priesthood;

nominally it is Roman Catholic, but it has been incorporated in and made partly subservient to the traditional system;

5   ceremonial relationship.

The study of the historic elements of the social identity of the village and a comparison with historic data reveal the absence of some of the important elements of the ancient Tarascan social system. The pre-Spanish hierarchy of priesthood, the ancient social classes and the original structure of kinship have entirely disappeared.

Of course, the culture and daily life of Ihuatzio today also have aspects which cannot be considered as contributions to the community's identity. These aspects include most of the community's material culture, its (popular) scientific knowledge, and, to a great extent, the Spanish dialect spoken by the villagers in their intercourse with mestizos and occasionally between themselves.

Notes to Chapter VIII

[1]   Nutini, 1961.

[2]   The calpultin are directly and closely connected with the organisation of festivals (cofradía). Every calpulli organises the festivals and ceremonies once in every *ten* years. The three largest barrios are divided into two groups of lineages, so each of these acts once in every twenty years. Nutini considers the social organisation of Contla as a remnant of a very old, probably pre-Nahuatlacan pattern. His arguments in favour of this view are not very convincing. Apparently, when he wrote his article he was ignorant of the contents of the Padrones de Tlaxcala del siglo XVI (Doc. no. 377. Biblioteca del Museo Nacional de México). The historic data collected in this document justify the conclusion that the historic social organisation of Contla considerably resembled that of other Nahuatlacan communities.

[3]   cf. Carrasco, 1961.

[4]   Códice Ramírez, 1944; pp. 126-128.

5 Anderson and Dibble, 1952, III, p. 54: (modern spelling) "Aw semololiwtiwi' in kanpa tlein kichiwa', in a'so pololli, tepantli, kwemitl, apantli kichiwa', motkitiwi', anoso moxe'xeloa. Aw kwawtla wi'konkwi', konmama' in kilwia' kwikatlawilli". See also Sahagún, 1955, I, p. 323.

6 Sahagún, 1955, I, p. 326: "... para que nuestro hijo tenga cargo de barrer y limpiar la casa de nuestro señor".

7 Códice Ramírez, 1944; p. 158.

8 Idem, p. 130.

9 Durán, 1951, p. 86.

10 Idem, p. 87.

11 Pomar, 1941, pp. 26-28.

12 Idem, p. 29.

13 Anderson and Dibble, 1952, III, pp. 67-68: (modern spelling) ".... a'mo tlakamekayotl motta, sa kwalnemilise', wel ye' motta, wel ye'motemoa: in kwalnemilise', in chipawak iyollo', in kwalli iyollo', in iknoyo iyollo' in tlapakaihiyowiani, in tlatepitswiani, in tlatlayolikwiani, in a'mo mosiwiani, in yollochikawak, in yollotetl, in yollochichik, in tepe'pepetlani, in temakochoani, in tetlasotlani, in tetlayokuliani, in teka chikani, imawki iyollo, in mitoa teutl iyollo, in tlateumatini, in teuimakasini in chokani, in tlayokwiani, in elsi'siwini. Aw inik walpewa i, ok itoka, 'tlamakasto(n)', niman ye' 'tlamakaski', niman ik 'tlenamakak', ye mawisti i, niman ik unkan ano i, in mitoa ketsalkoatl".

14 Códice Ramírez, 1944, p. 141.

15 See for instance: Anderson and Dibble, 1951, II, pp. 137-138: Chonchayokakaliwa (3-Atemostli), Panketsalistli festival; and Sahagún, 1955, I, pp. 195, 219, 222. The relations between Tenochtitlan and Tlaltelolco are another point to remember.

16 cf. Van Zantwijk, 1963 b.

IX　　　　　　　　　　*socio-economic development*
　　　　　　in relation to social and cultural identity

This final chapter is devoted to the relationship between the partly autochthonous Indian identity of Ihuatzio as described in this study and the difficulties
encountered in the execution of development projects in this village. Before
our investigations were started some Crefal experts had suspected the existence
of such a relationship. In fact this was one of the reasons for making this study
of Ihuatzio.

Before considering the problems encountered in the village in the light of the
results of this study, more should be said about the underlying purposes of the
development programmes.

Of course, its nature and limited resources prevented Crefal from carrying out
spectacular social and economic development projects on its own account; it
is also doubtful whether this was what the Crefal Director had in view and
whether it would have the approval of the Mexican government. Yet, from
1962 Crefal had pretended that some form of real community development
might be achieved in Ihuatzio in co-operation with the central government's
Development Brigade.

It is important first to consider what the term 'community development'
actually means.

The Economic and Social Council of the United Nations Organisation has
published an official document containing the following provisional operational
definition:

"The term 'community development' has come into international usage to
connote the processes by which the efforts of the people themselves are united
with those of governmental authorities to improve the economic, social and

cultural conditions of communities, to integrate these communities into the life of the nation, and to enable them to contribute fully to national progress".[1]
This definition is commented upon in the document itself as follows:
"This complex of processes is then made up of two essential elements: the participation by the people themselves in efforts to improve their level of living with as much reliance as possible on their own initiative;
the provision of technical and other services in ways which encourage initiative, self-help and mutual help and make these more effective. It is expressed in programmes designed to achieve a wide variety of specific improvements".[2]
So according to this document real community development can only be realised if two factors occur jointly, or can at least be combined, viz.:

1 a greater participation of the community than hitherto both in devising and in executing plans, but always in co-operation with a higher authority;
2 The objectives aimed at by the community and the higher authority should be made to fit a cultural, social and economic policy which is directed towards national integration. Also the co-operation between community and higher authority may not be confined to a few incidental cases, but should extend over a wide field of activities.

This interpretation by the author of the above cited texts reveals more fully the political character of the definition, for it restricts the term 'community development' to those controlled processes of development which strengthen or extend the power of national governments and other forms of nationwide organisations. It clearly gives existing political units priority over cultural, social or economic units.
The formulation of the operational definition of community development has been based on an objective acceptable to present-day governments, viz. complete national integration.
Yet it is not exclusively based on political motives; it also shows some influence of social scientific thinking recognisable in two related aspects of the definition: the emphasis laid on the sociological concept of *community*, and on active participation in the development process by the members of the community as an *organised social group*. The whole philosophy of community development as it has up to now been worked out reveals this influence. At first this 'philosophy' seems to have a simple and logical starting-point: communities with a low standard of living and bad hygienic conditions, whose members share a

number of traditional patterns of organisation and cultural expressions have to be helped in a way avoiding their disintegration and promoting, as far as possible, the useful contribution of the traditional forms of organisation to the community's development. This is a subject which is very near to the heart of many sociologists and social-anthropologists; their idea of community development is the promotion of gradual social and cultural developments and the prevention of too sudden changes which cause confusion in the community. In general they are in favour of social evolution, not social revolution, for a social and economic development planned in advance is incompatible with revolutionary actions.[3] These advocates of 'community development' assume that the community concerned will get a chance to develop and change without disappearing as a social entity, at any rate within a short time.

Another view also plays an important part in the philosophy of community development. It is the idea that it is possible to achieve a complete blending of the several cultures and social groupings within a national territory, eventually resulting in a new integrated national culture and society. Often this idea entirely dominates the other, which aims at the development of the community itself. Thus it often sacrifices the protection and strengthening of the community involved to the achievement, at a higher national level, of the idea of total integration. In the republic of Mexico this ideal is supported by a great confidence in the possibilities of so-called applied social anthropology. It is assumed that it is possible effectively to direct the progress of national integration, to control the blending of cultures and social processes in general in a way which is sure to lead to the ultimate goal. This view profoundly influences the planning of development projects in the predominantly Indian parts of Mexico, under the direction of the Instituto Nacional Indigenista (i.n.i.). The Director of this Institute, Dr. Alfonso Caso, expresses this idea in the following quotations: ". . . . there is a consensus of opinion that all acculturation processes can be directed, that they can be planned in advance, not with a view to enabling the stronger community to dominate the weaker, but to avoid the disorganisation and exploitation of the weaker community by the stronger".[4]

If there has ever been an agreement on this general definition, there have always been differences of opinion both in Mexico and elsewhere on the way in which the process of 'acculturation' or cultural change should be planned in advance.

Alfonso Caso knows only one way: ".... the only scientifically correct and at the same time the only just and human way. There is no other way to solve the indigenous population problem but this: the indigenous communities must be incorporated into the great Mexican society; these communities have to be reformed; they should be made familiar with what already exists in other parts of the country. .... Assuming that the problem is not a racial one, but one of cultural lag, the policy to be followed should be to change the negative aspects of indigenous culture into positive ones, and to preserve all the positive and useful aspects of the indigenous communities, their public spirit, their sense of mutual support, their traditional art and their folk-lore".[5]

Like the United Nations definition of community development, the above-quoted formulation of the purpose of development projects in the Indian areas containes more subjective criteria, and does not give a clear idea of what is meant by the development of such areas, as it is capable of different interpretations.

Caso's statements are evidently based on the same idea that underlies many studies of acculturation: the concept of a culture as consisting of elements which can be replaced by others or changed without drastic effects on the rest of that culture. (The same attitude leads to consideration of the Indian cultures today as mixtures of indigenous and Spanish elements). It is difficult to assume that this idea is generally valid. A drastic change in the economy of a community, for instance, will as a rule result in great social changes. If a rural Indian community is urbanised through a rapid process of industrialisation, it runs the risk of losing much of its traditional public spirit. Even if the national government should introduce a planned socio-economic development of the community, it is very doubtful if a 'positive' element such as traditional public spirit will function in the new social situation. If it fails to function properly, it will cease to be a 'positive' element.

The question arises of whether it is possible to realise a blending of cultures in the way advocated by Alfonso Caso. In the author's opinion it is, to a certain extent, indeed possible. Many culturally heterogeneous countries have ethnical minorities with a high social and economic level, which have nevertheless preserved important traditions, a language and a literature of their own. Such countries are for instance India, the u.s.s.r., Switzerland, and the Netherlands. But in these cases it is better to speak of a 'development with the preservation of a form of cultural identity rather than of a 'development with the preservation of positive aspects'. The first formulation is more dynamic, because it includes the new aspects and their specific characteristics; furthermore it avoids the use of such a vague term as 'positive'. Caso has not made it clear if he actually means a 'development with the preservation of the cultural identity of the community'. He strongly emphasises the necessity of incorporating the Indian communities into the general national Mexican society. According to him the 'positive' aspects of the indigenous cultures: public spirit, mutual support, indigenous forms of art, folklore, should not primarily contribute to the preservation of the Indian identity, but should rather help to enrich the national identity. If his statements are to be understood in this sense, the question arises of whether he does not grossly overrate the possibility of directing development processes. Caso's ideal of progress is a selective one: he selects the 'positive' aspects of two cultures with the purpose of preserving them for the benefit of the ultimate integrated national society. His writings are not explicit about the way in which he proposes to achieve this; they do not contain any general survey of the way to realise his undoubtedly noble ideas. The inmediate results of the practical methods followed by I.N.I. today, which the author has been able to observe in several places in Mexico are still far from the realisation of this ideal. Apart from anything else, Caso's idea is indeed a meritorious one: the incorporation of the Indian minorities into the national society should be achieved without discrimination against the indio. But a policy of selection, which aims at changing 'negative' and preserving 'positive' aspects will not suffice to achieve the end. This concept is hardly applicable even in planning the integral handling of integration problems, since 'positive' and 'negative' aspects are interdependent. Progress should always be viewed as a complex of interdependent processes of development.

What is progress? The author has described the concept of progress as "the advance towards desired ends".[6] Thus the signification of the concept depends on a wish to achieve particular ends and on the people who express the wish, and aim at its fulfilment. Progress means different things to different people. What is distinct progress to one person need not be regarded as such by somebody else. Serious problems in community development occur where the opinions of the community with regard to its own progress differ from those held by the governmental authorities. And even if these opinions agree, there may be many problems, mostly technical ones, but in such cases there is always every reason to hope that a solution can be found.

Development problems may differ in nature and size, varying from community to community and from situation to situation. When the government and the community concerned have different ends in view, difficulties are as a rule greater than when they differ simply with regard to the priority of campaigns and works to be executed.

In Ihuatzio both categories of problems were encountered. Its Indian identity means that the people have certain ideas on progress which deviate from and in some cases conflict with those held by the municipal, state and federal authorities. Even when a community and the national authorities are in agreement on certain objectives to be achieved, they often disagree with regard to the urgency of the realisation. Such differences may sometimes also arise between the various higher authorities.

The four executive village chiefs and three Hurámutich' were asked to give their idea of progress. They agreed on the following points:

1   with regard to their culture they desired an extension of the traditional religious system and the termination of anti-religious influences in public education.

2   Socially they aim at a better fulfilment of cargos. They would like individual members of the community to be more public-spirited; they want less freedom for the young, and the re-introduction of the Gwatapera in its later, chiefly colonial, form.

3   Their wishes in the economic and technical field were: a better equipment, and physical extension, of the ceremonial centre; more land, both in individual and communal ownership; irrigation works and better agricultural implements; the construction and equipment of a health centre.

As to politico-administrative matters, five of the seven men stated that one of the most ardent wishes of the population of Ihuatzio was for their village to be separated from the municipality of Tzintzuntzan. The other two did not mention it.

To these village chiefs and principals progress means the advance towards the realisation of these and some other objectives. These objectives are chiefly connected with their traditions. Noteworthy is their wish to enlarge their landed property. Prosperity and security are still associated with considerable landed property. In this connection it is interesting to note that successful chicken-farmers in the nearby island of Yunuén appeared to invest their earnings from the small farms in pieces of land on the mainland, which were then kept fallow.

Only part of the wishes mentioned above are in agreement with those of the government, e.g. those concerning agricultural improvements (by the use of better tools and if necessary by irrigation) and the establishment of a health centre. The objects which are given priority by the government, are of secondary or lesser importance to the chiefs and principals of the village.

Government authorities are in favour of strengthening the existing political-administrative units, the municipality of Tzintzuntzan among them. They want to expand public education and through it to propagate the political and social philosophy of the government party. They aim at increasing the ties that connect Ihuatzio with regional and national social, economic and political units, and consequently they try to eliminate those structures, forms of organisation and traditions which impede the advance of developments directed towards this end. Thus the higher authorities are in principle opposed to the cargo system, and to the strong influence of the traditional village chiefs appointed through the system; they also consider the competitive dual pattern of organisation as undesirable.

Community development in the sense expressed in the definition by international organisations, which often finds wide acceptance on a national level, also in Mexico, implies active co-operation between communities and higher authorities, their social and economic services in particular. This co-operation cannot be achieved, however, before wide agreement has been reached on practical problems between the authoritative leaders of the local community and the representatives of the higher governmental bodies and their services.

We have already seen that the situation in Ihuatzio offers little scope for such agreement; but the most serious difficulties are not the direct result of this lack of agreement. Most of the resistance to official government intervention is a direct result of its being a threat to the position of the traditional village chiefs. They can expect no personal advantage from co-operation with the present higher authorities. Since these authorities are in favour of stronger national institutions with the consequent extension of their own powers, the village chiefs can expect little more than a weakening of their position. The traditional chiefs derive their social functions chiefly from a section of community life which is not approved of by the government authorities. Its expansion and intensification does not agree with the government's ideas on progress, and will therefore never receive government support.

Thanks to the prudence of the development brigade the situation in Ihuatzio was relatively favourable. The government officials showed a full understanding of the position of the traditional chiefs and sought their co-operation, which they consider important enough to make some concessions in favour of the improvements desired by the chiefs. Yet such co-operation was hardly interesting for an Acha Maroata Santa Kruxiechani (August Lord of the Holy Crosses), as it constituted a danger to his position as a high dignitary, protected by external leaders of lower rank from too direct and dangerous outside contacts. For then he would run the risk of being degraded to the position of unofficial leader of the community, allowed to co-operate with a governmental official, who will of course assume most of the official and formal aspects of authority. Moreover such a condominium is always regarded by the government as a temporary, transitional solution. 'The August Lords of the Holy Crosses of the people that live here' fully realise this, and they as well as their predecessors have always realised this, as long as they had governments whose views on matters of progress clashed with the foundations of the Indian identity of the village. This awareness of danger is also demonstrated in the fairly unimportant external representation of the community, often by external chiefs of lower rank, which means in fact a limitation of social communication. In this way the village has long been able to maintain most of its Indian identity amidst a strong current of cultural, social and economic forces, which flooded this part of Michoacán, in many places eliminating most of the indigenous aspects of the communities. As we have seen before, Ihuatzio also had a small group of people, the agraristas, – now no more than 3 per cent. of the population – who favoured the modern trends. This small minority together with the followers of the P.R.I., who comprise less than 5 per cent. of the population, are probably the only people in the village whose ideas on progress agree with those of the government authorities. Members of the agrarista group are almost exclusively elderly men who played an active part in the riots of the nineteen-twenties; therefore the movement of the agraristas is likely to lose even more importance in the course of time. Other opponents of the traditional chiefs disapprove of some aspects of the ancient system, but want to retain some essential elements of it. This was also true of the modernist from the Kapitan wapánekwa, who tried to become Alkande without fulfilling the prescribed number of commissions, and advocated the introduction of many reforms. He wanted a reduction of the power of the traditional Principales and was an advocate of State education, but he also wanted the restoration of the Gwatapera, more collective labour for the wapánekwecha, a higher status for the Wandárich', a strengthening of some traditional religious institutions, etc.

The eighteen, mostly younger, men who had ignored the 'advice' of the Hurámutich' of joining the co-operative society of chicken-farmers, which had been founded and was controlled by Crefal, in 1962 provided further evidence of the power of the traditional system. At the large annual meeting of the society considerable profits were paid, and Crefal made an attempt to persuade the representatives of the various villages to spend a large portion of the money on the execution of improvements in their communities which were deemed necessary by Crefal or the Government. Many delegations complied with the request, but the eighteen men from Ihuatzio followed the advice of their Principales and placed all their profits at the disposal of the ceremonial centre for the construction of waterworks for the priest's residence and other improvements to the building. The next year they paid one thousand pesos for the construction of a health centre; this was also done with the consent of the principals. The question may be asked what were their motives. Only some of the eighteen men who had been the first members of the society in the village had joined it purely for economic reasons. Most of them had other motives as well, connected with the traditional system. Some frankly admitted that they needed the income from the chicken-farms for the fulfilment of commissions, their main consideration being that these earnings would make them less dependent on the support of relations and ceremonial relatives. They denied that their refusal to follow the 'advice' of the principals was due to a desire to undermine their power. They forgot, however, that the dependence on ceremonial and blood relations, which they were so eager to avoid, is in fact one of the important elements of their system of social control; and it is this social control which preserves the traditional system and with it the power of the chiefs in Ihuatzio[7].

Fairly strong discipline is maintained among the younger generation by the chiefs and older members of the community in general. But it is clear that this constitutes a weak spot in the traditional organisation. For if discipline is not strictly upheld, it is immediately in danger of crumbling, because the young will become more and more interested in activities which increase their independence. Once this process has started they will rise on the social ladder in ways other that the traditional ones, and this tendency will in its turn cripple the cargo system. In Ihuatzio this process has hardly started, but the first signs of it are already noticeable and the principals are worried about it. They might be able to keep the situation under control, but the increasing intensive contacts with the 'hostile' world outside enhance the danger of the young people receiving the active support of the Turíxecha, who encourage them to neglect their duties within the cargo system, sowing the seed of doubt in their minds with regard to the sacredness of the ancient religious and social system. This is another reason why the government officials who want to contribute to the development of the community meet with profound distrust on the part of the Hurámutich'. These officials are known to be people who prefer to seek contact with the most susceptible members of the community: the young men. The young man of Ihuatzio has these alternatives: to strive after wealth and incur the opposition of the community, or to strive after the fulfilment of cargos and remain a poor man in terms of money, but receive prestige and influence in reward. Most of the young men in the village lack the courage to go the first, anti-social way alone and passively resign themselves to the inevitably heavy task. But if the Turíxecha promise to lend them a helping hand and invite them to follow the first, more selfish, course the temptation may prove to be too great.

The 'august Lords of the Holy Crosses' are not alone in their struggle to defend the Indian identity. They are supported not only by the older men, who have all invested part of their earnings in the cargo system, but also by a great majority of the women. The women, as mothers, imbue their children with the values and norms of the traditional system, not simply because they were told the same things when they were young. As the author has remarked in passing in chapter VI, the women of Ihuatzio have a personal interest in the maintenance of their traditions, and the more intelligent women are well aware of this. Remarks made by women from Ihuatzio showed their disapproval of the position of mestizo women. A woman whose husband liked to go to town to enjoy himself, was commented upon by other women in this way: "She is like a mestizo woman; she is no longer angry when J (her husband) does not spend the night at home". A middle-aged woman from Sagrado Corazón said: "A Purembe-woman (i.e. a Tarascan woman) always knows what her husband is doing; a mestizo woman only knows it when she sees him". To the women of Ihuatzio the only alternative to their place in the traditional system is the position of the downtrodden rural mestizo woman, who is exploited and has no say in economic matters, and, in contrast to the Tarascan woman, cannot expect conjugal faithfulness on the part of her husband. This does not mean, however, that the women of Ihuatzio are generally averse to economic and material progress in general. Like the men they want economic and material improvements, and even like to widen their field of knowledge, or, to put it more generally, to increase what Erasmus calls their 'positive control'.[8]

The problems of development projects in general and of community development in particular can be arranged according to two related aspects: the technical and the 'philosophical'.

There is little to be said about the technical aspect. Irrespective of the philosophy underlying a development programme, mistakes can be made in its execution and, with insufficient staff trained for development work, it may fail through technical errors and lack of social communication between government officials and the people themselves. When new development projects were introduced, the people, not only in Michoacán, but also elsewhere in Mexico, were often told of the great personal material benefit to be expected from the projects. Thus desires were aroused in the people's hearts which could not possibly be realised within a reasonable time. The government usually stressed the economic aspects of the project and often their officials were surprised to find the people sceptical about it, while communities with strong social and religious traditions appeared to be scarcely interested. The worst mistakes are made by badly paid and badly trained lower officials, although they often complain about the capricious redtape methods of their superiors, whom they accuse of upsetting or delaying the work they are doing. These so-called 'front-line workers' often cause a lot of trouble. Their own social background often tends towards ethnocentricity and paternalism. They often compare 'indios' with children. They are inclined to make promises which neither they nor their superiors will ever be able to keep. In Michoacán these lower officials have a social status within the community of Tuříxecha which is much lower than that which the traditional village chiefs with whom they have to co-operate enjoy in theirs. This stresses the subordinate position of the traditional and – according to the Tuříxecha – 'underdeveloped' Indian communities in comparison with the mestizo society.

Another grave 'technical' error is the fact that the great majority of government officials do not speak or even understand the indigenous speech of the district where they work.

During the last few years the interest in community development has given rise to a rapid increase in literature on the subject. Any attempt to relate this literature in general to the conditions in Ihuatzio is beyond the scope of this study. Some results of our study of Ihuatzio, however, can be compared with those found in some of the most relevant works in this field.

Hoetink recently made a clear statement that up till now the problems connected with development have been studied especially in the light of a modern form of 'simplified evolutionism': usually the presupposition is made that all over the world social and economic development will inevitably lead to the 'western' type of society.[9]

Simplified evolutionism generally leads to a disregard of the power of the cultural and social identity of the developing groups. Objection should above all be made to the 'simplified' nature or roughness of the argumentation mentioned by Hoetink rather than to its 'evolutionist' character. Since the study of the problems of development is aimed at indicating various possibilities of 'progress', with due allowance for inevitable evolutionary processes, it is natural for 'evolutionists' theories to be formed. Köbben, Erasmus and Pozas have done this, each in his own way.[10]

Ricardo Pozas is still an old-style evolutionist, and, according to western standards, his theory of evolution is a dissonant echo of what was staged long ago in Western Europe.

Erasmus might be called a new-style evolutionist. His set of concepts contains the 'closed' and 'open' communities as the first and final stages of possible, but certainly not always inevitable, evolutions. According to Erasmus a closed community has hardly any specialisation, and a limited 'positive control'. By this he means the process of continued development of knowledge. He also uses the concept of 'negative control', i.e. the control of social environment through law and sanction.[11] Erasmus pays much attention to the concept of 'prestige', which he considers to be determined by biological as well as cultural factors. In this connection he evolves, in addition to Veblen's concept of 'conspicuous consumption', the concepts of: 'conspicuous giving', 'conspicuous ownership' (or perhaps rather conspicuous acquisition of property) and 'conspicuous production or service'. In a primitive closed society conspicuous giving is the most important means of attaining prestige 'inasmuch as the variety of durable goods owned by its members is limited by their unspecialised labor".[12] As specialisation increases and the society gradually develops into a more open one, conspicuous ownership and conspicuous production assume greater importance. Erasmus also recognises a development which does not, or not directly, lead to an 'open' society: ". . . . we shall see how a limited degree of capital formation may take place in closed societies through coercive negative control of large quantities of unskilled labor rather than through the development of specialization and knowledge".[13]

"The Inca civilization mentioned previously with regard to capital formation is a remarkable example of the extent to which the closed society was able to develop through coercive control of unspecialized labor".[14]

It is tempting to relate Erasmus's theoretical reflections to the situation in Ihuatzio, especially because they are based on the results of American and particularly Mexican field researches. Applying Erasmus's concepts, we may say that in Ihuatzio conspicuous giving overshadows conspicuous acquisition of property and production, and the people are more occupied with negative control than with positive control. The question now arises if we should assume the cargo system (conspicuous giving and conspicuous service) to be an obstacle to any form of economic progress. Before answering this question one serious drawback of Erasmus's study should be pointed out. His theory supports one specific objective: the promotion of evolutionary processes which lead to 'westernization', to the formation of 'free', i.e. capitalist societies. Unlike some of his colleagues Erasmus (an American) frankly admits that this theory embodies some preconceptions. Yet he is perhaps not always aware of the 'ethnocentric' character of his theoretical observations, when he clearly places himself in the service of 'cultural imperialism' by speaking of "our influence as a persuasive leader among free nations".[15]

Returning to the question asked above, we may stay that the cargo system in its present form decidedly acts as an obstacle to the development of a village community into an open capitalistic system. It is dangerous, however, to measure the degree of westernisation by economic criteria only. In this connection it is worth noting that Ihuatzio has long ceased to be a closed community economically. The villagers sell tule products, tortillas, fish, wheat, beef-cattle and fruit on regional markets in the neighbourhood, where they buy clothes, household-articles, tools, fireworks, candles, medicine, radios, and sometimes food to replenish their own stocks. Their tule products (mats, baskets, and decorative articles) are for sale even outside Michoacán. National currency is in circulation in the village and there are considerable differences in wealth within the village. But conspicuous consumption is largely suppressed. People who feel inclined to it are held in check by the fear of being charged with expensive commissions. Relatively rich members of the community hide their riches or, when they set great store on prestige and personal status, they accept one or more cargos. Although economically Ihuatzio has been partly integrated into larger units, the results of their economic activities, the money earned, is still spent on things connected with the traditional social system. The pattern of expenditure continues to differ strongly from that of the mestizos. This difference is due to the social control which is still exercised within the traditional system. In this respect the social community of the Tarascans of Ihuatzio can indeed be looked upon as a 'closed' one. As long as it continues to be so, strong westernisation will not be possible. The cargo system is an obstacle in the way of 'westernisation', but does it act as an impediment to any form of economic development? The author agrees with Erasmus that it need not necessarily do so. If changes could be introduced into the cargo system so that negative control is strengthened and conspicuous giving is more and more replaced by conspicuous service and production, considerable capital formation might be the result. Such changes in the situation in Ihuatzio are not unlikely, considering the success of communal service by the wapánekwecha, which was introduced by the present Acha Representante (see chapter IV). Erasmus and many others, who are averse to 'imperative' negative control, will consider this an unfavourable development.

Köbben's ideas on problems of development are moderate and varied. He is of the opinion that 'westernisation' and the 'western example' are valuable, but he is also alive to the social and cultural identities of many 'development areas', which are retained in spite of the introduced changes.[16]

This leads the author to formulate a question which has to be answered with regard to development problems in a culturally heterogeneous country: what policy should be adopted by the country's rulers and the directors of development projects in respect of the cultural and social identities of the various underdeveloped groupings within the heterogeneous national population in question?

Some people in Mexico believe that the progress of a country implies complete integration of its population. The ultimate result must be one national identity; differences must be eliminated as quickly and as completely as possible. The same people often argue that there are no pure Indian cultures, only population groups still living partly in a pre-Spanish and partly in a colonial stage.[17] Those who hold this opinion confuse identity with originality; they identify typical aspects with autochthonous ones. But they also have a reasonable argument in favour of complete integration: cultural and social differences – for instance differences of language – are in a way obstacles to national developments, because they make it difficult to co-ordinate the national efforts and require greater financial means from national institutions: those of education and others. However, these advocates of equalisation often forget to ask how many sacrifices have to be made to achieve the form of integration favoured by them.

It is difficult to be certain just what Ihuatzio would lose, if its Indian character, its Tarascan identity should disappear and personal evaluations will almost inevitably qualify the assessment. The main elements of that identity, which are considered valuable by many people, including non-Tarascans are:

dedication to the public cause (voluntary or compulsory), modesty in daily intercourse (except on ceremonial occasions), tolerance and a preference for compromise in solving social conflicts shown by those villagers who adhere to the traditional system, and finally the relatively high social position of women.

With their identity the Tarascans would also be deprived of their pride in their great past, and their chiefs and principals would become mere farmers in every respect. Their wapánekwecha would be broken up into households, some of which might be connected by occasional ceremonial relations. The Tarascan language and the people's concept of the universe would also disappear.

Furthermore 'imperative negative control' might become considerably less important, which would greatly please Erasmus and many others.

Personal assessment of values will often determine the choice between a development with or without the preservation of identity. One thing, however, is certain: every attempt made either by members of the minority concerned or by outsiders to retain the existing traditional system entirely unchanged is doomed to fail, and is therefore undesirable from an objective point of view. It has already been said that many Hurámutich' in Ihuatzio certainly realise this. It would therefore be a great mistake to consider the traditional chiefs and principals merely as 'conservative' men, because they want to preserve the cultural and social identity of their community. When government intervention is aimed at eliminating this identity, the traditional chiefs and principals must usually adopt a conservative attitude to maintain their positions. This usually causes a long struggle at the expense of much human energy. Sometimes this struggle is necessary and inevitable, but not always. Any way of avoiding conflicts must therefore be taken. It is quite possible that the chiefs and principals would be much less pre-occupied with other than economic developments, if the village were helped to attain a 'heterogeneous' development, i.e. development as well as preservation of some forms of Tarascan identity.

It is undeniable that the cargo system with its conspicuous giving, on which a 'pasado' and his relatives spend a great deal of money, amounting to as much as four years' income for the richer ones and up to ten years' income for the poorer ones, prevents the making of investments needed for further economic developments. But it should be remembered that until recently there were probably fewer real possibilities for capital investment in means of production than today. A further decline of the cargo system in Ihuatzio is therefore quite likely as these possibilities increase. Unfortunately prospects are not very promising. The economic situation in and around Ihuatzio differs a great deal from that in the Mayo and Yaquí territories studied by Erasmus.[18] In the present circumstances the Lake Pátzcuaro basin is overpopulated, and it is not likely that the engineering works needed to better the economic conditions will shortly be executed. As long as there is no substantial material progress, the development brigade and afterwards the Instituto Nacional Indigenista will not be able to offer more than the kind of support which leads to conditions as found in the poor rural mestizo villages with their high degree of social disintegration. To most Tarascans this is, rightly, an alarming prospect.[19] Therefore Ihuatzio will remain 'in the shadow of its yácatas' for some time to come; its past will always separate the community from the national culture, until real economic or social and structural changes take place.

We must next consider how such drastic changes can be brought about in a community like that of Ihuatzio, and what part the government is to play. Programmes of elementary education and community development cannot bring a real solution. Erasmus's well-founded serious objections to this form of development have been clearly formulated.[20] The methods of community development are in fact based on the mobilisation and use of unskilled unemployed workers under the direction of some or less expert outsiders undertaking material and cultural projects on a local level and scale. It is exceedingly difficult to co-ordinate these activities regionally and nationally. The method has the advantage that productive use is made of unemployed labour which would otherwise remain idle, and that it allows the local identity of the community to be preserved. But it contains the risk of promoting the self-sufficiency of the community. If, for instance, the wapánekwecha should start a large-scale execution of public works, it might delay integration, because the authorities of larger administrative units might then be less inclined to extend their own services of public works to Ihuatzio. The only really effective solutions to the problems attached to the development of Ihuatzio are large-scale irrigation and industrialisation. But neither of the two has a great chance of realisation, because, considered from a national point of view, they would be too expensive in relation to the number of people who would benefit from them. For some time to come government investments in either of these directions will not be justifiable from an economic point of view. Limited irrigation might, however, be possible and might lead to a significant rise of the standard of living in Ihuatzio.

Once economic development gets into its stride, the government will also be able to give support in other respects. It would be highly desirable for the government to give actual support. If they should fail to do so, the majority of the Tarascan population of Ihuatzio, during their process of integration into larger units, will find their way to the lowest classes of the national mestizo population. This can be prevented by giving active support to some aspects of their *cultural* identity. In general it will not be sufficient merely to tolerate those aspects, however reasonable that may seem at first sight. Many government officials with more enlightened views maintain that if the Indian identity were neither promoted nor opposed, its 'positive' or useful elements would eventually survive. These people forget, however, that in a process of increasing national integration minority groupings will always be at a disadvantage, if their cultural identity is not supported, for the simple reason that its counterpart, the national culture, i.e. the culture of the majority or that of the dominant groups, always enjoys considerable official support. In a sense the refusal to support the *cultural* identity of ethnical minorities is always a mild form of discrimination, and it is often felt as such by the members of those minorities. When an ethnic minority recognises the discrimination, nativistic movements may arise, showing a preference for linguistic purism, as is now seen in some Aztec areas.

If the government succeeds in directing the development of the Indian minorities by strengthening and expanding certain aspects of their Indian identity, the individual members of the indigenous communities will retain their own cultural dignity, which will enable them to make more valuable contributions to the national culture than if, after losing their own identity, they should find their way into the lowest layer of the national society as culturally impoverished mestizos. The former is the only way to attain Alfonso Caso's ideal: the preservation or rather the development of the 'positive' aspects of the Indian cultures. The situation in Ihuatzio illustrates this point. Economic conditions in the village are hardly different from those in a rural mestizo community. But the inhabitants of Ihuatzio consider themselves better – and in a way they are right – than the mestizos, who live in similar material circumstances. They distinguish themselves favourably by showing greater discipline, by a stronger organisation and higher moral standards, in short by their cultural and social identity. On the one hand the catrines, the urban or urbanised mestizos, may ridicule this identity, on the other hand the Tarascans derive from their identity a certain status within the regional society. The mestizos of Pátzcuaro look down upon the people of Ihuatzio, but rate them higher than the poor rancheros, the rural mestizos, who live in the same circumstances as these indios. So in a greater regional context the identity of the Tarascans is in a way favourable to them. In a culturally homogeneous situation a person's status is almost entirely based on his economic power, descent and education; in a culturally heterogeneous situation the criteria are much vaguer. As the Tarascans, in their present economic situation, would no doubt be reckoned to belong to the lowest social class if they should give up their *cultural* identity, it is in their interest, even if considered in a wider context, to preserve their identity. Many mestizos exaggerate the hidden riches of the Tarascans, and do not know what to think of them.

As long as such an Indian minority remains economically weak, cultural difference is a favourable factor. Therefore directors of development projects should not aim at eliminating a community's identity as quickly as possible. On the contrary, by supporting that identity they will be able to help the Indian minority group to remove 'the deadlock' in their situation. Then the members of the group need not have fears of falling to the lowest social status.

The conclusions reached with regard to problems relating to the development of an Indian community such as that of the Tarascans can now be summarised as follows:

1   Economic development is most urgent and an indispensable condition for other kinds of development.
2   Increasing economic integration will involve an increasing social integration into larger regional or national units, and it is possible, at least partly, to guide this social integration.
3   If the government should aim at lifting a considerable part of the Indian population directly to the level of the social middle classes, it will have to give active and actual support to the development of certain aspects of the Indian identity, especially the language, literature, arts and, if possible, folklore, i.e. it is above all the *cultural* identity which has to be strengthened. Government support of the *cultural* identity will make it easier for the groups concerned to accept the loss of much of their *social* identity, which

is the inevitable result of increasing national integration. The feelings of regret caused by the introduction of structural changes will then be alleviated by the strengthening of their own cultural dignity and the consciousness of a great past. This does not mean that the Indian *social* identity should in any case be eliminated. The political as well as the social and economic national conditions will decide to what extent it will be possible to incorporate that social identity into the national society.

Development problems in Mexico are unique owing to the ambivalent policy of the mestizo rulers towards the Indian minorities. The strong nationalist feelings of the mestizo cause them to aim at a homogeneous national culture, and consequently at the elimination of the cultural differences within the republic. But their strong nationalist feelings also cause them to make, sometimes desperate and spasmodic, efforts to find a national cultural identity of their own. In their search for it they often come back to their own Indian background. The disappearance of the Indian identity would, indeed, be a great loss of their national identity. This is the dilemma of a heterogeneous development-country like Mexico. A solution is only possible if autochthonous, and therefore often 'underdeveloped' aspects of the culture are no longer confused with identity. Active government support of the Indian *cultural* identity need not be a check on economic progress and integration. Government support of some aspects of the Indian *social* identity will even allow them to remain functional. Such support is not likely always to promote a so-called 'free' capitalistic development. But since 1910 Mexico has got beyond the point of view that this is the only possible way. Furthermore it should be remembered that today development aid is not only given by the 'free' capitalist countries, but such help is also offered by states and peoples whose investments are based on 'imperative negative control', conspicuous production and services. Development aid has, in fact, been rendered for some years from those quarters with undeniable success also in a Latin American country. As soon as the Indian minorities become aware of this alternative, which often fits their identity better, many Latin American governments who continue to aim at national uniformity will have disturbing times to face. But there is good reason to hope that at least Mexico will be spared the prospect which is the subject of a cynical folksong:

"Dicen en toda la nación O, madre mía Guadalupana, que está ya muy cercana la nueva revolución".	"Throughout the country it is said, oh, my dear Mother of Guadalupe, that the time is very near, indeed, for another revolution".

Notes to chapter IX

[1]   Official Records of the Economic and Social Council, twenty-fourth session, agenda item 4; Annexes, Geneva, 1957. Annex III of Document E/2931, twentieth report of the Administering Committee on Co-ordination to the Economic and Social Council; p. 14.

[2]   Idem.

[3]   There are, however, students of social science who consider disintegration and abrupt changes as inevitable consequences. Ricardo Pozas even looks upon them as positive and desirable developments. cf. Pozas, 1961, pp. 41, 42.

[4]   Caso, 1958, p. 36.

[5]   Idem, p. 103.

[6]   Van Zantwijk, 1963a, pp. 70, 71.

[7]   The agraristas, the member of Kapitan and, to a lesser extent, the chicken-farmers were dessentients of the type that Barnett refers to as 'the discontented' (cf. Barnett, 1953, pp. 381-385). The motives put forward by the Kapitan and the chicken-farmers do not suggest that these dissentients are really as susceptible to outside modernising influences as they are said to be. They appear to be so only to a limited extent. In some cases they prove to be as fervent defenders of their cultural identity as the conservative or traditionalist members of the community.

[8]   Erasmus, 1961, p. 102.

[9]   Hoetink, 1965, pp. 5, 6.

[10] Cf. Köbben, 1964, chs. 3, 4, 5; Erasmus, 1961 and Pozas, 1961.

[11] Erasmus, 1961, p. 102.

[12] Idem, p. 121.   [13] Idem, p. 103.   [14] Idem, p. 131.   [15] Idem, p. 168.

[16] Köbben, 1961, p. 93. cf. also p. 79: "The conservative ideas (of the Agni) cannot be explained completely as selfishness. Another factor which is certain to play a part is their pride of their own great past and their need to preserve in the modern world a face of their own".

[17] This standpoint was recently, in August 1964, publicly defended by the Mexican delegation to the 36th International Congress of Americanists. Even a man with such a great appreciation for indigenous cultures as Luis Villoro persists in defending the ideal of national cultural uniformity; however, he wants the Indian element to play an important part in it. cf. Juan Comas, 1964; pp. 171-209.

[18] Erasmus, 1961; part III (chs. IX-XII).

[19] cf. Aguirre Beltrán, 1952, pp. 280, 281; in the municipality of Aguilila, for instance, twenty per cent. of all people who died in 1949 died violent deaths.

[20] Erasmus, 1961; pp. 93-95 and 320-322.

appendix 2

GLOSSARY OF THE PRINCIPAL INDIGENOUS TERMS, TITLES AND NAMES

In general the pronounciation of indigenous words used in the text follows the rules for the pro-
nunciation of Spanish words; however, with the following additions and exceptions:

h a uvular fricative;
ř a flapped r, a sound between r and l;
tl a lateral fricative beginning with a plosive; a common Nahuatl sound;
ʌ a checked close central vowel, between Spanish u and i;
x a palatal fricative;
' a glottal plosive.

Some of the Aztec terms and words used in the text are spelt according to the old spelling of Chimal⁻
pahin, which is based on the Spanish spelling. This has been done especially with terms taken from
old chronicles. On the whole, however, preference has been given to the more logical new spelling.
Both spellings are still in use in Mexico today.

Acha	title, in general use for Tarascan chiefs (meaning: Lord; plural: Achaecha or Aches, as in Cherán). Cf. Acha Hefe, Acha Representante, etc.
Acha Alkande	one of the village chiefs in Ihuatzio, entrusted with the direction of the traditional religious organisation; head of the cargueros (see p. 182).
Acha Hefe (Jefe)	head of the local police, and representative of the municipal authorities in several of the villages discussed in this study. Official title: Jefe de Te-nencia.
Acha Katahpe	another indigenous name for the Acha Hefe in Ihuatzio. (cf. also: Katapi and Katáhpecha).

Acha Maruata
  Xantakruxiechani

"August Lords of the Holy Crosses", title of the old village chiefs and principals of Ihuatzio, the Hurámutich'. Sometimes "of those who live here" is added (Acha Maruata Xanta Kruxiecha ixu anápuecha).

Acha Representante

familiar title of the Representante de la Comunidad Indígena in Ihuatzio. His indigenous title is: Orétspetin Hurámuti Maruécheri.
He is the supreme external village chief.

Acompañantes

the five commissioners of San Isidro in Tzintzuntzan, under the direction of the Mayordomo of that saint.

agrarista

advocate of the Federal Government's land reform plans in the state of Michoacán. They are often associated with the 'devil' (cf. Carrasco, 1952, p. 49).

akwitse

serpent, the Tarascan symbol of death; formerly associated with the town of Pátzcuaro.

Alférez

a title of one of the helpers of the Moro Capitán and of one of those of the Soldado Capitán in Ihuatzio.
b one of the Cargueros de la Cruz in Tzintzuntzan;
c one of the Cargueros de la Judea in Tzintzuntzan;
d title of two cargueros of San Diego in Quiroga.

Alkalde (Alcalde)

the superior of the Kiengui in Angahuan; entrusted with the organisation of six festivals.

Alkande, Alkandi

(also: Acha Alkande), title of one of the village chiefs in some Tarascan communities, e.g. Ihuatzio and Pamatácuaro.

Anátakuri,
  Angátakuri

a in the 15th and 16th centuries title of the highest official below the Kasonsí.
b today in San Jerónimo Purenchécuaro the title of the three helpers of the Capitanes (Captains) of the patron saint.

Anyítakwa

the indigenous title of the semaneros in Angahuan, charged with duty periods of a week in the community hall, which is called Yurixo.

atlatl

Aztec for spearthrower.

atole

(from Aztec atolli), a drink made from fruit juice or cocoa mixed with maize flour.

Ayudantes

the helpers of a carguero (commissioner).

Awándaro

heaven, one of the three parts of the Universe.

barrio

(Spanish for village ward, hamlet, village) a term used for different social groupings, which are usually, but not always, connected with a certain area. cf.: wapánekwa, wapátsekwa and calpulli.

Biskal	(from Spanish: Fiscal), title of the Petahpe of Angahuan (see under Petahpe)
bracero	migrant workman; farm labourer migrating for some time (from a few months to 2 or more years) to the United States or to other parts of Mexico to earn a living.
Cabeza	one of the two chiefs of a barrio in Tzintzuntzan; with an indefinite tenure of office (usually for life).
Cabildo	administrative body in some Tarascan villages (Cherán, Chilchotla), consisting of all the old village principals (Principales, Aches, Tarépitich').
calpulli (kalpulli) (plural: calpultin)	social groupings within Aztec village communities; they are connected with certain areas, and may or may not have marriage-regulating functions; they had communal lands, and a community hall or ceremonial centre of their own (kalpulko); with other kalpultin they belonged to a common larger ceremonial centre.
calzón	(Spanish for trousers, kneebreeches), in Michoacán white cotton trousers, often with embroidered legs, sometimes with legs tied up above the ankles; traditional Indian garment; to go 'de calzón' to wear the traditional Indian dress.
Campanita	female bell-ringer, one of the young helpers in the Kenguería of Tzintzuntzan.
Capitamoro	one of the Wánanchatis or Roseras of Chilchotla, who has to carry a floral piece during processions.
Capitán (Kapitán)	(Spanish for Captain, leader), title of many commissioners (cargueros) in several Tarascan villages; they are always connected with a saint, sometimes the patron saint (Capitanes de San Francisco in Ihuatzio, of San Jerónimo in Purenchécuaro, of San Diego in Quiroga); not to be mixed up with Kapitan (without stress mark), the name of a wapánekwa in Ihuatzio or of one of its members. In Tzintzuntzan in former days the title of barrio chiefs comparable with the Urecha in Ihuatzio.
Capitanía	'Captainship'; the task of a Capitán; also 'Captaincy' as an institution, e.g. the Capitanía of St. Francis.
Caporal	title of two commissioners in Purenchécuaro, who have to perform so-called 'penal cargos' (commissions which do not bring prestige as a reward). Each of them is head of 6 Vaqueros and contributes to the celebration of Christmas and the preparations for it.
Cargadoras	title of female (married) functionaries in the kenguería of Tzintzuntzan.
cargo	in Tarascan villages a task to be performed within the framework of the traditionally ceremonial and religious organisations; the usual reward is social prestige.

carguero	a man who holds a cargo.
catrín (katrín)	nickname used by Lake Tarascans for urban mestizos and for Tarascans who dress like towns-people.
Chichimeka' (Chichimecs)	the Aztec name for some, ethnically not always related population groups or tribes, who led nomadic or semi-nomadic lives and came from the north of the present Mexican territory. They included the numerous northern tribes which spoke Uto-Aztec languages, as well as the Otomíes or Otonka'.
Chichiwa	title of a carguero in Chilchotla entrusted with part of the preparations for the Christmas celebrations and with the performance of some rituals at Twelfth Night.
Chuniechúkwaro	the Tarascan term for the underworld, the realm of the dead, one of the three parts of the universe.
cofradía	originally a Spanish term used for an organisation of people who devote themselves to a common task; in some places in Michoacán it is used to denote the cargo system or parts of it.
Colector	title of some functionaries in several Tarascan villages; they are always charged with collecting moneys for traditional festivals; cf. Ihuatzio, Purenchécuaro, Pacandan, Cherán and Chilchotla.
Comisionado	In Cherán a helper in a barrio; he plays a part in the preparations for the festival of St. Francis.
compadrazgo	ceremonial kinship, an important social institution in the rural villages of Michoacán.
compadre	'co-father', a term used for a male ceremonial relative of the same or an older generation than that of the speaker (women are called comadre = 'co-mother'); cf. Kumbe.
Comunidad Indígena	Indigenous Community, an institution which dated from colonial times; it controlled the lands in common ownership of the community and had certain obligations towards the colonial authorities. When the country gained independence, the official distinction between indios and mestizos was abolished. The Indigenous Communities had then lost the basis of their existence. When president Juárez introduced his land reform plans he wanted to abolish collective land-ownership, and representatives of the Indigenous Communities were appointed for the period of transition (cf. Representante de la Comunidad Indígena).
Consejero	title of three deputy chiefs in the village of Pamatácuaro; they assist the Alkandi and are his representatives in the village wards.

copal	from Aztec kopalli; a kind of resin burnt at several ritual ceremonies (incense, sacrificial smoke).
coyote	from Aztec koyotl; prarie wolf; originally the village god of Ihuatzio or his 'fellow-being'; see Hiwatse.
cristianos	a group of dancers in some villages, acting as counterparts of the 'moros' (e.g. in Quiroga).
destino	Spanish: 'destiny'; the term is used in Ihuatzio and some other Tarascan villages to denote occupations and the occupational groups.
Diputado	Spanish: deputy; title of the chief helper of the Mayordomo de la Soledad in Tzintzuntzan. (cf. Tiputádox).
Echerendo	the earth, one of the three parts into which the Tarascans divide the universe.
Ehpu	barrio-chief in Pichátaro, comparable with an Urétspeti in Ihuatzio and Cabeza in Tzintzuntzan.
ejido	in former times in Spain the common village grounds just outside the village (often pastures); today in Mexico an institution founded as part of the Federal Government's land reform programme. The term comprises the communal arable lands and/or pastures and also the board which exploits these grounds, either on a co-operative or a non-co-operative basis.
Eneani	one of the three groups into which the Wakúxecha were divided.
ereta, ireta	Tarascan for village.
Escribano	*a* helper of the Mayordomo de la Soledad in Tzintzuntzan; *b* helper of the Mayordomo de la Kenguería in Tzintzuntzan.
Fiscal (Fiskal)	title of a traditional official in some Tarascan villages (cf. Chilchotla, Angahuan, Pichátaro), usually entrusted with a task in connection with the worship of the Holy Virgin. (see: p. 182: Biskal).
gabán	in Michoacán: a blanket with a hole for the head; it can be used as a cloack and/or as a decorative article of dress (also called tilma and zarape).
Gabriélecha	the members of the San Gabriel wapánekwa in Ihuatzio.
gringo	nickname for United States citizens; sometimes also used for other foreigners, especially Europeans.
Gwanancha	a girl belonging to the Gwatapera (cf. Wananches).
Gwatapera	originally a community hall, a home for Tarascan women and girls, where the latter were educated in preparation for marriage; in the meantime they

also performed all kinds of services under the direction of female priests. Later on the term came to be used for the community halls which were founded in the Tarascan area by Don Vasco de Quiroga, who called them hospitales.

hayákwaro	Tarascan for territory.
hánguekwa	in: ma kwahta hánguekwa, hingun hánguekwa: household, conjugal family, those who live together.
hoskoecha	Tarascan for: stars.
Hoskok'eri	'Big Star', Venus.
Hospital	see Gwatapera.
huaraches (waraches)	indigenous sandals.
Huitzilopochtli	see Witsilopochtli.
Hurámuti	Tarascan title of an old 'pasado', one of the village principals of Ihuatzio (plural: Hurámutich').
Hwankrúsecha	Tarascan form of the term used to indicate the members of the Juan Cruz wapánekwa in Ihuatzio.
Irecha	Tarascan for: prince, king; another title for the Kasonsí.
Ireri	the title of the most important wife of the Kasonsí, always one of the nearest relatives.
ireti, hireti, ereti	a people, population.
Iᶒᴧts'ᴧ	'the Wrinkled One', title of the leader of a dance by women, which takes place in Ihuatzio on December 16th. He is the man who was the Ureti of the wapánekwa on duty until he relinquished office on December 12th.
Jefe	*a* short for Acha Hefe in Ihuatzio; (see: Jefe de Tenencia)
	b Spanish title or word referring to the Urétspeti, the wapánekwa chief, in Ihuatzio.
Jefe de Tenencia	in Michoacán: the representative of the municipal authorities in villages belonging to the municipality (not in the municipal capital); the official title of the Acha Hefe in Ihuatzio.
Juan Cruz	one of the nine wapánekwecha in Ihuatzio (cf. Hwankrúsecha).
Juez	'judge', justice of the peace, a lower municipal official in Michoacán; in Ihuatzio: the official title of the Acha Alkande.
Kámbiti	title of a commissioner and official in Angahuan who bears the costs of the Holy Week, directs some ceremonies, and is the head of the Tsᴧtsᴧ'ki hatsirati.

Kapitán	see Capitán.
Kapitan	one of the nine wapánekwecha in Ihuatzio or a member of that wapánekwa (plural: Kapítanich').
Karachakape	title of the commissioner of San Roque in Chilchotla.
Kasonsí	title of the highest official in the Tarascan empire, the head of the Wakú-xecha, king of Tzintzuntzan.
Katahpe, Katapi	official who has to maintain peace and order (cf. Ihuatzio, Chilchotla); plural: katápecha.
Katáhperakwa(ro)	'prison', police-cell.
katrín	see catrín.
Keni, Keng(u)i, Kieng(u)i, Kweni	title of an official entrusted with a task in connection with the ceremonial centre of the community; his position is an important one in Cherán, Angahuan and in Pichátaro; in Ihuatzio he is only a subordinate of the Prioste.
Kénikwa	divine service which was held in the Kenguería of Tzintzuntzan at 3 a.m. on Saturdays.
kumbe	Tarascan corruption of the Spanish word compadre 'co-parent'; plural kumbeecha, term used to refer to ceremonial relatives.
kura	*a* grandfather (in Old Tarascan); *b* priest (plural: kuracha).
Kurikaweri	'the Great Fire', the tribal god of the Wakúxecha, the chief god in the Tarascan pantheon.
Kuríndure	title of the head of the honey-gatherers in Chilchotla.
Kuritiecha	provincial priests in the Tarascan empire.
Kwerahperi	'Creator', the chief god of the Tarascans today. (cf. Kwerawáhperi).
Kwerawáhperi	'She who creates in her womb', the name of the supreme creating Goddess in the original Tarascan religion; she was especially worshipped in Tzina-pécuaro.
Luis Miguel	one of the nine wapánekwecha in Ihuatzio or a member of that group (plural: Luis Miguelecha).
Mandones	'commanders', title of six commissioners in Tzintzuntzan, who came in pairs from three special wards.
Maříkwecha	'girls', term used to indicate the married women of the wapánekwa on duty in Ihuatzio who on December 16th danced with the Iřʌts'ʌ.

mayóhtsikwa	Tarascan term for extended family, lineage.
Mayor	*a* title in Angahuan used for villagers who have been commissioners of the patron saint and Moro-dancers; *b* the Spanish title of the Petahpe of Chilchotla.
mayordomo	term used for the commissioners of some saints in Tzintzuntzan, Cherán, Chilchotla, and some other villages. This term, which is in common use in other parts of Mexico, is little heard in Michoacán, where the term carguero is much more common.
Melchor, Merchor	one of the nine wapánekwecha in Ihuatzio or a member of that group (plural: Merchorecha).
Mesa de Campo	title of the ex-Soldier and ex-Moorish Captains when, in the year after they have completed their term of office, they assist each other's successors and lead them during some ceremonies.
Moro-Capitán	Moorish Captain, one of the two Captains of St. Francis in Ihuatzio, entrusted with the safe lkeeping of the biggest image of the saint.
moros	'Moors', name for dancers, dressed like Moors, in several Tarascan villages, often connected with the patron saint of the village and with the worship of the saint; usually they are the 'pagan' counterparts of the soldados or cristianos.
náhuatl (nawatl)	the official language of the Aztec empire; the language of the Nawatlaka'.
nahuatlaca' (Nawatlaka')	'people of the law; people who speak náhuatl'; a term used to refer to the Aztecs and the ethnically related tribes together.
Naná Kutsi	Mother Moon or Lady Moon (nana = mother, elderly woman in general).
Okámbeti	head of a group of some twenty-five houses (sections of the territorial wards) in the Tarascan empire and at the beginning of the colonial era (plural: Okámbecha).
Orénaříkwecha	the oldest and most influencial men in the wapánekwecha in Ihuatzio; in each wapánekwa one of them acts as Urétspeti.
Oreti	see Ureti.
Orétspeti	see Urétspeti.
Orétspetin Hurámuti Maruécheri	'Ruler of the August Chiefs', indigenous title of the Acha Representante of Ihuatzio.
pasado	'he who has passed'; a term used to indicate those men who have completed all the cargos of the cargo-hierarchy.
pastorela	moralising traditional popular play with a religious strain.

patron	'owner'; Santo-patrón = patron saint (sometimes patrón for short).
Pendompari	title of the female standard-bearer of the Wánanchatis of Chilchotla.
Petahpe	a commissioner and official in the villages of Chilchotla, Angahuan and Pichátaro; also called Fiscal.
Petámuti	title of the Supreme high-priest in the Tarascan empire.
petate	from Aztec petlatl = tule mat.
petatero	maker of petates, tule-weaver.
plaza	square, village-square, open space near the most important church in a town or village.
Principales	'Distinguished men'; in colonial times a term used to refer to the members of the indigenous nobility; principals.
Prioste	title for different officials in several Tarascan villages; head of all the lower commissioners, supervisor of collective labour on behalf of the community (cf. Ihuatzio, Purenchécuaro, Cherán); in Tzintzuntzan one of the commissioners of the Kenguería, with a comparatively low rank.
Priostería	in Ihuatzio the official residence of the Prioste.
Purépecha	'Visitors', 'parvenus', 'strangers'; name for the free 'citizens' not belonging to the nobility (soldiers, farmers, fishermen and artisans) in the Tarascan empire; originally it may have referred to the Tarascan-speaking inhabitants of the islands and shores of Lake Pátzcuaro, who did not belong to the Wakúxecha; later used for the other subjects as well; today: the name by which Tarascans prefer to call themselves (singular: Purembe).
Regidor	Spanish: 'Ruler'; a) official municipal executive (a kind of alderman); b) traditional office in some Tarascan villages (Chilchotla, Angahuan).
Representante de la Comunidad Indígena	see Acha Representante and Comunidad Indígena.
Rezador	'man or woman leading in prayer'; title of some traditional helpers in the divine service; sometimes also called Rezadores del Rosario (of the Rosary); (compare Yunuén).
Rivera	one of the nine wapánekwecha in Ihuatzio or a member of that group (plural: Rivérecha).
Roseras	Spanish name for the Wánanchatis in Chilchotla.
Sánduri	one of the nine wapánekwecha in Ihuatzio or a member of that group (plural: Sándurich').
Sahumador(a)	female thurifer, a helper in the Kenguería of Tzintzuntzan; always a young girl.

San Gabriel	one of the nine wapánekwecha in Ihuatzio (see Gabriélecha).
santa, santo	'saint', the santos of the Tarascans today are, however, gods; diminutives expressing respect and friendliness are: santita, santito.
Sargento	'Second in command', title of the helpers of some commissioners in a number of Tarascan villages. (Quiroga: 2 Sargentos de San Diego; Tzintzuntzan: Sargento de la Cruz, Sargento de la Judea; Ihuatzio: Sargento del Moro, Sargento del Soldado).
Semanero	'Servant of the Week', Spanish name for the Urecha in Ihuatzio and Purenchécuaro, and for the Anyítakwas in Angahuan.
Sinarquismo	extreme right-wing political movement, with followers among orthodox Roman Catholics, especially in the Mexican states of Guanajuato, Jalisco and Michoacán; official name: U.N.S. (Unión Nacional Sinarquista).
Sinarquista	follower of Sinarquismo.
Soldado-Capitán	'Soldier-Captain', the head of the Soldados in Ihuatzio and one of the two Captains of St. Francis; entrusted with the safe keeping of the three materially small images of the patron saint.
Soldados	term used in some Tarascan villages for dancers and commissioners in the service of a saint, usually the patron-saint.
sʌrukwa	lineage, line of descent.
Taras, Thares, Taré	idol; also the name of the god of hunting of the Wakúxecha, comparable with the Aztec Mixcoatl.
Tarénpenya	indigenous title of a principal in Angahuan.
Tarépeti	indigenous title of a Principal in Chilchotla.
tareri	farmer (plural: tarecha, tarerich').
Tariata-k'heri	'Great Wind', the name of a mountain, immediately north of Ihuatzio.
Tatá	father, sir.
Tatá Cura	'Father' or His (Your) Reverence.
Tatá Huriata	Father Sun.
tequila	alcoholic drink, made from agave juice.
therúnchekwa	indigenous term for cargo (commission); a distinction is made between: therúnchekwa sapichu (minor commission) and therúnchekwa k'eri (major commission).
Therúnchitiecha	indigenous name for the cargueros (commissioners), common for instance in Ihuatzio and Pichátaro.

Teruhtsikuri	title of the chiefs of village wards in Purenchécuaro.
Teskatlepoka (Tezcatlipoca)	the commonest name for the supreme god in the Aztec religion (meaning: 'He makes the Black Mirror glitter').
Tiputádox	(Tarascan corruption of the Spanish word Diputados = delegates); term used to indicate the seven Captains of the saints who, like St. Francis, are honoured with village festivals.
Tonantzin	Aztec for 'Our Mother'; originally one of the names of the Aztec goddess of the Earth; now commonly used for Santa María de Guadalupe.
Topil	Aztec for 'staff', 'sceptre' (topilli); today used in several Aztec villages as the title of the keepers of peace and order (assistant policemen); in Chilchotla today the title of a helper of the Mayordomo del Hospital.
Tsakapu-hireti	'People of the Obsidian', one of the three groups into which the Wakúxecha were divided.
tule	from Aztec tullin or tollin, a reed suitable for making mats and baskets.
tuříx	'the black one'; a nickname used by the Tarascans of Ihuatzio for non-Indian strangers (plural: tuříxecha).
tsʌpahki	spearthrower, Aztec atlatl, still used by the Lake Tarascans.
Tsʌtsʌ'ki	'Flower', name of one of the nine wapánekwecha in Ihuatzio, and the term used for a member of that group (plural: Tsʌtsʌkich' or Tsʌtsʌ'kiicha).
Ureti	'First'; a) title of the external chief of a wapánekwa in Ihuatzio, entrusted with the organisation of the communal services of his group; b) title of the semaneros in Purenchécuaro; (plural: Urecha or Urétich').
Urétspeti	title of the chief of a wapánekwa in Ihuatzio, the head of the Orénarikwecha in that group and always a Principal or Hurámuti; (plural: Urétspecha or Urétspetich').
Úskuti	one of the nine wapánekwecha in Ihuatzio or a member of that group. (plural: Úskutich' or Úskuticha).
Vaquero	'cowboy', title of lower commissioners in some Tarascan villages; in Chilchotla, however, it refers to the leaders of the vaqueritas, where they are ex-cargueros with a relatively high position.
Vaqueritas	'girls who drive cows'; helpers of the Vaqueros and Wánanchatis in Chilchotla.
Wakérox	Tarascan corruption of the Spanish word Vaqueros (see under Vaquero).
wakús, wakux	eagle; symbol of the Sun, Heaven and Tzintzuntzan.
Wakúxecha	'Eagles'; the name of the ruling 'Chichimec' population group in the Tarascan empire.

Wanakase	(from Aztec: weinakase = having big ears?), name of one of the three groups into which the Wakúxecha were divided; it had the highest status of the three; the Kasonsí always came from this group.
Wanánchatiecha	girls who care for the Holy Virgin (Ihuatzio, Pichátaro); in former times the title of the girls of the Gwatapera.
Wánanchatis	female relatives of the Vaqueros of Chilchotla, who assist the Vaqueros and the Regidores and who are in their turn helped by the Vaqueritas.
Wananches	*a* female helpers of the Prioste of Cherán; *b* girls caring for the Holy Virgin in Pamatácuaro.
Wandari	'Speaker', title of the men who know the traditional Tarascan formulas, ritual and ceremonial speeches and fulfil certain ceremonial functions in their village or wapánekwa. Considered by many people in Ihuatzio as 'priests' (Petámuti).
wapánekwa	semi-territorial group consisting of a number of patrilineages or parts of them in Ihuatzio (plural: wapánekwecha).
wapátsekwa	Old Tarascan term for village- or town-ward.
waruri	fisherman (plural: warucha, warúrich').
Wichariri	title of the Katapi of Chilchotla, when he acts as dog-whipper.
Witsilopochtli (Huitzilopochtli)	'Humming-bird of the left side', the tribal god of the Mexi'ka' and later of all Aztecs.
Xarátanga	one of the names of the Tarascan Moon Goddess, who was especially worshipped in Xarákwaro (cf. Naná Kutsi).
Xunganda	title of the female leader of the Wananches in Cherán.
Xuhrku	Tarascan raincape made from palm leaves.
xurihka	term referring to indigenous midwives and female healers in Michoacán.
yácata, yákata	Tarascan term referring to a temple containing tombs; royal tomb; not to be confused with other temples which are also called yacáta by the mestizos today, their correct name however, being echekwahta.
Yurixo	'Place of the blood', or 'Place of the Virgin'(?) name of the most important communal hall in Angahuan.
zarape	see gabán.

appendix 3

Este estudio es el resultado de una investigación hecha por el autor y algunos de sus estudiantes principalmente en la comunidad tarasca de Ihuatzio, Mich. y además en unos pueblos cercanos donde se realizaron pequeños estudios comparativos. Esta investigación se efectuó en parte dentro del programa del Centro Regional de Educación Fundamental para el Desarrollo de la Comunidad en la América Latina (Crefal). El mencionado centro es una escuela internacional de adiestramiento para personal directivo de proyectos regionales de desarrollos socio-económico y cultural en la América Latina, administrada por las Unesco. En el Crefal el autor tenía a su cargo la cátedra de ciencias sociales entre noviembre de 1960 y noviembre de 1963. La investigación se prolongó por casi la totalidad de este período de tres años.

Las circunstancias en la cuales se hizo la investigación fueron solamente en parte favorables. La colaboración grande de la Dirección del Crefal y el entusiasmo de los estudiantes facilitaron el estudio, pero la desconfianza de la población a un lado y las interrupciones de la investigación a consecuencias de la clases y de los viajes de estudio que se efectuaron en el ramo del curso ordinario del centro al otro lado, tenían su efecto negativo.

Originalmente el objetivo principal de la investigación era encontrar la explicación de la resistencia a los modestos proyectos de desarrollo socio-económico del Crefal que existió en el pueblo. Cuando la investigación se profundizó y poco a poco fue descubierta la complicada organización social de Ihuatzio, se sintió la necesidad de estudiar detalladamente el fondo histórico del pueblo tarasco y de la comunidad de Ihuatzio en particular. De esta manera el estudio obtuvo una considerable dimensión etno-histórica y después resultó posible interpretar mejor las fuentes históricas sobre la base de algunos fenómenos actuales.

El pueblo de Ihuatzio está situado a la orilla norte de la parte sureste del lago de Pátzcuaro, la cual a veces es llamada Seno de Ihuatzio. El pueblo se encuentra frente a las colonias de Pátzcuaro al lado opuesto del mencionado seno. Al norte del pueblo todavía se ven las ruinas de los centros ceremonial y religioso del antiguo Hihuatzio o Coyu(hua)can que antes de la Conquista era una de las tres cabeceras del estado tarasco.

II   Fondo histórico

El estudio del fondo histórico prehispánico de los tarascos de la región lacustre tiene que basarse casi exclusivamente en un solo documento histórico: *la Relación de Michoacán*. Esta Relación del año de 1541, escrita por un autor anónimo, contiene los relatos de los funcionarios tarascos de Tzintzuntzan que sobrevivieron a la Conquista. En estos relatos se describen bastante detalladamente las instituciones políticas y sociales en el nivel estatal. Lastimosamente la Relación suministra pocos datos sobre la organización social de los pueblos y de los barrios.

La historia de la formación del estado tarasco conserva un carácter predominantemente legendario hasta más o menos dos generaciones antes de la conquista por los españoles (1522). Los datos históricos más evidentes y más importantes son los siguientes:

Tres agrupaciones tribales de diferentes estirpes étnicas se juntaron en una sola ordenación, a saber: el estado tarasco. Estas tres eran:

1 Los *huacúxecha* (águilas), una tribu llamada '*chichimeca*', probablemente hablante de una lengua uto-azteca. Estos se convirtieron en el grupo dominante, aunque llegaron más tarde a Michoacán que las otras dos tribus.

2 Los isleños del lago de Pátzcuaro, hablantes de una lengua antigua que después sería la lengua gubernamental del estado tarasco.

3 Los *michhua'que'*, probladores de ascendencia *nahuatlacatl*, hablantes de un dialecto náhuatl. Ellos formaron el grupo dominante en varias pequeñas unidades políticas de carácter semi-tribal que ya existían antes de que llega-

ran los *huacúxecha*, migrando desde el norte. Los centros más importantes de los *michhua'que'* eran Tzintzuntzan y Taríaran. (La migración de uno de estos grupos de *nahuatlaca'* hacia Michoacán fué descrita en el Lienzo de Jucutacato).

Los *huacúxecha* estuvieron divididos en tres grupos o estratos: *huanacase*, *Tzacapu-ireti* (los del pueblo de Tzacapu, actualmente Zacapu, Mich.) y *eneani*. Los *huanacase* (tal vez '*hueinacaztin*' = 'los que tienen orejas grandes') eran los principales de la tribu; ellos formaron una clase de nobleza. Los jefes más altos de la tribu y después del estado pertenecieron a este grupo.

El héroe legendario y fundador del estado tarasco era *Taríacuri*, hijo de un jefe *huacux* y de una señora principal de los isleños. Como jefe de un barrio o *huapátzecua* de Pátzcuaro se mostró activo y ambicioso. Tuvo un éxito parcial en su lucha con sus diversos rivales dentro y fuera de la tribu. Finalmente, apoyado por sus sobrinos *Hiripan y Tanga'xhuan*, logró poner toda la region bajo el dominio de los *huacúxecha*. Se formó un gobierno tripartito, parecido a las ordenaciones políticas toltecas y aztecas. Las tres cabeceras eran: Ihuatzio o Coyu(hua)can, bajo el dominio de *Hiripan*; Pátzcuaro, gobernado por *Hiquíngare*, un hijo de *Taríacuri* y Tzintzuntzan donde mandó *Tanga'xhuan* I. En aquel tiempo Ihuatzio era la cabercera principal.

Los isleños y una parte de los *nahuatlaca'* de la región se asimilaron y pasaron a formar un estrato medio en el nuevo estado, el de los *purépecha*, la gente común y libre. Entretanto los *huacúxecha* ya habían aceptado la lengua tarasca y entonces ya se iba a destacar la nueva nación tarasca como una unidad cultural independiente.

Los tarascos ya pronto conquistaron casi todo el territorio del actual estado de Michoacán y partes de los actuales estados de Jalisco y Guanajuato. Los *huacúxecha* se establecieron dispersados por todo su imperio. Explotaron las fuerzas productivas de sus nuevos vasallos, sobre todo de los de la tierra caliente.

En el estado tarasco predominaron los mismos principios organizadores que fueron los más importantes entre los aztecas:

1 El principio dualista:

    a en diferentes niveles del sistema gubernamental tarasco se encontraron parejas de funcionarios, uno cumpliendo con funciones internas, el otro con funciones externas (dualismo complementario).

b   en varias unidades sociales existieron ordenaciones de tipo competitivo
en las cuales las dos partes quedaron ligadas mediante rivalidades institucionalizadas o conflictos reglamentados.

2   La división tripartita:
Las tres capitales o cabeceras del estado, la ordenación tripartita entre los
sacerdotes y otras organizaciones siguieron este sistema.

3   La división cuadruple:
el estado estuvo dividido en cuatro partes, cada una bajo el gobierno de un
'cacique de los términos del estado'.

4   La división en siete partes:
esta es la combinación de la división triple y la cuadruple. Fuera del nivel
de estado se encontró también en algunos pueblos como Pátzcuaro y
Curínguaro.

Una institución interesante y específica para los tarascos era la *Guatapera*, una
casa de educación para las señoritas *huacúxecha*, que servían allí antes de casarse
con un oficial militar.

Muy importante entre los tarascos fué la organización de los gremios. Los
jóvenes eran adiestrados por sus padres o por sus hermanos mayores. En
general los oficios deben haber sido hereditarios. La organización de los
huapátzecuecha (barrios) probablemente coincidió con la de los gremios. Tal vez
esto explique la falta de datos sobre una organización tarasca semejante a la de
los *calpultin* entre los aztecas.

El matrimonio era preparado por los padres de los contrayentes o por los
amantes mismos, pero estos siempre necesitaban el consentimiento de sus
padres y tenían que ser originarios del mismo barrio. El pueblo en general
practicaba la endogamia territorial, mientras que los *huacúxecha* en particular se
casaban dentro de sus linajes.

Como se entiende, tanto de la Relación como de la tradición popular, el antiguo Ihuatzio estuvo dividido en dos grandes unidades territoriales. Además
la población se dividió en nueve grupos sociales, cada uno con su propio
adoratorio o sub-centro ceremonial. Siete de estos nueve grupos estuvieron
compuestos por *huacúxecha* y los otros dos fueron formados por *purépecha*.

La ordenación política tarasca fué destruida por los conquistadores españoles.
Estos suprimieron la religión autóctona, eliminaron a la nobleza *huacúxecha*
destruyeron una parte de la organización social y de la cultura. Después por la

intervención de Don Vasco de Quiroga, se restableció el orden público. Entretanto solamente los *purépecha* habían sobrevivido a las catástrofes de la Conquista. Ellos se retiraron dentro del territorio reducido de la nación tarasca, el que además tenían que compartir con los colonizadores españoles. Los tarascos o *purépecha* perdieron el dominio sobre sus colonias antiguas en la tierra caliente. A consecuencias de ese su economía cambió. Don Vasco reorganizó sus gremios y reformó la *Guatapera*, adaptándola a las nuevas instituciones religiosas. La población se redujo hasta el 30% del número de habitantes de antes de la Conquista. La época colonial y el primer siglo de la independencia pasaron sin otros cambios profundos. La Gran Revolución (1910-1920) tenía su influencia en el sentido de que Ihuatzio sufrió algunas pequeñas acciones militares. Además llegaron al pueblo varios fugitivos, algunos de los cuales se quedaron definitivamente. Los conflictos más serios ocurrieron entre quince y veinte años más adelante, cuando dentro de la población agraristas y tradicionalistas se pelearon con el motivo de dominar a la comunidad. En Ihuatzio los tradicionalistas ganaron. En los años treinta el General Cárdenas formó el nuevo municipio de Tzintzuntzan. Ihuatzio fue separado de Pátzcuaro e incorporado al nuevo municipio. Desde este momento los de Ihuatzio riñen con los tzintzuntzeños sobre los límites de sus tierras comunales.

III   *Agrupaciones dentro de la comunidad actual*

La familia chica actual de Ihuatzio se compone de todas las personas que conviven en una sola casa. Es la unidad básica dentro de la comunidad. La mujer más anciana de la familia chica guía las labores domésticas y la economía de la casa. Supervisa hasta todas las actividades comerciales de los otros miembros, incluidos los hombres. El hombre más anciano es el jefe de la familia que la representa hacia afuera. Es miembro con derecho de voto en su *huapánecua* (barrio 'ceremonial'). Cuando no vive ningún hombre adulto en la casa, la mujer de más edad (en este caso una viuda) desempeña esta función.
En general los tarascos de Ihuatzio viven según el sistema parilocal (o virilocal). Consideran la descendencia patrilineal como de una importancia particular, aunque también reconocen el parentesco bilateral. De esta manera existen en el pueblo patri-linajes y familias grandes de parientes bilaterales. Los primeros forman la base para la organización de los *huapánecuecha*; las últimas

son consideradas en relación con la regulación de los matrimonios: se prohibe el casamiento entre parientes hasta el quinto grado.

El compadrazgo tiene rasgos específicos. Hay compadres de bautismo o de pila y de voto. En Ihuatzio se buscan los parientes ceremoniales con preferencia entre los familiares de la esposa. Así el compadrazgo entrelaza los *huapáne-cuecha*.

La comunidad de Ihuatzio se divide en nueve *huapánecuecha* o barrios 'ceremoniales'. La gente del pueblo los considera como conjuntos de un cierto número de patri-linajes. Sin embargo esta representación es idealtípica. En la realidad uno no pertenece a cierto *huapánecua* solamente por su ascendencia paternal, sino más bien por su calidad como ocupante de cierto solar o sea, como habitante de cierto territorio. Aunque ninguno de los *huapánecuecha* actuales tiene un solo territorio cerrado, los jefes de cada uno de estos grupos saben perfectamente cuáles solares pertenecen a su *huapánecua* y cuáles no. De un hombre que, por ejemplo, se establece en el solar de su suegro y después hereda la casa y el solar, se espera que aceptará sus obligaciones frente al *huapáne-cua* de su suegro y que dejará el suyo. Por esta y otras razones en el curso del tiempo varios linajes se dividieron sobre dos, tres o más *huapánecuecha*.

Los nombres de estas agrupaciones de jefes de familia son los siguientes: Rivera, Juan Cruz, *Kapitan*, Luis Miguel, *Tsatsa'ki*, Melchor, *Úskuti*, *Sánduri*, y San Gabriel. Los melchores y los gabrieles son considerados como grupos extraños (como lo fueron dos grupos en el tiempo de Hiripan). Los primeros cuatro *huapánecuecha* predominan en el centro del pueblo, los *tsatsa'kich'* viven muy dispersos y los últimos cuatro *huapánecuecha* predominan en los extremos oriental y occidental del poblado.

Cada uno a su turno se encargan los *huapánecuecha* del servicio en el centro ceremonial. Cada servicio dura una semana. El año ceremonial se inicia el día 12 de diciembre. En este día empieza Rivera con el primer servicio que dura hasta el sábado siguiente. De aquel día en adelante se cambia cada sábado según el orden en que arriba fueron mencionados los *huapánecuecha*. Desde hace varios años los jefes del pueblo se sirven de los *huapánecuecha* en las obras públicas también.

Actualmente, igual como antes de la Conquista, Ihuatzio está dividido en dos grandes barrios territoriales: Sagrado Corazón en el este y Ascensión en el oeste. Existen rivalidades institucionalizadas entre los dos barrios. Los dos funcionarios más altos en la jerarquía de los cargueros son relacionados con los dos barrios. Todavía la gran mayoría de los hombres (casi el 90%) se casa con una mujer de su propio barrio.

Se encontraron restos de tres gremios o grupos de profesionales; los pescadores, los petateros y los labradores.

Existen en el pueblo unas agrupaciones femininas con objetivos religiosos.

Hay tres grupos políticos en Ihuatzio: los sinarquistas, que actualmente tienen la simpatía de más o menos el 30% de la población; los que apoyan al Partido Revolucionario Institucional que forman menos de 5% de los habitantes y el pequeño grupo de los agraristas, el resto del movimiento derrotado a fines de los años treinta, entre los cuales se cuenta un 3% de los lugareños. Más de 60% de la población no muestra ningún interés político, ní en los niveles federal y estatal, ní tampoco en el nivel municipal.

IV Los Cargueros y los Jefes

En Ihuatzio nadie puede ser jefe sin haber cumplido con ciertas tareas en relación con la vida religiosa-ceremonial de la comunidad. Para que se pueda ejercer una función directiva primero hay que pasar por ciertos 'cargos'. Existe una complicada jerarquía de cargos y solamente los hombres, en general ya ancianos, que pasaron por toda esta jerarquía (los que son 'pasados') son elegibles en los puestos más altos del gobierno tradicional. Los que cumplieron con un cargo o dos no pueden ser Principales, solamente pueden actuar como subjefes. De esta manera la jerarquía de los jefes y subjefes coincide en gran parte con la de los cargueros. La misma jefatura es considerada como un 'cargo', una obligación pesada. El jefe no obtiene muchos beneficios materiales de su oficio, al contrario le cuesta más de lo que le da. Pero el buen jefe es remunerado por la comunidad con prestigio, con un alto 'status' social; la gente le rinde mucho homenaje.

El gobierno del *huapánecua* es formado por dos extremos de la jerarquía de jefes. El jefe 'externo', el que representa el grupo hacia afuera es el *Ureti* (el Primero), un subjefe en general muy joven, un recién casado o a veces hasta un adolescente soltero. Muchos consideran el oficio de *Ureti* como 'el primer cargo chico', otros lo llaman "una primera condición para que se pueda aceptar un cargo". El jefe 'interno', el que ejerce la autoridad dentro del grupo, pero que no lo representa en el contacto con los de afuera, se llama *Urétspeti* (jefe). Este es casi siempre un anciano 'pasado'. Preside el consejo de los ancianos del *huapánecua*, compuesto por los que son llamados *Orénaïcuecha*.

El *Ureti* se encarga de organizar los servicios de su *huapánecua* en el centro ceremonial cuando llega su semana. Él y su esposa se ponen a la disposición del *Prioste*, el jefe de todo el personal del centro ceremonial. El *Ureti* sirve durante un año. En general el *Urétspeti* tiene su oficio por el resto de su vida.

Otros cargos 'preparatorios' son los de los *Quenich'* y *Huaquérox*, (Vaqueros), ayudantes del *Prioste*. En un grado más alto se encuentran los Ayudantes de los *Tiputádox* (Diputados). Todos sirven durante un año.

Los primeros verdaderos cargos, los 'cargos chicos', son los de los *Tiputádox* que ya reciben el título de Capitán. Hay siete *Tiputádox* que son encargados de organizar las fiestas de los siete santos que son venerados aparte del santo patrón, San Francisco. El *Tiputado* más importante es el Capitán de Guadalupe, que organiza la fiesta de la Señora de Tepeyac el día 12 de diciembre, día en que los de Ihuatzio cambian sus oficios y sus cargos. Los *Tiputádox* también sirven durante un año. Guardan la imagen de su santo en su propia casa. Después de haber cumplido este cargo uno puede ser elegido como *Acha Hefe* (Jefe de Tenencia). Este tiene como subalternos a un suplente, a un secretario y a diez *Catáhpecha* (encargados del orden), uno por cada manzana de 40 casas. Estos subalternos no forman parte de la jerarquía de los cargueros.

De más o menos el mismo nivel que los *Tiputádox* son los dos Alféreces y los dos Sargentos. Son los ayudantes de los dos Capitanes de San Francisco. Los cargos de los Capitanes de San Francisco son complementarios y son considerados como "los cargos grandes". Ellos organizan las suntuosas fiestas comunales entre el 4 y el 6 de octubre en honor del santo patrón. Se distinguen el Moro Capitán y el Soldado Capitán. El Moro guarda una imagen grande del santo, que no obstante su tamaño material, es considerada como chica. El Soldado guarda tres pequeñas imágenes del mismo santo, todas de unos 20 centímetros de altura. Sin embargo la gente las llama respectivamente "la grande', 'la mediana' y 'la chica', añadiendo que "el (santo) más chico es el más peligroso".

El Moro y el Soldado siempre salen de diferentes barrios. Cuando en cierto año el Soldado es del barrio de Sagrado Corazón, entonces al año siguiente el mismo barrio produce al Moro y así continúan alternativamente. Aparte del apoyo de su Alférez y de su Sargento los dos Capitanes de San Francisco obtienen la asistencia de un Mesa de Campo. Este es un Capitán de San Francisco del año pasado. El anterior Soldado es Mesa de Campo del actual Moro y viceversa, de modo que los dos siempre son del mismo barrio. Después de cumplir con la tarea de Mesa de Campo uno es considerado como 'pasado'.

Los 'pasados' son eligibles como Jefes del pueblo. Hay tres oficios dentro del poder ejecutivo tradicional del pueblo:

1 el *Prioste*, el jefe de los *Urétich, Quénich', Huaquérox* y de las organizaciones femininas; es el funcionario que vive en la *Priostería*, una casa comunal dentro del centro ceremonial, junto al templo y al curato; sirve durante un año;

2 el *Alcande*, a veces llamado 'Juez', el jefe de los verdaderos cargueros, el jefe interno principal del pueblo; sirve por un período de dos años;

3 el *Acha Representante* u *Orétspetin Hurámuti Maruécheri*, el jefe supremo externo, que representa la comunidad hacia afuera; el jefe de las tierras comunales; su oficio dura siete años, en general es reelegido y queda en función hasta su muerte.

Los tres jefes son responsables frente al consejo de todos los ancianos 'pasados', los Principales. Este consejo se compone de veinte personas más o menos. Los tres jefes ejecutivos y los miembros del consejo de ancianos llevan los títulos tarascos de *Hurámuti* ('El que manda') y de *Acha Maruata Xanta Crusiecha ixu anápuecha* ('Altísimo Señor de las Santas Cruces de los que viven por aqui'). Estas Santas Cruces son pequeños adoratorios de los *huapánecuecha* en forma de cruz, de los cuales solamente quedaron unos pocos después de la destrucción de la *Guatapera* hace 25 años.

Al lado de las jerarquías mencionadas existen los *Huandárich'* (Oradores) que son considerados como 'sacerdotes' (tradicionales o paganos). Ellos conocen las fórmulas tradicionales en lengua tarasca que se usan durante las ceremonias. Tienen mucho prestigio.

El cura, el sacerdote católico es muy ambicioso y por su carácter una de las personalidades marcadas de la comunidad. No le gusta el sistema tradicional, pero se encuentra encapsulado por las instituciones sociales indígenas. A veces se producen conflictos entre él y los jefes. La comunidad se considera propietaria de la iglesia.

V *La gente de Ihuatzio en su Universo*

La cosmovisión de los tarascos de Ihuatzio tiene un carácter propio muy indígena. La ideas e instituciones cristianas fueron incorporadas en la vida religiosa tradicional. Varios conceptos básicos y esenciales de la religión autóctona sobrevivieron a la Conquista y al régimen colonial hasta en la actualidad. Como ejemplos se pueden mencionar el concepto de tres estratos cósmicos: el cielo, la tierra y el tártaro o el infierno subterráneo y las ideas claramente politeístas que existen respecto a los santos.

La vida religiosa está íntimamente interrelacionada con la vida social de la comunidad. Los conceptos religiosos se expresan en la organización social. La oposición Sol-Luna se expresa mediante la rivalidad institucionalizada entre Soldado y Moro. El dualismo femenino-masculino se reconoce en la oposición de los dos barrios, en la agrupación de mujeres frente a los hombres durante las ceremonias, etc.

Los santos son más bien dioses. Los San Franciscos del Moro y del Soldado son considerados como diferentes santos.

Se celebran muchas fiestas en el pueblo. Cada fiesta se acompaña de un ritual o ceremonial elaborado y a veces suntuoso, razón por que los cargos con costosos. Las fiestas más importantes son: la de San Francisco, las siete de los *Tiputádox*, la del *Irats'a* (16 de diciembre), la de Expiración, la de Santa Marta y el día de los muertos.

En Ihuatzio la existencia de ideas mágicas se muestra con frecuencia. Creen entre otras cosas que los ancianos y sobre todo los 'pasados' tienen fuerzas ocultas considerables y que las pueden usar para mantener su autoridad. Ocurrió todavía en 1963 que un hombre que se negó a aceptar un cargo sufrió, junto con sus familiares, contratiempos catastrofales, que por la población en general fueron interpretados como consecuencias de la intervención mágica de los *Hurámutich'*.

VI *Contactos sociales con el mundo externo*

La comunidad de Ihuatzio no es cerrada en el sentido económico, pero sí lo es hasta alto grado en el sentido social. Además gran parte de los resultados de las actividades económicas, la mayor parte del surplús económico, es consumido en el ramo del sistema de los cargos y de las fiestas religiosas.

Hay varios contactos con otras comunidades tarascas principalmente de tipo tradicional. Ocurren escasos contactos eventuales con otros grupos indígenas, como aztecas, otomíes, yaquis y otros.

Regularmente los de Ihuatzio entran en contactos superficiales con los mestizos, a los cuales ellos llaman '*catrines*', o '*tuříxecha*' ('negros' ¡sic!). El último término lo usan también para todos los extranjeros, 'gringos', europeos, etc. Los contactos con el estado y la federación son escasos y superficiales. Con la municipalidad de Tzintzuntzan existe un contacto antagónico.

Las relaciones con "los del Crefal" eran bastante malas. Los *Hurámutich'* fueron alarmados por el apoyo dado por el centro a un líder rebelde durante los años 1957 a 1958. Este líder, un *Huandari*, que quería abolir el sistema de los cargos, tomó parte en un curso para líderes organizado por el Crefal.

El cura, no obstante sus rivalidades con los *Hurámutich'*, se mostró oponente del Crefal también, porque los expertos del centro le negaron un crédito para su gallinero en el atrio de la iglesia. Tanto el cura como los jefes esperaron del Crefal una acción dirigida en contra de la vida religiosa.

VII   El propio carácter socio-cultural tarasco

No hay que confundir lo propio del indígena con lo autóctono. El propio carácter socio-cultural de los tarascos contemporáneos es solamente en parte autóctono. En el curso de los siglos la cultura y la sociedad tarascas han tenido un desarrollo propio y hasta cierto punto autónomo. Se han desarrollado nuevos aspectos sociales y culturales que también contribuyen al carácter propio de la nación tarasca, ya que aún por estos aspectos los tarascos se distinguen de los mestizos o sea, de la actual cultura nacional mexicana.

El estudio del carácter propio de una entidad étnica tiene una utilidad doble. En primer lugar facilita una interpretación más profunda y más adecuada de las fuentes históricas que hablan del pueblo en cuestión y que en general describen la realidad social de una manera idealtípica. La segunda utilidad de la investigación del carácter propio consiste en los datos explicativos que produce acerca de las oposiciones y resistencias que dentro del grupo existen en contra de ciertos tipos de cambios socio-económicos. Las dos implicaciones del carácter propio socio-cultural son tratadas en los últimos dos capítulos.

Con el motivo de distinguir claramente lo que es específico para Ihuatzio en particular y para que se perciba el propio carácter socio-cultural de los tarascos en general se hizo una serie de estudios comparativos en otras comunidades de la región. Mediante trabajo de campo se recogieron datos sobre San Jerónimo Purenchécuaro, Cucuchucho, Yunuén y La Pacanda y por medio de las publicaciones de otros autores o por comunicaciones personales fueron comparadas las comunidades de Cherán, Angahuan, Pamatácuaro, Pichátaro, Chilchotla, Tzintzuntzan y Quiroga, las tres últimas ya siendo comunidades predominantemente mestizas, pero con algunas importantes influencias tarascas.

Esta comparación bastante amplia hizo posible determinar diez aspectos diferentes del propio carácter socio-cultural de los tarascos:

1 La fuerte relación entre ancianidad y autoridad.
2 La relación entre prestigio social y cumplimiento de cargos juntamente con la interpretación de los oficios públicos como obligaciones frente a la comunidad.
3 La importancia del principio organizador dualista en la vida social. Son muy extendidas tanto las organizaciones dualistas de tipo antagonista como las del tipo complementario.
4 El cambio de funciones de modo periódico entre dos partes de una entidad (oficios que cambian alternativamente entre dos barrios, etc.).
5 La tripartición, que se muestra tanto en algunas organizaciones sociales como en la cosmovisión.
6 La cuadripartición, las divisiones en siete y en nueve partes, que probablemente deben ser estudiadas en el ramo de una investigación de antiguas ordenaciones regionales.
7 La territorialidad como base de varias instituciones sociales, muchas veces con cierta relación con el parentesco (barrios, *huapánecuecha*, etc.).
8 La existencia y el funcionamiento de una casa comunal como eslabón entre el templo y la comunidad.
9 La existencia de ciertas formas de trabajo colectivo en servicio de la comunidad.
10 El encapsulamiento de la iglesia católica en el propio sistema religioso-ceremonial indígena con el peligro latente de un conflicto entre jefes tradicionales y el párroco.

VIII   Los elementos autóctonos en el propio carácter tarasco

Por el hecho de que la Relación de Michoacán suministra una visión global de la sociedad tarasca prehispánica la posibilidad de comparar las instituciones y grupos actuales con sus equivalentes antiguos está limitada. Sin embargo aquí nos ayudan las fuentes históricas mucho más detalladas de un pueblo vecino, relacionado con el tarasco por una historia común, el pueblo azteca. Una comparación de las instituciones sociales actuales de Ihuatzio con las antiguas aztecas muestra la existencia de similitudes sorprendentes. Naturalmente hay que tomar en cuenta las diferencias que existieron entre aztecas y tarascos, pero de todas maneras los resultados de la mencionada comparación parecen significativos y facilitan fijar, aunque sea hipotéticamente, los siguientes elementos autóctonos de la vida social de los tarascos actuales de Ihuatzio:

1   los *huapánecuecha* y su labor colectiva en servicio del pueblo;
2   los cargos en el sentido de obligaciones públicas;
3   el gobierno como cargo, dividido en funciones internas y externas;
4   la posición alta de los ancianos en la vida social;
5   la división de la comunidad en dos grupos rivalizadores;
6   el control social mágico.
7   la regulación del matrimonio;
8   la cosmovisión y varios conceptos religiosos.

Otros aspectos del carácter propio de Ihuatzio tiene una base autóctona más o menos amplia, pero ya fueron modificados en el curso del tiempo:

1   la posición social de la mujer;
2   la lengua tarasca;
3   los 'gremios' o 'destinos';
4   los 'sacerdotes' tradicionales (*Huandárich*);
5   el compadrazgo, que siendo de origen hispano aquí se organiza según modelos suministrados por el sistema social tradicional.

Algunos elementos importantes del sistema social autóctono desaparecieron casi completamente o se debilitaron mucho, como la jerarquía de los sacerdotes, la estructura original de estratos sociales, los gremios y el sistema prehispánico de parentesco.

Por supuesto en la cultura y en la vida social actuales se encuentran aún aspectos que no contribuyen al carácter propio, como algunos conceptos científicos y religiosos y la lengua castellana.

IX   *La promoción del desarrollo socio-económico y el carácter propio*

En colaboración con instituciones gubernamentales el Crefal trató de efectuar en Ihuatzio un modesto proyecto de desarrollo de la comunidad. El intento fracasó por varias razones:

1   El concepto del desarrollo de la comunidad, como fué propagado por las Naciones Unidas tiene un carácter predominantemente político. Aparte de su fundamento político (integración nacional bajo la supervisión del grupo en poder) tiene una base sociológica: la idea que la comunidad tiene un valor grande y que por eso no debe desintegrarse. Este idea parece por lo menos en parte equivocada.

2   Desarrollo de la comunidad no puede realizarse cuando las ideas que existen dentro de la comunidad acerca del progreso no coinciden con las que las autoridades gubernamentales tienen al respecto. La discrepancia en este sentido que separaba a los *Hurámutich'* y las autoridades era demasiado grande.

En la luz de las ideas de Alfonso Caso sobre indigenismo y de algunas teorías modernas del desarrollo socio-económico de los paises 'subdesarrollados' (por ejemplo la de Erasmus, 1961) se deja reconsiderar la situación en Ihuatzio y en la zona tarasca en general:

1   El sistema de cargos en su forma actual obstruye el desarrollo económico, pero se puede adaptar hasta cierto punto a las exigencias del futuro mediante el aumento del trabajo colectivo y la disminución de los dones ostentativos.

2   Los *Hurámutich'* no son simplemente conservadores; ellos quieren ciertos cambios y mejoramientos también, pero no quieren perder la única recompensa para los sacrificios que hicieron en servicio de la comunidad. Desean guardar su poder y la consideración del pueblo.

Para las autoridades gubernamentales una cuestión fundamental es cuál debe ser su actitud frente al propio carácter socio-cultural de las minorías étnicas. Muchas personas en los círculos gubernamentales desean la eliminación de las diferencias culturales y de organización social que existen en el país. Estas personas quieren una sola cultura nacional. Sin embargo, integración nacional no significa necesariamente uniformidad cultural. Varios paises en el mundo (Rusia, la India, Suiza, Holanda) muestran que la heterogeneidad cultural es compatible con la integración nacional. Un argumento justo en contra de la heterogeneidad cultural es que cuesta dinero (por ejemplo la diversidad idiomática). Pero los partidarios de la uniformidad olvidan facilmente que su política social es costosa también por las resistencias que deben ser vencidas. En el caso de México además se puede observar que eliminando su propio carácter indígena el pueblo mexicano pierde una parte esencial de su propio carácter nacional también.

Nuestra conclusión respecto a este problema es la siguiente:

1 El desarrollo económico de la zona tarasca es muy urgente. Para lograrlo se debe eliminar o reformar una parte del propio carácter social de la población indígena.

2 Para evitar que los indígenas se vuelvan mestizos en estado de pauperismo socio-cultural hay que apoyar activamente al desarrollo de su propio carácter cultural. Favoreciendo al desarrollo de su cultura propia el gobierno les da cierta recompensa por lo que pierden en el terreno social. De esta manera el indígena adquirirá plena conciencia de su dignidad cultural. La falta por parte del gobierno de estimular activamente el desarrollo del propio carácter cultural indígena se puede interpretar como cierta forma de discriminación, ya que el desarrollo de la cultura 'nacional' o sea la del grupo dominante, siempre recibe el apoyo oficial. Al prestar apoyo al propio carácter cultural y hasta donde sea posible al propio carácter social indígenas no siempre se promoverá el desarrollo en la dirección de la sociedad 'libre' capitalista y abierta. Pero desde la Gran Revolución en México pocos creerán que este sería el único camino posible.

bibliography

List of abbreviations used in the bibliography

A.A.	=	American Anthropologist.
A.A.A.	=	American Anthropological Association.
A.I.	=	América Indígena, magazine of the I.I.I.
I.A.	=	Ibero-Americana.
I.A.I.B.	=	Ibero-Amerikanische Bibliothek zu Berlin.
I.H.	=	Instituto de Historia (U.N.A.M.)
I.I.I.	=	Instituto Indigenista Interamericano.
		(Interamerican Indian Institute)
I.N.A.H.	=	Instituto Nacional de Antropología e Historia (México).
I.N.I.	=	Instituto Nacional Indigenista de México.
I.S.A.	=	Institute of Social Anthropology (S.I.)
I.U.	=	Imprenta Universitaria (U.N.A.M.)
M.A.M.H.	=	Memorias de la Academia Mexicana de Historia.
R.M.E.A.	=	Revista Mexicana de Estudios Antropológicos.
S.C.N.	=	Semenario de Cultura Náhuatl (I.H.; U.N.A.M.).
S.I.	=	Smithonian Institution.
U.C.P.	=	University of California Press.
U.N.A.M.	=	Universidad Nacional Autónoma de México.

I Sources and publications cited:

AGUIRRE BELTRÁN, GONZALO:
  1952: Problemas de la Población Indígena de la Cuenca de Tepalcatepec. *Memorias del I.N.I.* Vol. III; México.
  1953: Formas de Gobierno Indígena. I.U.; U.N.A.M. *Colección Cultura Mexicana 5;* México.
  1957: El Proceso de Aculturación. U.N.A.M. México.

ANDERSON, A. J. O. and DIBBLE, CH. E.:

1952: Florentine Codex; Book 3: The Origin of the Gods. *University of Utah;* Santa Fé, New México.

ARCHIVO MUNICIPAL DE LA CIUDAD DE PÁTZCUARO 1560-1960 (unpubl.)

Pátzcuaro, Mich. and partly (microfilm) in I.N.A.H., México.

ARCHIVO GENERAL DE INDIAS IN SEVILLA: Doc. Mex. Just. siglo XVI, XVII.

BAAL, J. VAN:

1947: Over Wegen en Drijfveren der Religie. Amsterdam.

1960: De Magie als Godsdienstig verschijnsel (Inaugural speech delivered in the State University of Utrecht); Amsterdam.

BARNETT, H. G.:

1953: Innovation, the basis of cultural change. New York.

BEALS, RALPH, L.:

1946: Cherán, a Sierra Tarascan Village. S.I.; I.S.A. no. 2; Washington D.C.

BORAH, WOODROW and COOK, S. F.:

1960: The Population of Central Mexico in 1548. An analysis of the Suma de Visitas de Pueblos. I.A. no. 43. U.C.P.; Berkeley and Los Angeles.

BRAND, DONALD, D.:

1951: Quiroga, a Mexican Municipio. S.I.; I.S.A. no. 11: Washington D.C.

CARRASCO, PEDRO:

1952: Tarascan Folk Religion. Tulane University; New Orleans.

1961: El Barrio y la Regulación del Matrimonio en un Pueblo del Valle de México en el siglo XVI. in: R.M.E.A. XVII; pp. 7-26; México, D.F.

1963: Los Caciques Chichimecas de Tulancingo. U.N.A.M.; I.H.; S.C.N., Vol. IV, pp. 85-91; México, D.F.

CASO, ALFONSO:

1956: Los Barrios antiguos de Tenochtitlan y Tlatelolco. M.A.M.H. Vol. XV, no. 1, pp. 7-63; México, D.F.

1958: Indigenismo. I.N.I.; México, D.F.

CHIMALPAHIN, CUAUHTLEHUANITZIN;

1949: Diferentes Historias Originales. In: *Corpus Codicum Americanorum.*

1952: Vol. III, 3 parts (published and provided with an introduction by E. *Mengin*); Copenhagen.

1958: Memorial Breve acerca de la fundación de la ciudad de Culhuacan. Quellenwerke zur alten Geschichte Amerikas aufgezeichnet in dem Sprachen der Eingeborenen; Stuttgart. (Aztekischer Text mit deutscher Uebersetzung von Walter *Lehmann* und Gerdt *Kutscher*).

1963: Die Relationen Chimalpahin's zur Geschichte México's. Teil I: Die Zeit bis zur Conquista 1521. Text herausgegeben von Gúnter *Zimmermann*. Universität Hamburg. Abhandlungen aus dem Gebiet der Auslandskunde.

Band 68 – Reihe B (Volkerkunde, Kulturgeschichte und Sprachen) Band 38; Hamburg.

CÓDICE RAMÍREZ or Relación del Origen de los Indios que habitan esta Nueva España según sus Historias.

1944: Mexico, D.F.

COMAS, JUAN:

1964: La Antropología social aplicada en México. Trayectoria y Antología. I.I.I. México, D.F.

COOK, SHERBURNE, F. and BORAH, WOODROW:

1960: The Indian Population of Central Mexico 1531-1610. I.A. no. 44. U.C.P.; Berkeley and Los Angeles.

CORONA NÚÑEZ, JOSÉ:

1957: Mitología Tarasca: México D.F.

DURÁN, FRAY DIEGO:

1951: Historia de las Indias de Nueva España e Islas de Tierra Firme. 2 vols. and atlas; México, D.F.

ERASMUS, CHARLES, J.:

1961: Man takes control, cultural development and American aid. Minneapolis.

FOSTER, GEORGE, M.:

1948: Empire's Children, the People of Tzintzuntzan. S.I.; I.S.A. no. 6, Mexico.

1961: The Dyadic Contrast: A Model for the Social Structure of a Mexican Peasant Village, in: A.A. Vol. 63, no. 6. A.A.A.

GILBERTI, S. F., R. P. FR. MATURINO:

1559: Diccionario de la Lengua Tarasca o de Michoacán, México. (Facsímile v. E. Ramos Meza: Colección Siglo XVI no. 9) with an introduction by José *Bravo Ugarte;* Mexico, 1962.

GÓMEZ DE OROZCO, FREDERICO:

1940: Crónicas de Michoacán. *Biblioteca del Estudiante Universitario no.* 12.

(1954) U.N.A.M.; México. (2nd ed.: 1954).

HOETINK, H.:

1965: Het Nieuwe Evolutionisme (Inaugural speech delivered in the Dutch University of Economics and Social Sciences, Rotterdam); Assen.

IXTLILXOCHITL, FERNANDO DE ALVA:

1952: Obras Históricas. 2 vols.; México D.F.

KÖBBEN, A. J. F.:

1964: Van Primitieven tot Medeburgers. Assen.

LEÓN, NICOLÁS:

1904: Los Tarascos. 3 vols.; Mexico.

LEÓN-PORTILLA, MIGUEL:

1956: La Filosofía Náhuatl, estudiada en sus fuentes. U.N.A.M.; México, D.F.

(1959) (2nd ed: 1959).

1962: Ley Orgánica Municipal del Estado de Michoacán, published by the Constitutional Governor of the State, Lic. David Franco Rodríguez and the Secretary General of the government, Lic. Roberto Estrada Salgado; Morelia, Mich. 8th September 1962.

(1904, 1908) Lienzo de Jucutacato (see: Léon, 1904 and Seler, 1908).

LUMHOLTZ, CARL:

1903: Unknown Mexico, a record of five years' exploration among the tribes of the western Sierra Madre, in the Tierra Caliente of Tepic and Jalisco and among the Tarascos of Michoacán. 2 vols. London. (Spanish translation: El Mexico Desconocido, 1904).

MATEOS HIGUERA, SALVADOR:

1948: Códice Arantza in: 'Tlalocan' II-4, pp. 374-375; México, D.F.

MEDINA, RAMÓN:

(1962- Sapichu Wandantskwa Hiwatse Eréteri (A short history of the village of Ihuatzio) or
1963) Manuscrito Medina, a collection of texts on the history, customs and folk-lore of Ihuatzio, partly in Tarascan, partly in bad Spanish; recorded by Ramón Medina. (unpublished, 15 type-written quarto-sheets).

1963: (with R. van Zantwijk) Dos Textos en tarasco de Ihuatzio in: 'Tlalocan' IV-2, pp. 161-163; México, D.F.

MENDIETA, FRAY GERÓNIMO DE:

1945: Historia Eclesiástica Indiana; México, D.F.

NACIONES UNIDAS (United Nations)

1960: Documentos Oficiales del Consejo Ecónomico y Social, 24th periódo de sesiones; Anexos (Ginebra, 1957), Tema 4. Anexo III del Documento E/2931, 20th Informe del Comité Administrativo de Coordinación al Consejo Económico y Social. Reprint: New York.

NUTINI, HUGO, G.:

1961: Clan organization in a Nahuatl-speaking village of the State of Tlaxcala, Mexico, in: A.A., vol. 63, no. 1 (Febr. 1961).

OROZCO Y BERRA, MANUEL:

1960: Historia Antigua y de la Conquista de México; 4 vols. México, D.F.

PLANCARTE, FRANCISCO, M.:

1954: El Problema Indígena Tarahumara. I.N.I. Memorias V; México, D.F.

POMAR, JUAN BAUTISTA:

1941: Relación de Texcoco. In: Relaciones de Texcoco y de los Señores.
(1964) de la Nueva España (*Pomar* and *Zurita*); México, D.F.
(Also in A. M. *Garibay*: Poesía Náhuatl, U.N.A.M.; México, 1964).

POZAS ARCINIEGA, RICARDO:

1961: El Desarrollo de la Comunidad. Técnicas de Investigación Social. U.N.A.M.; México, D.F.

REDFIELD, ROBERT:

1941: The Folk Culture of Yucatan. University of Chicago Press.

1944: Yucatán, Una Culture de Transición (translation by Julio *de la Fuente*); México, D.F.

RELACIÓN DE LAS CEREMONIAS Y RITOS, POBLACIÓN Y GOBERNACIÓN DE LOS INDIOS DE LA PROVINCIA DE MECHUACAN, HECHA AL ILLMO. SR. D. ANTONIO DE MENDOZA, VIRREY Y GOBERNADOR DE ESTA NUEVA ESPAÑA.

1541: Reproducción fascímil del Ms.c. IV 5 de El Escorial (José *Tudela*, José *Corona Núñez*, (1956) Paul *Kirchhoff*): Aguilar; Madrid. (Generally referred to as: 'Relación de Michoacán').

RELACIÓN DE TANCÍTARO:

1580: (in 'Tlalocan', with comments by Ignacio Bernal no. 3, pp. (1952) 205-235.

RENDÓN, SILVIA:

1950: Aspectos de Ceremonias Civiles Tarascas. in: A.I. Vol. X, no. 1.

ROJAS GONZÁLEZ, FRANCISCO: BARRAGÁN AVILES, RENÉ Y CERDA SILVA, ROBERTO DE LA:

1957: Etnografía de México. Síntesis Monográficas. U.N.A.M., Instituto de Investigaciones Sociales; México, D.F.

RUÍZ, EDUARDO:

1935: Michoacán, Paisajes, Tradiciones y Leyendas; México, D.F.

SAHAGÚN, FRAY BERNARDINO DE:

1955: Historia general de las Cosas de Nueva España. 3 vols. (Introduction, notes, etc. by Miguel Acosta Saignes); México, D.F.

SCHULTZE-JENA, LEONHARDT:

1957: Alt-Aztekische Gesänge. Quellenwerke zur alten Geschichte Amerikas, aufgezeichnet in den Sprachen der Eingeborenen; I.A.I.B. (herausgegeben von Gerdt *Kutscher*); Stuttgart.

SELER, EDUARD:

1908: Die Alten Bewohner der Landschaft Michuacan; in: Gesammelte Abhandlungen zur Amerikanischen Sprach- und Alterthumskunde, Vol. III, pp. 33:156; Berlin.

1927: Einige Kapitel aus dem Geschichtswerke Sahaguns. Stuttgart.

SIMÉON, RÉMI:

1963: Dictionnaire de la Langue Nahuatl ou Mexicaine. Graz.

SMITH, WILLIAM, C.:

1961: Hens that laid golden eggs, in: International Development Review. Vol. III, no. 3, pp. 2-5; Washington, D.V.

SOLÓRZANO PRECIADO, AURELIO:

1961: Contribución al conocimiento de la Biología del Charal Prieto del lago de Pátzcuaro, Mich.; México, D.F.

SWADESH, MAURICIO:

1957: Terminos de Parentesco comunes entre Tarasco y Zuñi; México, D.F.

TEZOZOMOC, F. ALVARADO:

1949: Crónica Mexicayotl; I.U. (U.N.A.M.); México, D.F.

1539: Titúlo de Tierras de Cherán Hatzícurin.

(1952) (drawn up by Pablo Qhamondage); in: 'Tlalocan', Vol. III-3, pp. 238-245; México, D.F.

TORQUEMADA, FRAY JUAN DE:

1723: Los 21 libros rituales y Monarquía Indiana; 3 vols.; Madrid.

(1943) (Facsimile-ed. México, D.F., 1943).

VILLA-SEÑOR Y SÁNCHEZ, JOSEPH ANTONIO DE:

1746: Theatro Americano; descripción general de los Reynos, y Provincias de la Nueva España y (1952) sus Jurisdicciones; 2 vols.; México, D.F.

ZANTWIJK, RUDOLF, A. M. VAN:

1960: Los indígenas de Milpa Alta, herederos de los Aztecas. Royal Institute of the Tropics, no. 135: Dep. C.P.A. no. 64; Amsterdam.

1962: La Paz Azteca, la ordenación del mundo por los mexicas, in: Estudios de Cultura Náhuatl III, pp. 101-135; U.N.A.M., S.C.N.; México, D.F.

1963a: Las Ciencias Sociales y el Desarrollo de la Comunidad, una introducción C.R.E.F.A.L., Pátzcuaro, Mich.

1963b: Principios Organizadores de los Mexicas, una introducción al estudio del sistema interno

del régimen azteca, in: Estudios de Cultura Náhuatl IV, pp. 187-222; U.N.A.M., S.C.N.; México, D.F.
1963c: Leyendas Nahuatlacas. I.N.I. Nuestros Cuentos No. 6. México, D.F.

ZURITA, ALONSO DE (OR ZORITA):
1909: Historia de la Nueva España. Vol. I (the only vol. published); Madrid.
1941: Breve y Sumaria Relación de los Señores de la Nueva España (Pomar and *Zurita*); México, D.F.

II Other literature consulted:

BASALENQUE, P. FRAY DIEGO:
1886 (1714): Arte del Idioma Tarasco, México.

BASAURI, CARLOS:
1940: Los Tarascos in: La Población Indígena de México, Vol. III pp. 503-578; México, D.F.

BUITRÓN, ANIBAL:
1961: Community Development in Theory and in Practice. in: Community Development Review. Vol. 6, no. 3, Sept. 1961 Community Development Division: International Cooperation Administration.

CHAVERO, ALFREDO:
México através de los siglos. 3 vols.; México ,D.F. (undated but about the end of 19th century).

CLAVIJERO, F. JAVIER:
1958: Historia Antigua de México. 4 Vols.; México, D.F.

COMAS, JUAN:
1957: Principales Aportaciones Indígenas Precolombinas a la Cultura Universal. I.I.I.; México, D.F.

ESPINOSA, FRAY ISIDRO, F. DE:
1945: Crónica de la Provincia Franciscana de los Apostoles San Pedro y San Pablo de Michoacán; México, D.F.

FERNÁNDEZ, JUSTINO:
1936: Pátzcuaro; México, D.F.

GIBSON, CHARLES:
1964: The Aztecs under Spanish Rule. A History of the Indians of the Valley of Mexico, 1519-1810; Stanford, California.

GOMÉZ ROBLEDA, JOSÉ et al.:
1943: Pescadores y Campesinos tarascos; México, D.F.

HAYES, SAMUEL, P. JR.:
1959: Measuring the Results of Development Projects; a manual for the use of field workers. U.N.E.S.C.O.; Paris.

HISTORIA DE LOS MEXICANOS POR SUS PINTURAS (ANÓNIMO):
1941: in: Relaciones de Texcoco y de los Señores de la Nueva España (*Pomar* and *Zurita*); México, D.F.

KIRCHHOFF, PAUL:

    1947: La Historia Tolteca-Chichimeca; Anales de Quauhtinchan; Fuentes para la Historia de México I; México D.F.
    (In conjunction with Heinrich Berlin and Silvia Rendón).

    1955: Quetzalcoatl, Huemac y el fin de Tula, in: "Cuadernos Americanos" XVI, no. 6, pp. 164-196.

    1961a: Das Toltekenreich und sein Untergang. in: Saeculum XII, Heft 3; Bonn.

    1961b: Der Beitrag Chimalpahins zur Geschichte der Tolteken. Sonderdruck aus: Veröffentlichungen des Museums fär Völkerkunde zu Leipzig; Heft II; Beiträge zur Völkerforschung. Hans Dann zum 65. Geburtstag; Berlin.

KRICKEBERG, WALTER:

    1956: Altmexikanische Kulturen; Berlin.

LEHMANN, WALTER:

    1938: Die Geschichte der Königreiche von Colhuacan und Mexico. Quellenwerke zur alten Geschichte Amerikas I; I.A.I.B.; Stuttgart, Berlin.

LEWIS, OSCAR:

    1960: La Antropología de la probeza. (Cinco Familias); México, D.F.

MACARRO, SEBASTIÁN:

    1952: Relación de Tancítaro. in: "Tlalocan" III-3;
    (1580) pp. 205-235; México, D.F.

MALINOWSKI, BRONISLAW and FUENTE, JULIO DE LA:

    1957: La Economía de un Sistema de Mercados en México. Acta Antropologica; época 2; Vol. I, no. 2; México, D.F.

MENDIETA Y NÚÑEZ, LUCIO et al.:

    1940: Los Tarascos, monografía histórica, etnografía y economía; México, D.F.

MIRANDA, JOSÉ:

    1952: El Tributo Indígena en la Nueva España durante el siglo XVI. El Colegio de México; México, D.F.

MOTOLINIA, FRAY TORBIA DE BENAVENTE:

    1956: Historia de los Indios de la Nueva España; México, D.F.

    1946: Noticia Histórica acerca del Estado de Michoacán (anónimo); Secretaría de Educación Pública; México, D.F.

NACIONES UNIDAS (United Nations):

    1955: El Progreso social mediante el Desarrollo de la Comunidad. Dirección de Asuntos Sociales; New York.

    1941: Origen de los Mexicanos (anónimo); in: Relaciones de Texcoco y de los Señores de la Nueva España (Pomar and Zurita); México, D.F.

PASO Y TRONCOSO, FRANCISCO DEL:

    1930-1942: Epistolario de Nueva España (1505-1818; 16 vols; México, D.F.

SAAVEDRA, R.:

    1925: En Tierra de Tarascos. in: Magazine de Geografía Nacional. Agosto. México, D.F.

SALAS LEÓN, ANTONIO:

    1956: Pátzcuaro, cosas de antaño y de hogaño. Morelia, Mich.

SPICER, E. et al.

    1952: Human Problems in Technological Change. New York.

TOUSSAINT, MANUEL et al.:

    1942: Pátzcuaro. U.N.A.M. México, D.F.

VELAZQUEZ GALLARDO, PABLO:

    1947: Dioses tarascos de Charapan; in: Revista Mexicana de Antropología IX-2; México, D.F.

VEYTIA, M.:

    1944: Historia Antigua de México. 2 vols. México, D.F.

WEST, ROBERT, C.:

    1948: Cultural Geography of the Modern Tarascan Area, S.I., I.S.A. no. 7; Washington, D.F.

WHETTEN, NATHAN, L.:

    1948: Rural Mexico. Chicago.

index